13 Ways of Looking at Student Teaching

13 Ways of Looking at Student Teaching

A Guide for First-Time English Teachers

Mike "Wiggs" Rychlik and Pamela Sissi Carroll

HEINEMANN
Portsmouth, NH

Boynton/Cook Publishers, Inc.
A subsidiary of Reed Elsevier Inc.
361 Hanover Street
Portsmouth, NH 03801–3912
www.heinemann.com

Offices and agents throughout the world

© 2003 by Michael Rychlik and Pamela Sissi Carroll

Library of Congress Cataloging-in-Publication Data
Rychlik, Mike.
    13 ways of looking at student teaching : a guide for first-time English teachers / Mike Rychlik and Pamela Sissi Carroll.
        p. cm.
    Includes bibliographical references.
    ISBN 0-325-00551-6 (alk. paper)
    1. Student teaching—United States.   2. English language—Study and teaching (Secondary)—United States.   I. Title: Thirteen ways of looking at student teaching. II. Carroll, Pamela S.   III. Title.
LB2157 .U5R93   2003
370′ .71—dc21   2003009956

Editor: Lisa Luedeke
Production editor: Sonja S. Chapman
Cover design: Jenny Jensen Greenleaf
Composition: House of Equations, Inc.
Manufacturing: Steve Bernier

Printed in the United States of America on acid-free paper
07 06 05 04 03 VP 1 2 3 4 5

CONTENTS

PREFACE

Thirteen Ways of Looking at Student Teaching is an attempt to help preservice and beginning teachers navigate and even thrive within the zone of discomfort and uncertainty that they will, inevitably, inhabit for several months. The book operates at three interrelated levels to speak to preservice and beginning teachers and to those who are involved in their preparation to teach:

1. It reveals the kinds of struggles that beginning teachers of English and language arts face, as presented in the letters they wrote during their early classroom teaching experiences (and thus it paints a lively—sometimes frightening, sometimes comical, sometimes poignant—picture of what those who are preparing to teach can expect when they enter today's classrooms in the role of teacher).

2. It addresses those specific actual problems and concerns, through the advice of a veteran teacher of English, Mike Rychlik, with whom the beginning teachers corresponded during their early teaching experiences.

3. It expands the view of specific problems and concerns to situate them within a larger conversation about English education, through the experience-based reflections and theory-based comments of Sissi Carroll, a teacher educator.

Throughout, we are primarily concerned with the question of what you—student teachers and new teachers—can expect when you enter the teaching profession, and what we can do to prepare you to enter successfully. We want to help our readers uncover their fear of the unknown elements of teaching (Will I be able to earn students' respect? Will they like me? Will I know more about the subject than they do? Can I continually create interesting lessons? Will they be cooperative, or will chaos reign in my classroom? How tough do I have to be? Will they see through me? Can I smile before Christmas?). We want to help preservice and beginning teachers enter the profession with attitudes and reflective habits of mind that will enable you to find and keep your professional footing.

This is a book that is about helping new teachers recognize and give serious thought to the realities of today's educational institutions, and about supporting you as you set and work toward high expectations for your adolescent students, colleagues, school environment, and yourselves. Although it is not primarily a book about specific teaching and learning strategies and lesson plans, those are included, as they were in the original student-to-teacher correspondences, where they illuminate a point.

We are also concerned with finding ways that teacher educators can invite their students into the professional conversation—as full and equal, though less experienced, participants. *Thirteen Ways of Looking at Student Teaching* is a book that prompts experienced teachers and teacher educators like ourselves to remember our own initial misgivings about the profession and our roles within it, and that updates our memories so that the context of today's schools, today's adolescents, become central in our thoughts.

Mike Rychlik and Pamela Sissi Carroll

ACKNOWLEDGMENTS

Special thanks to all the FSU students who contributed to this text: Keri McComb, Robert Oakley, Susan Elizabeth Wilson-Corwine, Robin Grey, Jessica Sobon, Shari Ann Clay, Floyd Fishel III, Clebern R. Edwards II, Angela E. Fitch, Christopher E. Guarraia, Sarah Stegenga, Summer Flood, Matthew Guyton, Christina Hart, Pamela McClean, Rebecca Cappellini, Erica Wiczynski, Dawn De-Santi, Scott Whittle, Melissa Aherns, Gail Bridges Bright, Michelle Cejas, Ed Collins, Michele Hasselbach, George E. (Eddie) Lyle, Dawn Hughes, Jeanine F. Halada, and Molly Peck.

Huge thanks, as well, to Lisa Luedeke, Heinemann editor, who breathed life into our project and kept puffing, and to the anonymous reviewers whose advice was extremely helpful.

INTRODUCTION

During my own internship in 1982, I carpooled with two other prospective teachers to a rural area thirty-five miles south of Tallahassee, Florida. Despite the dull landscape of scrub pines, junk yards, Jiffy Marts, and trailer parks, the daily drive provided our trio with some therapy time. En route, we yammered, laughed, railed, and boasted about our classroom adventures.

Two weeks prior to graduation, though, we hit a snag. The sun was rising like a fuzzy peach that fine Monday morning when I picked up Tony—a fellow intern who had lucked into an ideal apprenticeship, working with creative writing and college prep classes under the tutelage of an innovative teacher. Consequently, Tony's experience had been relatively stress free. To his credit, Tony also had the "right stuff." He not only loved literature and writing, but he truly enjoyed the students. Naturally, we were giddy that morning. After all, our internships were winding down, and we were almost certifiable teachers.

When we wheeled into John's yard, though, our fellow intern's young wife stood waiting for us at the corner of the driveway. She looked exasperated and anguished. She couldn't get John out of bed. He wasn't ill; he was simply sick and tired of the entire ordeal.

John had been struggling within himself the entire semester. It wasn't the lesson plans, the stack of papers, the new state standards, or latest standardized test preparations that drove him to ruin. What had worn his enthusiasm to a nub was confronting the apathy and rage of his students. Hence, a mere fourteen days from the finish line, John refused to complete the mission. Simply put, he never wished to enter the portals of a secondary school classroom again.

Of course, Tony and I reasoned, begged, pleaded, and needled John to finish, get his degree, and graduate. Nothing we said could unhinge John from his position. He remained riveted to his conviction. His perpetual retort, "I know I never want *to try* and teach again."

Ironically, John had not failed; the system had failed him. Too often, education programs rely on theoretical text books that have little relevance to the primary question on aspiring teachers' minds: "What's it really going to be like in the classroom?"

When I began my graduate work in the fall of 1997, I hearkened to this parable of John because I was amazed by the number of master's degree-seeking students who had never taught. Typically, they were humanities or English majors who after years of unfulfilling occupations had decided to reenter academia for purposes of gaining certification. Consequently, class discussions often strayed from the heady texts that seemed far removed from the "get down and dirty world" of secondary schools. Repeatedly, the novices wanted to know what teaching kids was really like.

Battle scarred, I had a few answers. I had taught middle school in a minimum security, juvenile detention center for three years, and for ten years I had been an English teacher at Sail High School, which is one of the premier alternative programs in the state of Florida. As a result of my experience, the university hired me as a consultant for a distance learning project. Basically, I served as an e-mail version of "Dear Abby" for student teachers heading into the field for the first time. Each week, the students were required to e-mail their reflections to me. What ensued was a fascinating dialogue. Successes and failures were chronicled. Advice was humbly offered, and most often, it was warmly welcomed.

Early on, I realized the educational value of these exchanges. The very scenarios and situations that students in the English education classrooms yearned to explore were pouring into my electronic mailbox every day. Consequently, I downloaded the discourses, cut and pasted them, revised and edited them, tweaking them into historical fictional e-mail accounts, until I had amassed what eventually has become a "real-world" text about weathering an internship and exploring the art of teaching English.

To enhance the reader's experience, I enlisted the services of my mentor and friend, Dr. Pamela "Sissi" Carroll, to add a theoretical (but self-reflective) angle to my rantings and musings. The result is a spirited, theoretically sound, and practical vehicle for student teachers before they enter the classrooms—the book is also a reference for beginning and veteran teachers looking for inspiration. Each of the thirteen chapters covers a thematic aspect about teaching English. The topics include professionalism, content, class management, grading, and jazzy lesson ideas. The format is unique but simple—the students and I volley back-and-forth on a particular subject, grappling with various teaching approaches and principles before Sissi caps off the discourse by interjecting her "home spun" professional wisdom on the issues we raise. In addition, Sissi provides a professional reading list at the end of most chapters, so readers can further explore the subjects. This tri-level approach (student teacher, classroom veteran, education professor) gives the reader plenty of ideas and viewpoints to consider. It should be a welcome addition for colleges of English education to utilize for opening discussion, offering insight, and providing guidance for its prospective teachers.

By giving our new legion of teachers a heady dose of reality up front, it is my hope that the parable of John won't be repeated.

Respectfully,
Mike Rychlik

1   *Becoming the Teacherly Type*

In these exchanges, Melanie—a twenty-one-year-old college senior in the throes of an internship at a local high school—is overwhelmed by her entrance into the adult world of educational professionalism. She frets about being too friendly, dressing appropriately, and sharing her passion for pop culture with her students, while still appearing smart enough to teach the whiz kids in her AP class. In short, Melanie struggles with the instantaneous transformation from student to teacher.

Dressing and Acting the Part

Dear Mike,

One thing that I have encountered while preinterning are students asking me questions about myself. For instance, a student asked if I liked the group Fugazi, and I gave my response. Another student was wearing a T-shirt from a concert I had gone to, but I was not sure if I should ask him if he went also. What is the line as to how much personal information you can tell your students?

I have also been wondering about clothing and attire. While I have been preinterning, I noticed that some of the teachers are getting away from "business clothes" and even wear jeans. Do you know if this is the case everywhere, or is it something that only this county does? I don't think teachers should have to wear a suit, skirt, or dress to teach, especially since they are standing more than sitting, and since they have to work with students who are not necessarily the cleanest of people. Do you have any suggestions?

Melanie

Dear Melanie,

The key is to be professional. Of course, that's a relative term. Therefore, you will simply have to find out what the dress code is when you get your assignment. An important thing to consider, however, is the age difference between you and the students. If you're between twenty-one and twenty-five, you probably need to consider dressing a little more conservatively—just to better separate yourself from the students (especially if you're teaching at a high school).

At my school we have a rather lax dress code. I wear jeans most of the time, but I also wear polo shirts and a sports coat—just so I look more like a teacher than a student. I'm over fifty, though. One of my twenty-eight-year-old colleagues wears a tie every day, just to better illustrate the difference between his students and himself. Bottom line, it's a personal choice. I tend to think, though, you should not look like a student. Look like a professional, and act like one, too.

Nonetheless, I don't think there is anything wrong with talking to students about rock and roll. Of course, you can't tell them the dirty little secrets about some summer of love-fest when you followed the Grateful Dead or Phish cross-country in a micro bus. But, if you profess to dig Fugazi or even spin a relevant rock song to accentuate your lesson, that's totally in bounds. I had an intern who used a techno song to help him teach the thematics of *Romeo and Juliet*. The song was about the "forbidden fruit" of young love, and its message (and infectious rhythm) proved a very effective tie-in with the play. So don't be afraid to be yourself—just use good judgment, and remember that you're the adult now.

Respectfully,
Mike

Maintaining a Sense of Fair Play

Hello, Mike,

One thing that I've been concerned about so far is choosing favorites. I noticed my teacher has a few favorites, but it's odd because I haven't noticed any resentment toward them from other students. And, it seems like Mr. H. will do more for the student who stands up to him. If a student does not do an assignment, Mr. H. tells the student that it's too late, and it won't count. Now, if the student says "Okay," that's the way Mr. H. will leave it. But, if the student tells him "That's not fair," Mr. H. gives the student a second chance. I think he figures the student who stands up to him will have parents that will stand up to him regarding their child's grades. I really want to strive for a more consistent approach.

Melanie

Dear Melanie,

You've picked up on an important issue—consistency and fairness. You are going to have favorite students. Try as you might, that's a given. There will be students who make you giggle, who make you feel special, who make you feel proud, and who inspire you to think thoughtful thoughts. And there will be those students who irk you, shirk you, and snap your bean. However, you need to have fair policies (especially concerning work and grades) for all of your students. No single set of behaviors should change the way you conduct your business.

Flexibility, however, is important. Remember that we're dealing with young people. They will screw up from time to time (and so will we). What I've found to be most effective is to bend, but not break. In other words, stick by your standards and objectives and high expectations, but also remember you're dealing with human beings. Therefore, having a sense of humanity is essential for motivational purposes. To be honest, I've found myself cutting deals with more "trouble" kids (not whiners) than with my pet students. In a parent-student/teacher conference a few weeks ago, I initiated a deal with a senior who had stopped coming to school last semester because she had fallen in with a tough crowd of skipping drug abusers. She would've easily passed my class had she not quit coming to school. To get credit, she needed a B on the final, but she had flunked it because of her chronic absenteeism. In order to get her back on track, I gave her an opportunity to truly study the material and retake the final. She studied; she got her B; she received her credit; she's coming to school almost every day; she's got a much better attitude, and I am hopeful that she's going to graduate. Of course, not every story has a happy ending, and this young lady might crash and burn before the year is out. But given the circumstances, I looked at her situation and made the call. As they say, sometimes the carrot works better than the stick. Of course, I tend to use a carrot stick; it bends but it doesn't break.

Respectfully,
Mike

Shedding the Guru Image

Dear Mike,

I really like the AP English students, because they are very willing to participate in class. In fact, sometimes they say things that have me pondering for hours. I just hope that I can teach them something; they are smart, and I don't want to be criticized.

Have a great day!
Melanie

Dear Melanie,

Don't worry about trying to outsmart them. Believe me I've had plenty of whiz kids who wowed me with their amazing intellect and insight. That's why I give my students a syllabus on the first day of school that states "I don't have all the answers, and I am here to learn from you." This lays out the concept of a democratic classroom that empowers students to think as individuals.

For example—I taught the novel *The Catcher in the Rye* for several years before Holden's incessant question about "where the ducks in Central Park go for the winter" ever made any sense to me. On the surface, Holden's rant simply seemed like the ravings of a madman, but I felt compelled to ask for help. I just had to be honest enough to ask my students the question and admit my confusion. Luckily, a stellar pupil aptly named Hope finally made the connection for me.

"The park represents home," Hope said. "Subconsciously, Holden is trying to reconnect with the peaceful scenes he remembers with Allie in the park before life became complicated by premature death. The park is indicative of a time and place when Holden's life felt safe and made sense. Now that Allie's gone and it's winter, the fate of the ducks is representative of this loss of innocence."

Of course, who knows what Salinger really meant? Maybe he was just having Holden bemuse the elements for bemusement's sake, but Hope made a terrific connection for her classmates and for her old dog of a teacher.

Naturally, we can't expect our students to provide swell answers for everything. Sometimes they will stare at you with mouths agape and eyes glazed, and it'll be your task to jump-start them—so you must make sure you do your homework and be plenty prepared. During discussions, you will have to moderate, commentate, and breathe plenty of heady insights into the discourse. So be open and be amazed by the students' wonderful infusions into the Muse. That's what makes this so much fun.

Respectfully,
Mike

The Discussion Road Map

Dear Mike,

My first lesson went wonderfully (in my opinion). The night before, I called friends to get their input. I presented my lesson to my roommate, and I reread everything. Anyhow, the class had a great debate session, but I did stick to my questions. I guess as a beginning teacher, I will live by my lesson plans. I don't mind, though; I felt like they were my life support. Of course, I'd turn them over a few times so I wouldn't rely on them too much, but I kept turning them back over. I am just SO excited about getting into the classroom and leading lessons. It went really well.

Thanks,
Melanie

Dear Melanie,

It's great that you're writing out questions for your discussions. This enables you to have a road map of reference points to make sure you cover what you intended. As you've probably noticed from observing discussions—they easily meander and splinter off into some very strange directions (students love to spin a discourse into space). On the upside, many of these spontaneous excursions are truly essential to form a more perfect union in the community classroom. However, teachers (especially beginning ones) should always have some key points written down on note cards so that they can steer the class back on to the sacred paths of knowledge that they deem essential to the discourse. In other words—by having a game plan, you have a better idea of how to play the game.

Respectfully,
Mike

Thematic Units

Dear Mike,

I realize that I have to plan a lot, but I am freaking out about doing units. I can handle a lesson plan—no problem. But when it comes to these thematic units, I can feel the knot in my stomach. For the next grading period, I have to plan a four- to five-week unit and pick a theme, but I'm clueless.

Melanie

Dear Melanie,

Check out the literary anthologies available at your school. I guarantee if you thumb through a couple of them you'll get some ideas. Some of the best texts are arranged thematically. This will be a good place to begin arranging your unit and your ideas, especially if your school has limited materials. Just remember to integrate strategies à la vocab, grammar, writing, along with the literature. In other words, your Lit should serve as a jumping off spot for writing models, grammar lessons, and vocabulary work. Also check out the big, bound teacher's portfolios that go with the literature books. In them, you'll find a lot of ways to integrate all of these disciplines. Remember, though, these are just ways to get jump-started. The real fun comes when you begin to bring in outside materials that you dream up and weave together, such as music, lyrics, art, newspaper or magazine articles, TV, video, etc. And don't forget to tap into the students—empower them with some brainstorming activities and some choices. The more they are involved in the process, the more invested they will be in the upcoming adventures.

But don't fret about it. Embrace the challenge. Planning wise, thematic units are really the most important things we do. By connecting our lessons into focused themes, we help the students connect our classes to their lives. So seek themes with which they will connect. I guarantee that eventually you will have fun doing this because it makes teaching relevant, too. It connects them to you and you to them.

For example, I'm currently honoring Black History Month with a thematic unit on oppression. Of course, this isn't the only time of the year we read African-American writers (we do it all year), but the theme of oppression covers the plight of minorities, women, and teenagers as well. To begin the unit, I introduce the concept of causal analysis. This writing and critical thinking modality serves as an effective tool for considering the societal ills and political solutions for examining oppression. Simply put, why do these things happen, and what are their effects? We read essays, poems, short stories, lyrics, and raps; we watch videos, listen to music, and then analyze them all by breaking them down and using this causal chain rubric.

Just the other day we read the prologue to Ralph Ellison's *Invisible Man*, and after a great discussion, the students highlighted photocopies of the intro with different colors—one shade for causes and another for effects. Then they wrote causal analyses examining why Ellison's narrator felt invisible, and the range of effects such a feeling caused. They followed the causal chain by figuring out why the narrator felt compelled to "bump back" physically (with fisticuffs), and considered those effects. The spiritual objective? Role-play a little and get into the Invisible Man's emotional state of being. The writing objective? Causal analysis. Naturally, the grammar, mechanics, transitions, and spelling all followed suit and came into play once the students took their pens and pencils into their hands and fine-tuned their *Invisible Man* "monster-pieces."

Personally, I love teaching thematically. It brings the real world into the classroom, enabling us to see our community of learners as a microcosm of society—a working democracy. Consequently, it gets a bit dicey at times. Debates heat up. Students become overwhelmed by their passions. But therein the beauty lies. Our lives together become relevant, meaningful, and full of purpose.

Respectfully,
Mike

Respecting Physical Space

Dear Mike,

How much physical contact (if any) is acceptable? Occasionally, I have given kids a little hug when they do a good job, but a couple kids today sort of made me wonder if I'm sending out the wrong message. We were walking in the hall toward the media center when one of the boys kind of put his arm around my waist, while another boy grabbed my wrist and sort of fiddled with my hair. They were joking around that I was "their girl."

Since I really like these two boys, I didn't want to freak out. Still I felt extremely uneasy, and I finally told them that I would prefer if it they kept their hands to themselves, so they quit. They seemed a little offended and acted like they were just having fun and being friendly.

Did I do the right thing? I didn't want to overreact, but I wanted them to get the message that it wasn't okay. Still, it bothers me that my only recourse is to never have any physical contact with the kids. I think that it's important to show them how much we care.

Thanks,
Melanie

Dear Melanie,

When students are making inappropriate comments, advances, or gestures—you must set them straight. Consider it a teachable moment. Explain to them why it is inappropriate, then warn them that it must not happen again. If it does, report them to your supervising teacher and, if need be, to the office staff. Make sure that the students are reprimanded and dealt some form of appropriate punishment. With the help of your supervising teacher, you may even call their homes and get their parents involved. Never put yourself in a compromising situation. In other words, don't allow inappropriate behavior that makes you feel uncomfortable in any way to continue. Assert yourself by being up-front and firm. Young men especially need to learn the taboos about sexual harassment, and where better than in school?

In addition, always leave the door to your classroom open during one-on-one conferences with a student. Or better yet—step out into the hall with the student, so others can see you interacting. Unfortunately, we hear of teachers being falsely accused of improprieties with students from time to time. Therefore, it's best to be careful.

On the other hand, I must say that I am a proponent of pats on the back, high fives, and soulful hand shakes—especially when kids have done something really swell. That's a true sign of respect and compassion. So I wouldn't recommend becoming too cucumber cool or rigidly frigid. Of course, many experts and legal advisors would disagree—they recommend we keep a two-foot barrier between ourselves and our students. But I firmly believe that for many students a pat on the back from a teacher may be the only positive contact they have with an adult figure.

Respectfully,
Mike

Maintaining Your Own Style

Dear Mike,

I think I've come to a conclusion this week. Nothing profound. But I've identified another source of frustration. I don't think I like this interning thing. This is not to say it is not necessary, and I know I'm getting something out of it—but I'm getting antsy and craving my own class. Mr. H. is very good about giving me as little or as much flexibility as I want with my time in front of the class, but it is not time I look forward to. I think the pitfall of having such a dynamic, talented teacher is that the classroom is so particularly his. There is a very distinct tone to the room, a nearly tangible connection between him and his students. When I get up in front and speak or introduce something, I feel like I'm taking away from that relationship. I feel like I'm intruding and trying to demand something from students who have no reason to feel they owe me anything. Certainly the students are all very sweet and agreeable, but I feel like I'm being humored when I'm up there.

This is not helped by the fact that I look young for my age and could easily pass for a high-school student. Is this wrong? Should I not feel this frustration? I want so badly to have my own classroom, my own classes, my own established relationship with my own students. In the meantime, am I being unreasonable or naive or stubborn by not thoroughly enjoying this preinternship experience? Do you think I have a bad attitude?

Melanie

Dear Melanie,

Actually, you've hit on a great point—*You are you—And Mr. H. is Mr. H.*

In other words, his style is totally different than yours. Appreciate that. Nurture it. When you interact with the class, do so on *your terms*—not his. Involve the students in the kinds of activities and interactions that you feel are important and essential. Use *your own approach*. By all means, don't follow his lead and try to emulate his style—especially since it isn't yours. Be yourself. The way you interact with the young people is the signature of your personal style. It is an extension of who you are as a human being. Personally, I have a very offbeat, humorous, and dramatic teaching disposition. The last thing I'd want my intern to do is try to be like me (one of me in the classroom is enough). Just do what feels right and what's effective.

Nonetheless, you're still in a situation where the mentoring teacher has classroom rules. There will also be school rules. And furthermore, you will have your county, state, and national dictates, too. Therefore, you will have to do whatever the situation allows you to do (within reason).

As for curriculum, Mr. H. will pretty much be the determining factor, but it sounds like Mr. H. is allowing you some freedom. Embrace that.

Just believe in yourself, Melanie. The part of your journal entry I want to accentuate the most is the following quote: "I want so badly to have my own classroom, my own classes, my own established relationship with my own students."

Don't forget that. Remember how badly you want your own classroom full of students. That will prove to be the most motivating factor to help you overcome any aversion you may have with regard to being a guest teacher in a veteran's domain. Like it or not, the internship is a rite of passage that most prospective teachers must endure.

Respectfully,
Mike

FROM ANOTHER ANGLE

It seems that Melanie's primary concern might be paraphrased this way: What does it mean to be a professional, in the context of teaching English in a high school? She is also asking another question: What does authority in the classroom look like, and how can a young teacher gain it, keep it, and use it wisely?

Melanie asks Mike about her attire, about how much personal information she should share with students, and how to respond when she suspects that they have misinterpreted her teacherly caring for the rights to social or even physical closeness. With these questions, she draws attention to issues that are addressed, in various ways, by teacher educators, including Gordon Pradl and Bruce Pirie. And she reminds me of my early teaching experiences.

To begin a discussion of authority—how to get, maintain, and exercise it—I offer an embarrassing personal recollection. Because the story is true, I have often wished that I could write an apology to every single student I taught for the first three years of my career. I include it here because, though not all will admit it, I have a strong suspicion that most of us, like Melanie, have struggled to find where we fit in the classroom when, as continual learners, we first make the shift from student to teacher:

As an idealistic young teacher, I thought I would begin as one of those teachers to whom students warm up immediately and cooperate with instinctively. I was wrong. When I first began teaching high-school students, I was twenty-one and looked more like I was thirteen. Upon the advice of the principal who hired me, and the department chair who'd just accepted the resignation of the second teacher in my new position that year (it was late November; by that time in the school year, two veteran teachers of English had resigned in frustration because of the attitudes and apathy of the students, and the failure of the school administration to intervene for them), I tried to look older and authoritative. Like Melanie, I had been worried that I would be mistaken for a student, since I was not much older than the eleventh graders I would be teaching. I also feared that they would not take me seriously if they found out the truth about my level of intellect: I listened to the same radio stations they enjoyed, and watched a soap opera every now and then. I didn't view myself as an adult who possessed or could demand any type of authority.

My solution was to create a serious adult persona. I designed a teacherly look. I fixed my long, wild hair in a tight bun, donned matronly skirts and baggy sweaters, wore clunky shoes that made all kinds of noises as I clacked down the hallway. And I fought my natural inclination to smile whenever students were in the vicinity. I complemented the surface touches by beginning each class with the distribution of a list of rules—a long list which featured the word "Don't" more than any other word (Don't speak out of turn; don't chew gum; don't interrupt anyone; don't spit tobacco on the dictionaries in the back of the room; don't apply makeup or hair spray during class; don't forget your pen and paper . . .). In other words, I tried to impersonate a teacher about whom I had no firsthand knowledge. I believed that a stern appearance and demeanor were my best initial defenses against the chaos of a real classroom filled with older adolescents.

It should not have surprised me that two things happened during the first few weeks of my job. First, I realized that students saw through my act; they dismantled my posture as authority figure by undercutting it at every turn; some laughed out loud when I gave out my list of rules, while others merely began breaking each one. Some used foul language in responding to simple instructions, while others chose my classes for nap time. Further, I realized that students could simply refuse to try any of the inventive lessons that I'd spent hours planning for them, and that there was little I could do to insist on their involvement. I was miserable and ended most days sitting in my car in the teacher's parking lot, crying, and thinking that my parents had been right after all: I should've gone into pharmacology.

I wanted desperately to be that teacher to whom students come for advice as well as for formal education, the teacher with whom students share their poetry and aspirations for Ivy League universities. I longed to be the teacher whom students invite to their basketball games and speech competitions, to be a truly student-centered teacher (and I actually envisioned myself as that kind of teacher, even then). But I was failing—in a huge way. Soon, I could hardly communicate with the students at all, beyond assigning work and reminding them that they must pass English courses in order to graduate. I called parents, I ranted, I used the silent treatment, I graded furiously, and graded for nothing more than a bit of demonstrated effort. Nothing seemed to matter. The students and I were on different, and opposing, teams. What had happened to the student-centered teacher within me? Where was she? And who was this person who had taken her place?

Although I was not a good teacher, I was not a quitter. I continued to try to get through to my first group of students. Gradually, instead of crying about the situation, I got angry; as a result, I got tough. Nasty. One wrong word and I would send the student to the office (I lost standing with the vice principal in charge of discipline, who assumed that good teachers could handle their own discipline problems, but I was desperate.) One failure to turn in an assignment meant an F added to the test grade average (the "fairness and consistency" that Mike remarks on was not part of my grading equation at the time). I began to exude and exert some "authority" within my classroom, but it grew out of conflict, not cooperation. I was like a big bully on a playground; I tried to gain authority through terrorizing my students. But, I was still miserable.

I had always envisioned classroom authority as a by-product of cooperation. Yet instead of cooperation, I tried to rule as an absolute tyrant: I controlled what we studied, how we approached topics, what grading policies would be used for which assignments, how much time we would devote to aspects of the curriculum, and so on. I was uncomfortable in the classroom, and I am certain that the students were. They must have been so stunned that they quit fighting back; although I was unable to establish any rapport with my students (who would want to come to me with poems or problems?), I felt redeemed by the fact that I could at least get them quiet when I wanted to talk at (not with) them. And I regained my standing in the vice principal's eyes.

Still I wondered why the same students whose natural energy and curiosity I consciously squelched, would not eagerly get involved in discussions of *The Catcher in the Rye,* or not spend hours poring over the intricacies of the comparison-contrast essays. And I wondered why I felt so lousy at the end of each school day. Yes, they were "under my thumb," but I felt like an impostor. And I *was* an impostor: I had hidden my own teacherly identity— my teacherly essence—beneath a set of routines, a long list of rules, and a stern authoritative gaze; none of the features that described my teaching, those first months, was consistent with the teacher I'd dreamed of becoming, while I practiced and participated in teacher preparation courses.

The problem? Looking back, I realize that there was a Grand Canyon-sized gap, a serious disconnect, between what *I* thought it took to gain and use authority in the classroom, and what my *students* knew about shared responsibility for authority. This disconnect prevented our communication; it created a barrier that became almost impenetrable. Fortunately, a guidance counselor with whom I discussed my frustration and disillusionment suggested firm and rather drastic action. I was willing to try almost anything in order to demonstrate to the students that I was willing to work *with* them toward a remedy. With the encouragement of that sagacious school guidance counselor, I put my carefully developed lesson plans on hold, and devoted an entire week to discussions of goals and expectations (students' and mine) and ways that we could work toward achieving goals and meeting expectations.

The week away from the regular curriculum was well worth the time. For the first time, the students and I were on the same team. We were working together. We were sharing responsibility for deciding what the characteristics of their English classes would be (they explained how they saw my list of "Don'ts" as demeaning and childish, and created a short, reasonable set of "class policies" that were framed positively, for example).

Through that early teaching experience, I began to develop a sense of what a student-centered classroom—or to use Purves, Rogers, and Soter's (1995) more appropriate term, a "student-sensitive" classroom—can be: it demands shared responsibility for identifying problems, as well as for solving them; it requires a great amount of talk, and even more listening; it depends on all members showing respect for opinions that differ from their own. In the process of reinventing my first classes, I had begun to show signs of becoming the teacher I'd hoped to be all along. I did not have to turn over every decision to students in order to extend to them a sense of being participants in the classroom; I did not have to yield on curricular points that I felt ran counter to their best interest (they wanted to do two speech units and completely ignore research papers, but we found a compromise). I *did* learn the value of giving students some significant choices (which novel we would read in February, which kinds of response assignments would be available as the final project associated with the novel, and so on). And I learned that students want classrooms to work just as much as their teachers do.

Melanie seems to be asking Mike for advice regarding how far she has to distance herself from the adolescents whom she is to teach, in terms of her manner of dress and the content of conversations she has with students. She worries that they will read her as a friend and not respect her as an adult teacher. Hers is a legitimate concern. Adolescents commonly ask their young preservice teachers about the concerts, bars, churches, health clubs, restaurants, and shopping malls they frequent. And as a preservice teacher, you might feel flattered that the adolescents seem so interested in you as a human being. However, because you are a novice teacher, you sometimes may fail to recognize that adolescents ask personal questions in order to determine whether you are a potential member of their teenage club, or if you have already rooted in the adult world. It surprises many beginning teachers when they realize that adolescents appreciate uncovering clear boundaries between their world and their teachers'.

The related issue of physical contact is clearly defined by law, and should be practiced with stringent attention by all beginning teachers. After years of successful teaching, a teacher who has developed a reputation for being caring and nurturing, can usually afford to pat a student on the back in order express congratulations, or shake a student's hand to seal an agreement. However, as a beginning teacher, you have not had an opportunity to prove your motives. This reality means that you should avoid all physical contact, especially with students of the opposite sex. When I coached young swimmers and divers, I frequently hugged them when they performed well—after all, I had known the kids on my team, and their families, for years. But as a beginning teacher, I was just becoming acquainted with new students and knew none of their families. I simply could not be as expressive with those students as I had been with the kids I coached. I had to remember to separate myself from my adolescent students in terms of attitude, attire, behavior, and physical contact. Students need teachers who are adults, and they need adults whom they can trust. Mike is right on target when he advises: "Look like a professional, and act like one, too."

Sadly, the litigious nature of our society, and the poor judgments—and public accounts—of the teachers who have abused their relationships with students, have provoked a climate that demands absolute restraint. There is no safe middle ground here, at least for you as a beginning teacher of adolescent students.

Gordon Pradl, a teacher educator and former secondary-school teacher, situates questions like those Melanie raises within the context of the dilemma that teachers face when they try to establish a classroom environment in which authority is based on communication and cooperation. This requires that the teacher put himself or herself in the seat of the student, and, from that perspective, consider what will make learning compelling. Pradl recognizes that there are at least three ways in which teachers can respond to the question of sharing responsibility and authority with students: (1) we can insist on our own superiority as thinkers and knowers, and ignore students' input all together; (2) we can abdicate all responsibility for what students are taught and learn, and figuratively, if not literally, turn over our classrooms to students completely; and (3) we can try every approach we dream up in order to prove to our students that they are more important to us even than our own professional identity as the final authority in our classrooms. It is, of course, the third choice that Pradl recommends. Likewise, it is the third choice that Mike is pointing to when he advises Melanie: "Be open, be amazed at their wonderful infusions into the Muse. That's what makes this so much fun."

Bruce Pirie, a teacher of secondary-school English, drama, and media studies in Ontario, Canada, enters the conversation regarding authority in the classroom, and defining successful student-centered teaching, in *Reshaping High School English* (1997). Pirie recommends that we reject what he refers to as "the cult of the individual" as an educational trend that emphasizes the individual in isolation (Chapter 1); he suggests that we need to see students as individuals, but that we also must regard them within the context of a membership in a larger social group, or the "community" to which Pradl refers. Pirie reminds teachers that there are limits and dangers inherent in "the tendency to believe that everything important can be explained in terms of personal needs, understandings, and growth" (9). He offers a definition of classroom authority that focuses on "what happens between individuals and the rest of their world" (11). In this conception, a teacher and the students must share authority, since all have a stake in what happens within the classroom.

For Pirie, the teacher is one authoritative voice in the classroom, but, like the students, the teacher is only one member of a learning community, and thus the teacher is obligated to participate as a member, not the ruler, of the community. Mike provides Melanie with a sense of balance that all of us teachers need to consider when we begin to define our roles within the community of learners where we lead and grow:

Don't worry about trying to outsmart them. Believe me, I've had plenty of whiz kids who wowed me with their amazing intellect and insight. That's the point of doing this.

The finest books that speak to teachers about teacherly behaviors and expectations are those that recommend specific, tried, and proven strategies, and place them within a framework of a well-defined approach to instruction. The following are books that I recommend and use with my students, and to which they respond favorably; I think that you will find that each belongs on your teaching desk.

Milner, Joseph O'Beirne and Lucy F. M. Milner. 2002. *Bridging English,* 3rd edition. Upper Saddle River, NJ: Merrill/Prentice Hall. This is an ideal English "methods" course text book. With a knowledge of Milner and Milner's advice and carefully explained strategies, lists, and rubrics (which are frequently accompanied by samples of students' work) you will feel more confident of the direction of your own teaching. The Milners cover topics that range from oral language instruction to the SAT essay examination.

Christenbury, Leila. 2000. *Making the Journey*, 2nd edition. Portsmouth, NH: Heinemann. Christenbury, who served as President of the National Council of Teachers of English (NCTE) in 2001, is a professional who has spent years teaching secondary English, and years working with preservice and practicing teachers. Her metaphor of teaching as a journey is right on target; she encourages teachers to reflect on their actions and attitudes, and to keep students' interests, backgrounds, and cultures in mind as we plan and implement instruction.

Burke, Jim. 2003. *The English Teacher's Companion*, 2nd edition. Portsmouth, NH: Boynton/Cook Heinemann. The conversational tone with which Burke opens this book welcomes new teachers; it seems to say that feeling unsure and uncomfortable is alright, because Burke is there to serve as a guide. He proves to be a terrific guide—through curricular issues, changes wrought by technology, and issues related to the basics of securing a job and becoming professionally grounded. Like the others on this list, it is top-notch and will find a place on your desk where you will pick it up for ideas and reinforcement often.

2   *Demonstrating Decorum when Student Teaching*

In these exchanges, Larry—a rather headstrong intern—struggles with the structure of his mentor's classroom. Basically, he doesn't agree with his supervising teacher's management styles—behaviorally or academically. Since Larry wants to change almost everything, he battles his compulsion to confront his mentor about their differences. In the interim, he experiences rapport problems with her, and those problems exacerbate his dilemma when confronting his own fears as a novice classroom teacher, trying to sound scholarly in front of a pesky group of middle-school students.

Stifling the Urge to Take Over

Dear Mike,

My first day went as well as I could have expected. First period, Mrs. B. took the class to the media center, where I helped a lot of them begin research for their history project. Some students pretty much ignored me, but a few were polite. I was pretty pleased with that. Second period was not a good class. Mrs. B. said that it was as bad as it gets, and I hope so. Their behavior ranged from constantly talking and asking questions that were not needed, to falling out of their chairs and making unnecessary comments on every topic. One student came in late and dropped his late pass on the floor in front of Mrs. B.

The teacher countered by putting his name and the other disruptive students' names on the board and threatening to call their mothers, but it did not seem too effective. As a beginning teacher, what can I do to help? How much discipline should I use? Can I take the student out of the class? I really had no idea, but I felt like Mrs. B.'s tactics were not enough. As a teacher, I'm pretty sure that I won't tolerate those kinds of attitudes in my class. I felt bad for her.

Thanks for listening,

Larry

Dear Larry,

Rest assured, Mrs. B. will expect you to follow her behavior management system. And if calling parents is her final step, suggest to her that she help you follow through with those consequences if and when you personally have a problem with a student that reaches that point. Just be careful not to insinuate to Mrs. B. that she's not doing a good job. Explain to her that as a beginning teacher, you feel like you might need a little backup muscle every now and again. While she's teaching, though, don't intervene. Let her handle things her way.

Hopefully, Mrs. B. will be very approachable and open with you. That should prove a big plus. Keep her in your court by continuing to communicate with her. As the saying goes, "The only dumb questions are the ones you don't ask." Hey, maybe it won't even be a problem. At this point, you should start figuring out what's happening in the class, and then conjure up some interactive lesson plans that will inspire Mrs. B. to allow you to do some teaching.

Respectfully,
Mike

Redirecting Your Anger

Mike,

I got to teach a little and gave a vocabulary test, but it didn't go too well. I found that despite the complete ease with which I can talk to others and present myself in public speeches, I was still nervous in front of the class. During the test, I found that I read the words too quickly and that they sounded very stilted. I assume this is probably caused by my extreme nervousness. This is the first time since I have been here that I have been allowed to speak to the students in any formal setting. I find myself irritated because I feel that with more exposures to the real deal of teaching, I will settle right into the groove. Instead, I gave the appearance of an incompetent fool in front of the students, and I found myself directing my anger toward Mrs. B. who was "kind" enough to correct my test methods in front of the students.

Larry

Dear Larry,

Don't worry about the relaxation thing. That will come in time. Unfortunately, you've landed in a somewhat unrelaxed atmosphere and that won't help ease your tension—so just do the best you can.

I might suggest really rehearsing your spiel and shtick before you get up in front of the kids. When I'm driving alone in my car, I'm always practicing my rap, thinking out loud, and talking to the wind. Still, sometimes I feel like I'm doing that same thing when I'm yammering away in class in front of twenty-five blank, young faces.

As for your growing animosity toward the teacher—ease off, Larry. Decompress. You're only going to make things worse by focusing all of your angst in that direction.

Respectfully,
Mike

Using the Right Tone with Your Mentor

Mike,

I'm still having trouble getting an opportunity to teach anything, and as of yet, I haven't been able to do much of anything except give that vocab test.

I am afraid to push this teacher, as she is very firm about her control. And when I have shown even the least amount of assertiveness in the class, she has corrected me in front of the students. Though I feel this was inappropriate, it re-affirms my justification for my hesitation.

Larry

Dear Larry,

I've always found that phrasing things in a positive way usually garners support. I wouldn't phrase it so much in that you are "supposed" to begin teaching a class, but that you would really appreciate the "opportunity" to teach a lesson. Then go on to explain about your internship and how you would really like to have a little more experience under your belt before you actually move on to the next level.

Respectfully,
Mike

Winging It

Mike,

On Tuesday we discussed note taking. I stood at the front of the class and told everyone about how to take notes and what will be expected of them in the future while in their high school and college classes. We ended the class with them asking me questions they had on note taking and about high school and college in general. They came up with some very interesting questions such as: "Do you get detention in college?" "Can you chew gum in class?" and "What happens if you don't do your homework?"

My only complaint of the day is that Mrs. B. didn't tell me in advance what we were doing, so when I got there, she put me on the spot and said to the class "Now our intern is going to tell us a little about note taking and some of the elements of note taking."

Now keep in mind that this was news to me! I had prepared nothing and I had thought of nothing. My palms immediately became sweaty and my brain was working overtime. Fortunately, I handled the pressure. Otherwise, I would have been up the expletive creek! But I really did hate that she did that to me!

Sincerely,
Larry

Dear Larry,

If need be, share with Mrs. B. your apprehension about having to wing it. Maybe you could phrase it like this: "I really appreciate you giving me the opportunity to lead the class, but I wish I had been a little more prepared. I've got some really good ideas that I'd like to try."

Or: "If there are some specific things you'd like me to teach, such as a poem or short story or a writing or learning skill—just give me a little more notice. Since I'm new at this, I would feel more sure of myself if I had time to really prepare."

Whatever you do—don't back down from the opportunity to teach, but try and make it clear that you want to do a most excellent job and to maximize the opportunity by planning an engaging interactive lesson.

Respectfully,
Mike

Staying Optimistic and Being Prepared

Mike,

I took your advice and approached Mrs. B. about teaching a lesson. On Thursday, I am supposed to "have a discussion" about a short story we are reading. What Mrs. B. really wants me to do is stand at the front of the class and lecture. I do not want to do this. I have made a few suggestions, such as a circle where we all can discuss, but she will not hear of it. I know that these kids would love it if I gave them some leeway and let them open up and share their ideas. I don't want to be the dictator at the front of the classroom. I am at a loss as to what to do.

I would also love to do some sort of writing. These kids don't write; they barely even read in this class and my basic class has not read or written one single thing since I've been here. So far I have been unsuccessful in trying to add anything of myself into this classroom. Any suggestions?

Larry

Dear Larry,

Slow down. Mrs. B. is letting you teach, so don't rattle her.

Once you begin your lesson, though, style shift in increments. Do your discussion by disguising it as a lecture. In other words, start yammering, then occasionally ask for clarification and comment. Forget the circle, but try to integrate some real-world issues and themes from the text that will generate a real connection with the class. Phrase your questions to elicit more lengthy responses—no "yes" or "no" answers. Ask "who, what, when, where, why, and how?" type stuff.

And don't be afraid to share yourself with the class. Of course, use good judgment. Some things are sacred. Be bold and make personal connections to the themes and issues of the story. Comment personally on what it reminds you of or how it makes you feel. Ask them to do the same. Show interest in each student. Call on ones who don't volunteer. Ask them to respond to what someone else just said. Lectures easily evolve into discussions once teachers get their students really thinking, and if they call on all of their pupils to participate.

Above all, stay optimistic.

Respectfully,
Mike

Staying the Course

Mike,

We had a pretty good time on Thursday. I began the class with them asking me questions about my experiences in England, because this is where the story that they are reading takes place, and they asked me some great questions! Some I could not answer, such as "Why are their license plates so different?" For the most part, though, their questions were relevant and interesting.

Next, we discussed the story and we ended up only covering a few major themes and getting stuck on those. When I was asking them questions, they seemed a little surprised at first. I don't think anybody has really asked them how they felt about a story. They jumped on the opportunity, though, and made sure that I realized they did not like the story. They thought it irrelevant and pointless—not to mention dumb. I made sure that I asked them to back up their argument with examples, and some ended up changing their minds the more we discussed the story.

I have realized from this assignment that you cannot please everyone. Some thought the story was really short; some thought it too long. Some liked the characters; some hated them. I think maybe they would like it if I let them choose the story for a change, it would have to be appropriate, of course, but I think that I would probably be surprised with their choices.

These kids just want variety. They seem to like someone at the front of the room to talk to them for once, to ask how they feel, and to get them involved. I think that they would be better off with a more mature story than "The Widow and the Parrot," something they can relate to without all of the foreign mumbo jumbo that only confused them.

When I gave them Mrs. B.'s writing assignment, they were a little unhappy because it did not really relate to what we were talking about (I had hoped to talk further about the subject; it was about why animals sometimes do unusual things for their owners), but we ran out of time.

I wanted to change the topic of the assignment to something more relevant, but Mrs. B. does not like change on the spur of the moment, and I did not want to upset her. Although looking back now, I realize that I probably should have just gone ahead and changed the topic anyway. Once they got started, though, they seemed to enjoy themselves.

I won't be working with these advanced kids anymore, because they rotate every six weeks and their time is up. I just hope that Mrs. B. can give them more stimulating material in the future.

Overall, though, I have to say this has been an interesting experience (even though I'm not too crazy about Mrs. B.). On the upside, I have yet to say "God, I really don't want to go face those kids today." My kids, for the most part, seemed like they wanted to learn. They are much better than when I first got there, and now I am greeted every day that I am there. They tell me stories about their dogs, cheerleading, boyfriends, hair cuts. It's been fun.

Larry

Dear Larry,

Your candid responses to your experiences in England sounded like they went well, and the students seemed as if they were very interested. I've always found that students appreciate having teachers open up to them. Once again, we can't share the sordid details of our lives; however, since we continually require students to reflect about their views on issues and on their own lives, then why shouldn't we give them a little glimpse of ourselves every now and then? We can become more like real people to them, maybe even have a little impact on their collective consciousness. Obviously, I'm glad that you want them to express themselves, and that you are willing to share yourself with them. Believe me, that's essential.

As for "changing directions in mid-lesson," I have to side with Mrs. B. on that one. You should be a little careful of that when you're starting out. Stick to your lesson plans. If you hadn't run out of time and could have given them some of your personal connections to the writing prompt, it probably would have ignited some more thoughts in their little heads.

As for the "pleasing everyone" bit—forget about it. As you discovered, what these little darlings do the best is COMPLAIN. "This is boring" and "this sucks" are the battle cries of the whiners on the front lines. I really appreciate how you had them qualify their complaints with detailed analyses. Then, lo and behold, what happened? Some of them changed their minds and began to see the redeeming light of the literature.

Rest assured; this is the true nature of the beast. Giving the students choices about what they read isn't a bad idea, but it's not a panacea for enthusiasm. First of all, they probably won't agree on what to read. And once they've read it, the class slack factor will still beef, wheedle, and whine. So stick to your guns, and keep firing away with an armada of literary elements that you think are explosive enough to trigger their hearts and minds.

And stay positive! It sounds like Mrs. B. is finally giving you some leeway and letting you loosen up and grow. Maybe things aren't so bad after all. As for your musings about looking forward to seeing your kids every day, kudos, Larry, you're getting the gist of this teaching gig.

Respectfully,
Mike

Following Orders

Mike,

Today I came in early to talk with Mrs. B., and we discussed a quiz that I had made up and given to her for prior approval. Of course, she felt that the test was too difficult. After looking at the test again, I feel that the test is not too tough, but I will change it because she asked me to.

In class, I reviewed some vocab words with the students and gave them exercises. Once again, I found myself being nervous. It seems the realization that this is a class that I'm teaching rather than participating in—shakes me a little. Another factor I think comes into play is the fact that this is NOT truly my class, and I am trying to work within a predefined set of rules that I am uncomfortable with. I find myself wanting to do things differently, but I can't because I know the teacher would be furious if I TOOK OVER HER CLASS!

The next day, I collected (or should I say SHE collected) papers of MY assignment! I have trouble in this class because of the inability to gain ANY sense of control. I have found that I obviously bother my supervising teacher with my presence in the room. She told me that when I sit at the side of the class at the desk while doing my observations that it drives her crazy to see me there. I understand that she may be idiosyncratic and "little" things may bother her, but I feel it is more a reflection of her real feelings about my presence in the room. I have determined that she feels threatened by me, and this feeling is probably responsible for her resistance to my instruction within the class. I was rather put off when she began to collect "my" assignment and put it in "her" pile of work. I had to go ask her to see the papers, and she told me how she wanted them graded. This is very frustrating!

All in all, the papers were okay. Out of a twenty-point system, most probably scored between a sixteen and seventeen. It was good to FINALLY be able to see their work and get some feel for the REAL side of teaching—the results. Overall, I was pleased with the work done. Sadly, some simply didn't complete the work—even though what they did was very good.

Larry

Dear Larry,

An intern must realize that he/she is a guest in the house. In accordance, you are going to have to be obedient and follow the rules. As demeaning as it may seem, it's all part of your education. During my apprenticeship, I often felt that even as a rookie I was already a much better teacher than my mentor. However, I realized the ever present decorum issue. She was my boss, she called the shots, and I was continually required to do things her way. Obviously, I had grave reservations about some of her respective methodologies, but I buttoned my lip and followed suit. I was a good trooper. I made the grade. I played the game. I got my degree. I got a job and started teaching the way I wanted to teach.

What worries me about your current situation, Larry, is your reluctance to accept the inevitable. She runs this class; you don't. So quit trying to buck her system. Judging from the tone of your letter, it seems highly likely that your attitude is making her uncomfortable. Decompress and try to become a good first mate. Above all else, follow your captain's orders.

Respectfully,
Mike

FROM ANOTHER ANGLE

During the past sixteen years, the student teachers with whom I have worked have fallen into various combinations of these three categories:

1. those who are eager to learn more about teaching and adolescent students in the classroom setting, and who are well-prepared to work with their mentor teachers

2. those who are unsure of their academic and personal abilities in regard to the demands of teaching adolescents, and who are so frightened by the prospect of being held to professional standards as a teacher that they are living with the hope that their mentor teacher will continue to do most of the work in the classroom

3. those who want to take over the classroom from the moment they step into the door, sure that they can do a better job than the classroom teacher with whom they are paired, despite the imbalance between the student teacher and the mentor in terms of classroom experience

In which of these categories would you put yourself? Would your instructors and mentor teachers agree with your choice(s)?

Larry is clearly one of the student teachers who would fall predominantly into the third category. He is intelligent and takes time to reflect on his teaching performance, and those qualities are, of course, essential for the beginning teacher. But intelligence and reflection are not sufficient for beginning teachers. While Larry does take time to reflect on how he presented himself in front of the middle-school students, he does not seem ready to reflect on how he presents himself to his mentor teacher. He does not recognize that his attitude creates a barrier that prohibits communication with his teacher and the students. Nor does he recognize the problems inherent in his assumption that he would be better off if Mrs. B. would just let him take over and do things his way. Even if he believes, from the beginning, that her classroom management and instructional styles are ineffective, he could ask her to help him better understand the students in her classroom. He could weigh her insights and information with his own observations and expectations. Then he would be prepared to begin to make informed assumptions about the classroom, the students, and the effectiveness of the teacher. Instead, he rejects her work totally from the start, and then complains that she doesn't stand aside to allow him to demonstrate his talents. Hubris also causes Larry to keep the students in the class at arm's length. He doesn't express any interest in finding out who they are, and what their language arts class is like from their perspective.

It seems curious, at first, when Larry admits that, unlike other situations in which he speaks before a group, he feels especially nervous in front of the middle-school students. Yet I suspect that his nervousness grows out of the way he has defined his role in the classroom: he wants to be the perfect teacher. He is eager for students to see that he is able to teach substantive material in a way that piques and sustains their interest. (And he hopes that they will note how much better he is than Mrs. B. in achieving this melding of challenge and interest.) This desire to be perfect is one reason that I worry about student teachers such as Larry. Yes, we all want to be fine teachers even in our first year on the job, but this expectation of perfection ignores one truth: learning to teach is, above all else, a gradual process.

As a beginner, you might have a strong academic affinity for the subject matter that you will teach. Some of your colleagues, on the other hand, might be extraordinarily talented in designing creative ways of presenting new information to students. But I have never seen a student teacher or beginning teacher who was able to do every aspect of the teaching job well from the very start. If your expectations are that you will be perfect, you might find yourself resisting or rejecting constructive criticism, or failing to reflect on what you might have done better in planning, presenting, or evaluating a lesson.

A second concern that I have regarding student teachers such as Larry (those who assume that they have little to learn from veteran teachers) is that they tend to focus more on themselves than on their students. More often than not, they define success in terms of how comfortable they feel when presenting a lesson, or how well they cover a predesigned lesson plan of the day, or how quickly they grade a stack of essays. In reality, though, good teachers take cues from their students. You need to pay careful attention to your students' responses to literature, for example, in order to determine when they will benefit from further focus on one part of a study and when they are ready to move on to other issues. When Larry states, "We discussed the story and we ended up only covering a few major themes and *getting stuck on those*" (italics added), I see a teacher who is more directed by his agenda than by his students' responses to an assignment. I have to wonder, what did Larry hope to accomplish by teaching the "The Widow and the Parrot" (a story that he found too immature for the students, and toward which he did give them time to vent their dislike)? Although he had been told which story to teach, and how to present it, Larry could have begun the lesson with some sense of what he could help students gain by spending their time reading and studying the story. Instead, Larry appears to be preoccupied with getting through each step of his lesson plan, so that he can tell himself that he accomplished his goals as a teacher. How might his account of the literature have been different if he had been more interested in hearing what his students have to say about the story and their literary experience, in what the students have accomplished as learners?

I have to admit that Larry's exchanges with Mike also bother me for two other reasons, as well. First, I sense that his attitude (or should I say arrogance?) will prevent him from taking constructive criticism once he is a teacher. The best teachers I know are the ones who think of themselves as continual learners. Because our students are also the students of our colleagues, we can gain insights about how to work more effectively with our students when we are willing to talk candidly with faculty colleagues about what we are doing in our classrooms, and why. If we feel superior to them, too insecure to share our ideas with them, or fall anywhere in between those two extremes and try to work in isolation, we deprive ourselves of one source of professional development.

Second, I am bothered because Larry's stance toward Mrs. B. and her classroom suggests that he is interested in being a teacher who has all the answers, and will dole them out to students whom he deems worthy. Perhaps Larry, and the others who fall into the third category that I identified above—student teachers who are frustrated when they are not allowed to take full responsibility for a classroom from the start—will benefit from spending some time thinking about how they conceptualize what happens in an effective classroom. In *Engaged in Learning: Teaching English, 6–12* (2002), Kathleen and James Strickland provide some guidance when they contrast traditional classrooms, in which final products provide evidence of student learning and success, and constructivist or transactional classrooms, in which teachers and students work together as language learners and language users, and in which the process of learning is given as much attention as the final products of instruction:

> When we went to school the unstated but nevertheless well-known rules for conduct were that students sit quietly in their seats arranged in rows, eyes forward on the teacher and the chalkboard; students speak only when addressed and raise their hands to ask or answer a question; and, sometimes students would have to rise and stand next to their desk to speak when called on. . . . Information flows in one direction, from teacher to pupil, and any questions that are asked by the teacher are done to test the attention and understanding of the class.
>
> . . . A different set of rules for behavior exists in a constructivist, transactional classroom. . . . Since transactional classrooms have a different perspective on how language is used to negotiate learning between students and teachers, classroom rules are based on the premise that knowledge flows in two directions, between master and apprentice, expert and novice.

> Students sit in various arrangements, circles, small groups, rows, and some-times don't sit at all. Instead of confirming reception of transmitted information by repeating, rephrasing, or regurgitating the information back to the teacher, learning is certified through a negotiated transaction in language between students, teachers, peers, and texts. (18-19)

I hope that I have not sounded too hard on Larry or harsh in my assessment of his conversations about the prestudent teaching assignment. Like each of you who is reading this page at this moment, I am sure that he wants to be a good teacher. It is unlikely that he would continue in the teacher education program, at this penultimate stage in his undergraduate program, unless he wanted to help adolescents become better users of language, better thinkers, and more confident and competent people. I hope that Larry will continue learning what his roles as a teacher will include, and that he will develop a willingness to learn from the veterans with whom he will work, even when he doesn't agree with their approaches. As Mike suggests to him, his confidence and skills will grow, as long as his attitude supports growth. As he learns, he will be able to be himself, not the image of perfection that he seems committed to displaying at this point in time. Finally, I hope that he will reflect on his progress toward learning to teach, not only in terms of how he feels about his place in the classroom, but in terms of how he is learning to get his students involved in thinking, learning, and growing. And I hope these things for you, too.

Other books that might lead you toward thinking about how you view what does happen, and envision what might happen, in the classroom include these:

Baines, Lawrence and Anthony Kunkel. 2003. *Teaching Adolescents to Write: The Unsubtle Art of Naked Teaching.* Boston: Allyn & Bacon. Baines and Kunkel use writing as a medium through which adolescents—and their teachers—can explore life. The pedagogical stance that they promote, one of "naked teaching"—baring heart and soul before students—encourages us to think of ways that we can enliven our classrooms with activities that are "stimulating and enjoyable" and in which "emotion is not a dirty word" (vii). Baines and Kunkel call on teachers to take responsibility for serving as adult role models to adolescents, and provide us with ideas about how to accomplish that with sensitivity as well as panache.

Rief, Linda. 1992. *Seeking Diversity: Language Arts with Adolescents.* Portsmouth, NH: Heinemann. I return to this book again and again for its reminders that as teachers of young adolescents, we too can have high expectations of our students, and that our job is to help them reach those expectations. Rief's book is filled with examples of students' work and sounds of students' voices. She is a teacher who has learned to practice what she preaches, and to share her lessons and her beliefs in clear, compelling prose.

Golub, Jeffrey N. 2000. *Making Learning Happen: Strategies for an Interactive Classroom*. Portsmouth, NH: Boynton/Cook Heinemann. Golub's refreshingly playful voice resonates throughout this short book, encouraging us to find the difference between "motion" and "progress" (xv). Golub's pedagogy, one that values students' inquiries above teachers' prescriptions, is evident in the book's chapters, each of which is devoted to strategies for bringing learning alive in the classroom, and establishing environments that promote learning.

Milner, Joseph O'Bierne and Lucy F. M. Milner. 2002. *Bridging English*, 3rd edition. Upper Saddle River, NJ: Merrill/Prentice Hall. This book provides a comprehensive introduction to the roles and obligations associated with teaching English today. Milner and Milner do not shy away from the implication that teaching English can be an overwhelming responsibility, but they provide theoretical grounding about teaching and learning in general and in the English classroom, and present outstanding practices for those who accept the challenges of the profession.

Burke, Jim. 2003. *The English Teacher's Companion: A Complete Guide to Classroom, Curriculum, and the Profession,* 2nd edition. Portsmouth, NH: Heinemann. Our students carry this book with them into each field experience, including prestudent teaching and student teaching. In the text, Burke presents a student-sensitive pedagogy in a way that highlights his high regard not only for adolescent thinkers, but for the profession of teaching. This is a good book to turn to if you need to be convinced that you were on the right path when you decided that you wanted to teach English.

Christenbury, Leila. 2000. *Making the Journey: Being and Becoming a Teacher of English Language Arts*, 2nd edition. Portsmouth, NH: Boynton/Cook Heinemann. In this book, Christenbury, a former president of the National Council of Teachers of English and an unabashed proponent of classroom teachers, explains and demonstrates the importance of reflective teaching—of thinking about why we make the choices we make, and examining the impact of our actions and expectations. She sets a strong example to support the notion that learning to teach is a process.

3

The Grammar Monster

Like many interns filled with current theories about relevant teaching, Robin is shocked when she discovers that her mentor is still using grammar worksheets and vocabulary lists in isolation from literature and writing. Throughout her experience, she questions the effectiveness of such traditional approaches, while she integrates some novel approaches to making both grammar and vocabulary relevant to her middle-school students.

Playing with Grammatical Concepts

Hello, Mike,

Because of "far from promising scores" on the recent standardized tests, grammar instruction is being incorporated into an everyday occurrence. I'm not sure if I agree with the methods Mrs. G. is using, but it sounds like her supervisor gave her no choice. Each day a short sentence is written on the board. This week's focus is nouns and being able to distinguish between common and proper—concrete or abstract. Students are required to write the sentence down in their planners and complete the directions given. The grammar sentence is a tie-in to the day's worksheet they are to complete.

After watching how all this was done, I had to run the lesson myself as I was told. I know that the kids need the instruction, but I'd like to go about it in a different manner. Any suggestions?

Robin

Dear Robin,

Try to stay away from grammar exercises in the book. Incorporate grammar into writing minilessons that emphasize parts of speech, punctuation marks, dialogue, phrases and clauses, and combining sentences. Give the students some stimulating writing models and prompts, and then spend some "writing time" playing with the concepts. Put them in groups and give them blank overhead transparencies and have them come up with some examples to share with the class. Make a game of it, and they'll respond.

Take, for instance, your concrete and abstract nouns. Make a lengthy list of each kind, type them out, make several copies, cut each noun into a little strip, and have a paper bag with "concrete" written on one and "abstract" on the other. When you get to class, put the students in pairs and have them see who can sort the strips of nouns the fastest with the most accuracy. Or, simply put the students into groups of three and have them quietly brainstorm a list of concrete nouns for two minutes. Then have them pass their list to the next group to check the scores. See which group had the most accurate and extensive list. Repeat with abstract, common, proper, whatever. Students love to play and compete and learn.

Whatever you do—DON'T belabor the points with exercises that isolate one dumb skill after another in a series of worksheet activities. Guaranteed—the students won't retain much from that. And be sure to follow any minilesson with a writing activity. Remember—types of words and mechanical concepts are the tools writers use, so iterate the concepts with real practice. With abstract nouns, I usually have my general ed classes pick an abstract noun that best describes them, and then they have to write an expository paragraph that uses concrete details to illustrate their particular "abstractness" à la "How do I embody hopefulness or charity or love or benevolence or malevolence or slackness or lethargy or apathy or peace? Let me count the ways." Then I have the students write another paragraph about their generation or peer group. Of course, the students do a couple drafts and eventually, they read one (required) or both (for extra credit) essays to the class. It's a very interesting writing exercise that not only gets the students to self-reflect, but to stand up and share their musings about themselves and their generation's space in time. Over the years, I've heard some mighty inspiring stuff from my students. And that's why I like doing what I do.

Respectfully,
Mike

Combining Literature and Grammar

Dear Mike,

I'm always nervous about entering Mrs. G.'s classroom because she drills her students with grammar lessons from the book and worksheets. I don't want to overstep my boundaries, but I've tried to express that grammar can be taught interchangeably within literature instruction. Mrs. G. disagrees, saying that these kids can't learn that way. "They can barely read," she says. Funny how I disagree, but I've graded their tests and they can't even distinguish between a noun and a verb. Where do I go from here?

Robin

Dear Robin,

As I touched on last time—teaching grammar in isolation is not only ineffective but detrimental, as well. Contrary to popular belief, it impedes the writing process. Dwarfed and stunted, the writers become encumbered and bemused by the shackles of the rules and regulations and conventions concerning the correctness of their musings, so they refuse to muse. Therefore, your theory is sound. Teaching grammar should be integrated into the examination of literature and the process of writing.

For example, I always begin my unit on the novel *Cannery Row* by John Steinbeck with a grammar and writing minilesson. And why not? The entire first paragraph of the prologue is chock full of what I call "power nouns."

> Cannery Row in Monterey in California is a poem, a stink, a grating noise, a quality of light, a tone, a habit, a nostalgia, a dream. Cannery Row is the gathered and scattered, tin and iron and rust and splintered wood, chipped pavement and weedy lots and junk heaps, sardine canneries of corrugated iron, honky tonks, restaurants and whore houses, and little crowded groceries, and laboratories and flophouses.

On the flipside, Steinbeck's second paragraph is racked and stacked with power verbs. Here's a bit of it, but get a copy and check out the entire ditty.

> . . . [T]hey come running to clean and cut and pack and cook and can the fish. The whole street rumbles and groans and screams and rattles while the silver rivers of fish pour in out of the boats and the boats rise higher and higher in the water until they are empty.

To introduce the novel, I read the prologue aloud to the class. Then I put the students into groups and give them highlighters and photocopies of the text. Next, I talk to them a little about power nouns and verbs, and how really good writers strive to find these strong concrete words so they don't have to fluff up their prose with a lot of modifiers. The groups then highlight all of the power nouns in the first paragraph and the power verbs in the second one. After we've zipped through that tactile part of the exercise, we review and compare our notes. Then each group is given the task of writing a free verse poem that conceptualizes the setting and mood of *Cannery Row* as envisioned in these opening stanzas. Each group must use a minimum of ten power verbs and power nouns from our composite lists. At the end of class, we have a poetry show wherein each student must have a speaking part in the presentation. The results are always astounding, and the objectives are met. We learn how writers use power words to create a strong sense of place, time, and mood.

Thus, the students begin to see the grammar for what it really is—a series of tools and strategies that writers use to create "special effects."

Of course, this probably only deepens your distress, since your mentor seems to be a true believer from the evangelical "grammar book as the gospel" sect. But you needn't say, "Hallelujah!" Stick to your own beliefs.

Unfortunately, you might have to tough this one out, though, and do things her way. Teachers of this ilk usually aren't too flexible. They're firm in their convictions. However, I would suggest that you try to talk to her about presenting the same material in a slightly different way that will combine other disciplines (writing and literature). Have a concrete lesson plan and couch your suggestions in a manner that won't seem too judgmental or condescending.

Respectfully,
Mike

Jazzing Up the Exercises

Dear Mike,

I'm scheduled to "do my thing" on Monday. I am very excited about it. I took your advice and talked to Mrs. G. and we came up with a compromise. There wasn't much to be done for possessive pronouns versus contractions to make it interesting. So I made up an exercise that is a "fill in the blank" paragraph with each blank having a choice of two words. I think my attempt was pretty good; I tried to make the paragraph as silly and nonsensical as possible. I think this group of eighth graders really likes silliness. The similar paragraph that was in their grammar textbook was simply awful. It was about the duties of an ambassador! Who cares? The kids sure wouldn't!

Robin

Dear Robin,

Entertainment (especially silliness displaying comedic wit) with middle school or high school or even college kids is a plus and a must. Writing your own exercises shows creativity and a command of what's happening. It also exemplifies (in real terms) your complete understanding of the concept. In other words, you are actually using the grammatical concept in your own writing.

May I suggest that you have them do the same? Make them write a similar comedic or serious paragraph that illuminates their mastery of the grammatical concept. Have them use your paragraph as a model. After all, grammar and writing together forever is where it's at.

Respectfully,
Mike

Prescribing a Grammatical Cure

Hello Mike

This past week I had the opportunity to see some extraordinary things. Mrs. G. had me observe two unique classes. The first class was a self-contained special education class. The range of disabilities was astronomical. Ms. B. rattled off so many letters—ESE, ADD, ABC, etc.—of learning disabilities I didn't know one from the other. Anyway, during my time of observation, I witnessed the group of twenty as they tackled language arts. They were having problems with capitalization. It seems I can't get away from a behaviorist style of teaching grammar. Overall, it was interesting to observe students with varying abilities and disabilities work together.

The other class I observed was an ESL (English as a second language) class. Once again there was a wide variety of students whose primary languages ranged from Arabic to Japanese. The students were excited to show me what they knew. One thing I found interesting was the difference students displayed with the spoken word versus the written word. The students seemed fluent in English when speaking, but when it came to the written word the students struggled. I related it to babies. They know how to say Mama and Daddy—understanding how to use those words—but they have no clue how they are written.

Robin

Dear Robin,

The language thing is interesting. I was reading Mina Shaugnessy's book, *Errors and Expectations*, this week, and she was talking about how when kids with writing difficulties read back their own garbled texts, they orally read them in a more standard form. This indicates that the students have their own way to transcribe and order their thoughts. So while their rudimentary etchings might not make much sense to you or me, it makes sense to them. In other words, their lack of spelling, punctuation, and standard form inhibits their written communication. But their thoughts often make perfect sense. Thus, the writing process breaks down for them.

This ties into your grammar thing. What Shaugnessy's book suggests is learning how to spot trends of misuse in a student's writing so the teacher can prescribe specific diagnostics to attack the problems in their written communication. In other words, the mere isolation of grammar in a classwide blanket attack on RULES AND REGULATIONS won't address the *individual* student's particular problems or needs. That's why grammar and writing must not be taught in isolation from one another.

Anyway, I'm glad you're getting out a little and seeing some other scenarios—even if you are spotting some distressing trends within the context of the GRAMMAR MONSTER. See if you can explore some more.

Respectfully,
Mike

Combining Grammar and Real Writing

Hi Mike,

Last week was vocabulary and grammar. Mrs. G. worked on commas and quotation usage. She decided to take the sentences directly from their own writing that they had written in personal narratives and had them correct the grammar (pretty interesting). She also selected the words that they had misspelled, misused, and massacred the most as a class for the students to work on last week. The quiz consisted of sentences directly from their personal narratives. I found this to be a pretty nice way to incorporate grammar. The students seemed to really get quotations, but struggled (as always) with commas and possessives. By the end of the week, though, they seemed to have a better handle on the whole process.

Robin

Dear Robin,

No doubt about it—grammar with real student writing is the key to grammarian relevancy. Kudos to your mentor and to your reflection. It's also fabulous that she flipped on the rewind switch and went back over the skills that had eluded the students the previous week. Immediate remedial therapy is much more effective than waiting until the next standardized test or the final exam looms on the horizon. Maybe Mrs. G. isn't so bad after all.

As for the quotation and comma usage lesson, I have found that these objectives provide a wonderful opportunity to combine mechanics and grammar with creative writing. Obviously, this could easily be incorporated with Lit. For instance, I might have the class read a scene from a short story or novel excerpt that is dialogue intensive. In the follow-up discourse, the class analyzes how the author created character, not only through people's actions and mannerisms, but with their verbal interactions as well.

At that point, I put the students into groups, and they reexamine the text. Then I have each group come up with at least a half-dozen rules for punctuating dialogue. Amazingly, they create a thorough list just based on their observations from what they've examined. Each group writes their rules down and shares them with the class. From these lists, we come up with a master set of dialogue rules. Any rules that haven't been covered, I point out by questioning the class about the section of the story that exemplifies that particular situation. I have found that it is much more effective for the students to discover the rules than to simply read a list and momentarily memorize them. Of course for this exercise to be totally effective, you must find a story or scene that uses every example of quotation and dialogue rules. To guarantee this, I sometimes resort to writing my own scene that is usually based on a madcap classroom interaction with my students or my colleagues (this also models their assignment).

For their written assignment, I have each student write a creative dialogue using each type of dialogue and punctuation rule. The dialogues must be based on two or more members of the faculty. They can be funny, but not cruel or inappropriate. Naturally, these prove to be fun and entertaining because the students all know the "characters" in the stories, so when each member of the class reads his or her essay we have more fun. Once again, though, the main objective is met—the rules regarding mechanics and punctuation reinforce the writing process and the writer's intent.

Respectfully,
Mike

Making Vocabulary Relevant and Fun

Dear Mike,

In my observations I learned that I probably will not just hand out a vocabulary list with the words on it, and then have the students look up the definitions. I really don't think that the kids get the points of the words.

The lesson that went with the vocabulary words was "look up the words then write a sentence using them." I guess that is okay. However, I think that kids in today's classrooms get bored with that method quickly. I was thinking about things that would get me interested in these words. Maybe a song, a script for a favorite show, or a picture.

Thanks again,
Robin

Dear Robin,

I really like your ideas for incorporating the vocabulary into songs or TV scripts or pictures. I had an intern who conjured up a nifty vocabulary review by having the students write commercials for different products. First, she broke the list of twenty-five words down into groups of five. Then she put the students into groups and randomly dispersed the word lists. She had also come up with a list of goofy products (potato peeler, solar-powered electric hair curlers, air-cooled rayon slacks, etc.) that the groups randomly selected. The groups then came up with a TV commercial or skit that they performed at the end of the period. The intern was also specific with her objectives, emphasizing that the words had to be used in such a manner that it illustrated each one's meaning.

When I was in grad school, an ESE teacher came to visit our class, and she said that having the students create pictures is often a perfect way to imprint vocabulary meanings for students. She has her students create pictures to illustrate the meaning of the words, and she hangs the best one up for each word around the room for the week to iterate the definitions. Since a lot of the students with learning disabilities are very tactile or visual, this strategy really brings the words to light for them. The students also get very creative with their illustrations. For instance, one boy drew a bumble bee doing nine kindly acts for the word "benign."

Remember—having the students apply what we want them to learn and know in a creative and reflective fashion should always be our main objective. That's why I'm glad to hear that you have an aversion with the old "look up the words in the dictionary and write sentences with them" method of vocabulary work. Aside from the boredom, it's not very effective.

As a result, I model the vocabulary words of the week using my wit and skill before I ever have the students write with them. In fact, I prepare my vocabulary lists for my students with the preferred definition or definitions of each word, along with model sentences that show a "working knowledge" of the word. In other words, through the context of the vocab word, one can infer its meaning. Hence, they have a working model to help them comprehend and to eventually help them use the words.

Dictionary work as prescribed in ye olde "look up the words and write the definitions and write your own sentences" can actually kill the students' curiosity about this terrific source. I prefer to have my students play a dictionary game wherein the objective is to help them see the relevancy of the reference text. Give each student a dictionary, put them in groups, and then call out a word that is familiar, but difficult to spell. As soon as you've said it, the students race to find it in their dictionaries (and to get credit, they must find it, not just spell it off the top of their heads). Keep score, make a game of it, but the lesson's objective becomes "How do you find words in the dictionary when you're not sure how to spell them?" This exercise clues the students into some phonic options for various combinations of vowel sounds that may sound somewhat similar, but are spelled differently (negotiable, negligible). Plus, it's a fun, yet educational way to do it. Remember, the dictionary (like the grammar book) is a reference book we want students to respect and actually learn to LOVE to use.

Respectfully,
Mike

Combining Literature and Vocabulary

Hello, Mike,

Today we are starting on *Call of the Wild*. I am preparing a list of vocabulary words from the book, and each student will be given a copy of this list with the part of speech, definition, and sentence the word was used in from the book. Usually the words are written on the board with the definition after they've looked them up in the dictionary, but I thought if the students looked at the sentence from the novel that included the word before actually reading the book, maybe this would help their comprehension.

Robin

Dear Robin,

It's a sound idea to tie vocabulary with the literature. This not only helps the students understand what might be a difficult text, but it also shows them the "relevancy" of the words' usage.

Respectfully,
Mike

Requiring Thinking with Vocabulary

Dear Mike,

I can't wait to start doing this full time, you know, as a professional! Mrs. G. shared the vocabulary list I created with another eighth-grade teacher, so that was really neat. My latest project is a word search I created, using the vocabulary words. However, the words are not written on the sheet. The students must first write in the word next to the definition, which is not verbatim from the definitions they studied. The students must really think about the definition, and determine which word goes where. Also, I placed a few teasers in there which are very similar to the word, but slightly misspelled. The students will have to weed out these words to find the correct ones.

When the students are tested for vocabulary, they need to write out the word next to the definition. I think it's a good idea that the students have to also know how to spell the word. Mrs. G. also had them write stories using their words, which I really enjoy. The students got wildly creative with story ideas, and they were learning how to use the word, the definition, and the proper spelling.

Robin

Dear Robin,

I'm so glad you're hearing the teacher's call of the wild—"I can't wait to start doing this full time, you know, as a professional!"

And you have the makings of a true pro—you really care about having the students think critically and creatively. Plus, you are willing to examine and re-examine your approaches to reaching and teaching them. Kudos to you!

I like the vocabulary connections you're making (Mrs. G. is making some good ones, too). Of course, the usage of the words is the ultimate test. Therefore, having the students write a creative story is a wonderful way to teach them to properly use the word.

That's why I liked your word search idea. Honestly, I'm not a fan of the more traditional word searches. They seem like a waste of time. But I appreciated the way you mixed up the definitions in order really make the students *think*. Your little brain teasers will help them with their problem solving and critical think-ing skills, too. I'm also glad that you and Mrs. G. are working together. It's awe-some that she's showing off your exemplary work.

Respectfully,
Mike

FROM ANOTHER ANGLE

Preservice teachers are often surprised, like Robin was, to find that teachers continue to present "straight grammar" lessons in English classes in the twenty-first century. These preservice teachers are probably acquainted with the statement written by Richard Braddock, Richard Lloyd-Jones, and Lowell Schoer, in the 1963 National Council of Teachers of English report, *Research on Written Composition*:

> In view of the widespread agreement of research studies based upon many types of students and teachers, the conclusion can be stated in strong and unqualified terms: the teaching of grammar has a negligible or, because it usually displaces some instruction and practice in actual composition, even a harmful effect on the improvement of writing. (37–38)

Preservice teachers experience a frustrating mixed message when they take this learning into preinternships, then see that teachers continue to teach formal school grammar, and to teach it in isolation of other language-using skills and activities. We have worked with teachers who express many different reasons for teaching grammar in isolation. We do not intend to suggest that those who teach formal school grammar, in isolation, are bad teachers. The fact is that one group of teachers engages in formal school grammar instruction almost by default. These teachers have never questioned the assumption that grammar instruction leads to more effective use of written and spoken language. Most of these teachers view traditional grammar instruction as a job requirement: some feel the need to pass on the lessons that they were taught when they were in school. Others respond to pressure from the parents of their students, and from administrators, department chairs, and others outside of the classroom. Parents frequently implore teachers to teach "proper English."

A second group of teachers with whom our student teachers work believes that formal, isolated grammar instruction will improve students' skills and talents as writers. This group of teachers believes that, by doing a long series of skills drills, students will absorb language rules and begin to apply them appropriately. I suspect that Robin's cooperating teacher, Mrs. G., is likely to feel most comfortable with this cohort.

A third group of teachers argues that students who spend time studying formal school grammar improve their ability to think and engage in problem solving, in general. They base their rationale on the assumption that cognitive activity is good for the brain, much like physical activity is good for the body, in general.

And we have to acknowledge that a fourth and small group of teachers enjoys the relative ease with which grammar lessons, worksheets, and tests—with right and wrong answers—can be developed, presented, and graded.

Because you have made it to the point of student teaching, you realize that there are two courses of action that you will probably need to choose, simultaneously, regarding grammar instruction. First, you will need to learn how to make the best of the situation if your cooperating teachers—and your future colleagues and bosses—demand formal school grammar instruction, and thus ensure the perpetuation of the status quo. Second, you need to learn to work, subtly, toward making gradual changes in language instruction in your school. You need to be familiar with the body of research, theories, and best practices that demonstrate the benefits of a focus on grammar and usage that is different from the methods proposed in traditional school grammar models. (See the bibliography at the end of this chapter, for starters.) You can become the school expert regarding grammar study and language mechanics, integrating them in purposeful and meaningful ways, with instruction in the other language-using activities such as speaking, listening, writing, reading, and thinking.

Robin's experience with Mrs. G. demonstrates that experienced teachers, like those you may be working with, can be willing to change, when they see evidence that change is positive. Robin and Mrs. G. "came up with a compromise" when it was Robin's turn to teach language lessons. The compromise was simple: Robin took a worksheet, one of Mrs. G.'s old reliables, and remade it, adding a twist of whimsy that Robin designed specifically to pique the interest of their adolescent students. The lesson on possessive pronouns and contractions was accomplished, and the goals of both the traditional grammar teacher and less traditional, preservice teacher were met.

In an effort to effect change in grammar instruction, we often turn to the expertise of Constance Weaver, especially through her *Teaching Grammar in Context* (Boynton/Cook Heinemann, 1996). Weaver provides us with research-based examples of integrated approaches to language instruction to which she refers as "grammar in context" (1996). Weaver draws on a history of research to debunk myths associated with grammar instruction. She includes attention, for example, to Macauley's 1943 study that indicated that students do not retain information acquired in grammar lessons (1996, 16-18), Elly's 1976 study that found no real differences in writing ability that could be traced to the effects of either transformational grammar, reading-writing, or traditional grammar instruction, and McQuade's 1980 study that indicated that direct grammar instruction, in the form of a course on editorial skills, led to student writing that was characterized by self-conscious attention to correctness instead of expression of ideas (16–23). Weaver then offers alternatives to traditional formal grammar instruction that today's teachers can incorporate in wide-ranging language lessons. Some of the alternatives she offers include these ideas (paraphrased from pages 26–28):

1. Restrict grammar teaching to elective courses for students who are intrinsically interested in language study. This alternative assures that language study can occur at a linguistic depth that is meaningful, as opposed to the superficial type of instruction that is characteristic of traditional school grammar instruction.

2. Promote the use of grammatical constructions through reading, and point out examples of sophisticated language use in works that students read. This is the kind of strategy that Mike implements when he has students note Steinbeck's rich use of power nouns and verbs in the opening of *Cannery Row*.

3. Keep the use of grammatical terminology to a minimum, but use a wealth of examples of grammatical constructions, and spend more time helping students generate sentences than on helping them analyze sentences. Mike provides guidance for Robin in these areas, when he emphasizes the point that "the mere isolation of grammar in a classwide blanket attack on RULES and REGULATIONS won't address the students' particular problems or needs. That's why grammar and writing must not be taught in isolation from each other."

4. Focus on effective and powerful language use, including use of punctuation, instead of spending time solely on correct usage. Mike's suggestions regarding lessons on punctuation in which he describes "a madcap classroom interaction with [his] students or [his] colleagues" that students explore then use as a model for their own writing of dialogue gives Robin an example of Weaver's point.

5. Study dialects, as they emerge in movies, literature, and in the life of the school and community. Along with an emphasis on dialects, encourage English Language Learners to take risks as users of English, and provide an environment where they feel safe taking those risks. Allow them, on occasion, to teach their classmates something about their home language, so that they can be classroom experts. Robin saw ESL students learning in an atmosphere that promotes learning, and she notes that the ESL students "were excited to show [her] what they knew." The students in the multilingual class were far from acquisition of competence in spoken or written English. However, they were confident language users. They are therefore likely to acquire English, with opportunities of low-risk practice, feedback, and time.

We also rely on the work of Rei Noguchi, such as *Grammar and the Teaching of Writing: Limits and Possibilities* (NCTE, 1991), when introducing our students to new ways of approaching grammar learning and teaching. Noguchi presents what he terms a "writer's grammar" and reduces attention in grammar instruction to those features that are essential for writers, including the notion of sentence, subject, verb, and modifiers. His premise is that the ability to properly and easily use a variety of grammatical constructions can improve a writer's power and impact. Noguchi offers two reasons why his approach appeals to teachers and their adolescent students: it is practical, and its emphasis is on teaching students that they have stylistic choices from which to draw as speakers and writers. He uses the analogy that our job is to help students distinguish between when it is appropriate to wear jeans and sneakers, and when they need to dress in a suit and dress shoes. Then he adds, "The choice of style (or dialect, as the case may be) is no less significant in language, particularly in writing, where the nature of the medium heightens the assumption that addressers have taken the time to refine their message to meet the needs and expectations of the addressees" (Noguchi 1991, 30).

When Mike encourages Robin by saying that she "can still spark a kid's creative juices by integrating writing with grammar," he is suggesting the classroom application of the kinds of grammar instruction that Weaver and Noguchi recommend. Mike insists that she not "belabor" grammatical points "with exercises that isolate one skill after another in a series of worksheet activities" and that she "be sure to follow [instruction on a grammatical element] with a writing activity." In these suggestions, he is nudging Robin away from the influence of a supervising teacher who has relied heavily, at least in part, on traditional approaches. He is providing her with strategies for integrating grammar instruction with real language-use activities—activities that *matter* to secondary students because they help them become more effective and powerful language users.

Similarly, when Mike introduces the way he teaches the concepts of "power nouns" and "power verbs" through the analysis of the opening pages of Steinbeck's *Cannery Row*, he provides Robin with an explicit example of how literature study and grammar study can be integrated. This kind of lesson, when beginning teachers transport it into their classrooms, can lead to a change in the ways that we conceive of grammar instruction. Just as important, is that it can help our secondary-school students *and* their teachers explore the value of paying close attention to the ways we all use language.

My high-school English teacher, Mr. Pearson, marked our papers with an F if we made even one tiny error. One misspelled word meant an F. One dangling modifier, one misused superlative, one sentence fragment wrought the same grade: an F. Mr. Pearson's one-error-and-you're-out approach worked well for him; students who cared about their grades paid careful attention to him in class, and never took his assignments lightly. The other students vanished from class in a kind of natural selection process. As his student, I became meticulously careful about punctuation marks and the correct uses of "affect" and "effect," and could site the cases when "continual" was more appropriate than "continuous."

Mr. Pearson would be proud, I think, to know that I have grown up to be a person whose career depends in large part on my ability to use language. But my language is not perfect—it never will be. Students still giggle at the expressions I rely on, steeped in the rhythms of the North Georgia mountains, with Central Alabama intonations stirred into the blend. And a couple of years ago, after I finished speaking before an audience of 500 people at a national conference for English teachers, a woman approached me with what can only be described as a slanted compliment. She said, "You were great. I didn't really listen much to what you said, but the way you said it was so—cute!" Cute? I certainly did not aim to be cute in that context. I wanted, instead, to be taken seriously as a scholar. Language usage matters. It is unconscionable for teachers to pretend otherwise when teaching language lessons.

For most of us, positive, empowering, and even playful approaches and attitudes toward grammar instruction, as a part of the larger topic of language study, offer more potential. Grammar and language instruction can be infused with fun and curiosity and opportunities for growth. And teachers who are able to inject grammar and language lessons with the same kinds of creative enthusiasm as they bring to composition, literature, speaking, and thinking lessons, demonstrate what Mike calls "the makings of a true pro."

References you might like to read if you feel ill at ease regarding your preparation to teach grammar, or to participate in the profession's long-standing grammar debate, include these:

Noden, Harry. 1999. *Image Grammar*. Portsmouth, NH: Boynton/Cook Heinemann. This book offers an encouraging and different approach to traditional school grammar, in that it helps teachers learn to show students how their language can be displayed in ways that are similar to the ways a painter uses color and texture in paintings. My students have found the CD-ROM that accompanies the text very useful, too, because it provides over fifty specific grammar lessons and sample passages that help illustrate key points.

Weaver, Constance. (Ed.) 1998. *Lessons to Share*. Portsmouth, NH: Boynton/Cook Heinemann. Whenever I need help in finding a way to make grammar study accessible to students (university teacher-candidates or high-school students), I turn to Constance Weaver's texts. A theorist and researcher, Weaver has collected essays from teachers who testify to the power of teaching grammar as part of a broader curriculum of language study. From a chapter on ESL instruction to one on teaching from a whole language perspective at the university level, this collection offers thought-provoking essays and specific suggestions for classroom use. (This text also includes a chapter by Harry Noden on his concept of "image grammar"; see entry above.)

Simmons, John S. and Lawrence Baines. (Eds.) 1998. *Language Study in Middle School, High School, and Beyond*. Newark, DE: International Reading Association. This is a fine text for teachers who are interested in several different perspectives on ways that language study can be conceived and implemented in secondary schools. My favorite chapter is perhaps the one by sociolinguist Walt Wolfram, who discusses how to take advantage of what students already know about the ways their language works, even when they are speakers of "non-standard" dialects.

4 *Animated Literature*

In this dialogue, Laura—an idealistic intern with a passion for the power of literature—bemuses her encounters with a mentor who relies heavily on a non-stop barrage of classic novels and plays. Beaten down by predictable presentations and teacher-generated interpretations, Laura bemoans the plight of her uninspired students, as she tries to envision and plot her future plans to make literature resonate and sing.

The Reading Aloud Rap

Dear Mike,

Friday, we read *Gulliver's Travels*. The kids took turns reading aloud. It was so slow and boring. It was also *very* hot in the classroom and most of the kids were struggling to stay awake. I felt so sorry for them. They are going to be doing this for the entire month! HELP! How can these poor kids stand it? How else could it be done? Maybe novels are not good for this age (ninth grade). It takes so long to read aloud in class.

Myself, I don't pay attention to reading aloud for long periods. I think I would rather teach themes and use lots of different activities, readings, and writing. These kids do very little writing. As a matter of fact, they do little other than listening. They don't do discussions and never group work. They also sit in rows at tables to read. No one can see anyone else. Sitting in a circle might help a little. Maybe even some silent reading interspersed with some activities along with the reading aloud? It sure is going to be a long month for them. Wish me luck!

Laura

Dear Laura,

Literature is like music, and I dare say that few individuals will ever learn to appreciate classical music by listening to a room full of novice violinists squawking through Bach or Beethoven for an hour every darned day. If anything, the listener will tune it out and begin to abhor these geniuses even more. Hey, you, yourself, admitted as much. "Myself, I don't pay attention to reading aloud for long periods." Not when the performance is stumblebum city.

It's been my experience that low-level (and a lot of general skills) students massacre literature when they read it aloud. What it iterates to them is the two-fold lesson they've learned repeatedly in their public schooling experience—their reading skills are not up to par and they hate literature.

Think back to elementary school. Most of us fondly recall "story time" when the teacher would pick up a book and transport us to such faraway and magical places as Oz or Whoville. At that point in our lives, literature seemed wondrous—not burdensome or tedious. Somewhere along the assembly line of education, that readerly love all too often gets lost, and students begin to abhor reading. By the time these same students reach secondary school, many of them have quit reading for leisure or pleasure. That's why literature—especially the old classic stuff—is such a hard sell. As a result, teachers in general classes must deliver the goods. We must make classic Lit live and breathe. And by using the oral tradition, we animate and illustrate and pontificate our passion for the muse.

In addition, we must involve our students, though, by requiring them to truly think, to honestly respond, and to critically evaluate the themes and character motivations inherent in the Lit. By doing so, we offer our students the opportunity to come up with their own right answers and connections to the texts. We afford them the creative space to embrace or reject the writerly notions of Twain and Angelou, Cather or Shakespeare. Of course, once we give the students true latitude and leeway in their reflections, we must hold them accountable for how and why they think and reason and figure and respond in such unique terms and manners. In other words, responding to literature should be just as artistically and critically effusive and moving as the primary source of inspiration. And as literary crusaders, we have an obligation to doggedly defend our high-minded discipline by not denigrating our artistic endeavors into some multiple-choice, true-or-false grilling especially designed to check and quiz and pester our budding readers with the petty details of who did what, when, where, how, and with whom. Art and life are more noteworthy than that.

Thus, the problem isn't with *Gulliver's Travels*—it's with such a laborious and slow-paced presentation. Studies have shown that people actually learn to read better by listening and following along in a text. In Jim Trelease's book, *The Read-Aloud Handbook*, he suggests that reading aloud to students helps them develop and improve literacy skills—reading, writing, speaking, and listening. He also suggests that since young people listen on a higher level than they read, listening to other readers stimulates growth and understanding of language patterns and vocabulary.

That's why it is so important for teachers to read aloud to their classes! And if we're choosing a novel for the class to study, then the main objective should be for the novel to come to life. So we shouldn't beat that sucker to death by having students plod through material they haven't read beforehand and practiced. Hence, teachers have an obligation to become facilitators of the musicality of the muse. We should all strive to make the prose and poetics sing and soar and lift the spirit. You might also try using the assistance of audio tapes. Gary Sinese does a fine job with *Of Mice and Men*, and I'm sure there are capable tapes of *Gulliver's Travels*.

Of course, if the class is full of solid, independent readers (advanced, honors, college prep), then having the students read silently isn't a bad strategy at all. In general classes, though, you usually have a wide disparity of reading levels. So, if you assign a certain amount of pages for a class discussion, it may prove to be a challenge to keep some of the students up to speed. In addition, it's also very difficult for a lot of young readers to catch the subtleties of ancient texts without a teacher's guidance. And face it, Mr. Swift is not only ancient, but he was satirizing the politics of another country on another continent in another century. For students to totally buy into the experience, the teacher must help fill in the gaps.

Thus, a curriculum (or any curriculum) should be founded on student needs. That's what makes teaching English so exciting. Every student, every class, every year is unique. As a result, flexibility and adaptability become the "tuned-in" teacher's strength, while rigidity and predictability become his downfall. Obviously, you may not be in a position where you can alter your cooperating teacher's format. But if given the opportunity, you should try to incorporate some activities to accentuate the issues that the novel raises. Find some poems, newspaper articles, music, TV clips, artwork, or journal entries that thematically tie in with the book.

Remember—the best way to keep the class (and yourself) jazzed and totally on track is to continually be trekking with a multiplicity of insightful stimuli.

And finally, I'm not saying, "Kids should never read aloud." But when they do, they should read something with which they're familiar—a poem or lyric they've practiced, or a story they've already read, or better yet, something they've written for the class. Usually that will improve their delivery.

Respectfully,
Mike

Avoiding Meaningless Tests and Discourses

Dear Mike

I'm perplexed. The grades on the test over the novel were awful. It was an open-book test over *Gulliver's Travels*. The page numbers were given to them. I figured that after reading the material, having access to the book and notes and being given the page numbers to find the answers, they would have aced this one. They didn't! I don't understand why.

The students who seemed to be the most involved were the ones with the lowest grades. Perhaps their attention was feigned, and they really don't care. Perhaps their participation is another means of attention seeking. Perhaps grades are not a good enough reward. This last theory I suppose I can understand. Grades were never an incentive for me in high school. I didn't care, either. The difference was—I didn't pretend to, either.

After reading your last e-mail, I asked Mrs. M. if she did any activities or instruction that would relate the story to the kids personally. She stated that she is planning to do that later in the instruction. This seems to me to be of utmost importance and should be done at the beginning to make the students want to learn.

I believe all literature is written so that the readers may learn something about themselves and human nature in general. *Gulliver's Travels* is a prime example of this. The author was satirizing the government and human nature. Neither has changed that much. The government still promotes people for their ability to "suck up." They still show cruelty to the citizens and may as well "produce and eat the children" for they show no compassion to the people and are insensitive while they strive to succeed individually and as a nation. And human nature in general is still more inhumane than the horses in the land of the Houyhnhnms. These are the things I believe we, as readers, should be learning from great works such as *Gulliver's Travels*. We should be looking for similarities and symbolism to teach us something about ourselves. We should be seeing ourselves and realizing the need to improve ourselves and doing it!

This is where my question comes in. My goal for teaching is to help adolescents look at themselves, see the faults, and improve their lives, attitudes, and goals to become more humane individuals. I realize that everything I do, see, and experience, I see as an avenue to learn by and change myself to become a better person. In this way, I suppose I am very philosophical. Placing this way of approaching life into the classroom and the lives of the children I teach (not in a controlling manner, but rather with guidance and motivation) is what my husband claims is a desire to "save the world." I guess this is my goal. To save the world, one student at a time. If I can reach one—and that one becomes a better person because of my guidance and instruction—I have fulfilled my goal. I would rather reach many, though. This is my reason for wanting to teach. Am I wrong? Are my goals too idealistic? Am I too philosophical for this job?

Please reply!

Laura

Dear Laura,

Perhaps the page numbers and open books and notes weren't enough incentive to make the students care about the test. Obviously, the grades didn't seem to matter. Failure is acceptable. Which brings us to your main point. Why didn't they buy into this experience? I'll venture a guess that the test was more of a regurgitative explanation of who did what, when, and where. In other words, the students had to be able to successfully plot the plot like a dot-to-dot. Consequently, the students probably weren't required to put much of themselves on their papers. They weren't required to relate the material to themselves. They weren't required to have passion for their own ideas and connections to the text. Basically, they weren't really required to think. Sometimes, when we ask so little of someone—so little is given in return.

But, don't kid yourself.

I'm not sure if "all literature is written so that the readers may learn something about themselves and human nature in general." However, I do agree that
as secondary-school teachers, all (or most) of our instructional efforts should be
geared to "relate the story to them (the students) personally." These are your words,
Laura—and don't tell your husband I said this (or go ahead if you want), but you're
exactly right about everything you've said concerning your "reasons for wanting
to teach."

That's why teaching thematically is so important. It requires the teacher to
find literature that will help the student readers "learn something about themselves and human nature in general." For instance, I still teach *Grapes of Wrath* to
my eleventh-grade honors classes, even though it was required reading for jun-
iors way back in '68 when I was that same age. However, the themes of capital-
ism run amuck, the division of classes, the destruction of the environment, and
the spiritual struggles of a nation torn by wealth and poverty are all relevant today. It inspires the students to talk about how the Super Walmarts have run the
mom-and-pop stores out of business, and to bemoan the pesticides in the farm-
ing and food industries, and to ponder the lack of spiritual oneness in a nation
torn between haves and have-nots. We follow up *Grapes* by reading T. Coraghessan
Boyle's novel *Tortilla Curtain*. It's a terrific satire about yuppies and illegal immigrants in contemporary California, and it echoes many of Steinbeck's same themes.

As you can well imagine, this is important stuff for American students to
ponder. And in those wee hours of the daybreak on my way to school, I feel like
I'm tackling a significant task, trying to save the world, one student and one class
at a time. Am I wrong? Are my goals too idealistic? Am I too philosophical for
this job?

I don't think so, Laura. I'm just an English teacher taking my responsibility
and this opportunity seriously.

Respectfully,
Mike

Making the Bard Relevant

Dear Mike,

Thank you for the words of encouragement, but things on the old school
front have gone from bad to worse. We've finished *Gulliver's Travels*, and we're jumping into *A Midsummer Night's Dream*.

This is a class with a lot of "problem learners." The boys in the back kept
raising their hands to read, and Mrs. M. didn't seem to pay them any attention. If
they are interested enough to volunteer to read, she should call on them. I think
she is trying to get the "good" readers to read aloud. Sure the play goes better
with people who read aloud well but isn't our job to interest ALL students in learning? If these boys want to read Shakespeare—why not?

One African-American boy even said one day that Shakespeare wasn't for
black people. Mrs. M. told him about Othello, but we're not reading Othello! I

think it is important to let the African-American students partake in the play. Keeping students interested and busy also keeps them from disruptive behaviors.

Laura

Dear Laura,

1. How effective is this oral reading?
2. Is Shakespeare coming to life in the arena or is it falling on deaf ears?
3. How can you include the disenfranchised African-American kids in the classroom? Will equal distribution of oral reading parts bring rapture to their hearts?

Respectfully,
Mike

Dear Mike,

Answering your questions:

1. The oral reading seems to be going better this time around because she's relying on her best readers. Most readers and listeners seem to be "getting" it. If they don't, Mrs. M. does a summary on the overhead.
2. I guess Shakespeare seems to be coming to life for most of these kids. They fight over getting to participate. There is also very little "goofing off" while the reading is going on, which to me indicates that they are interested in the play.
3. The "boys in the back" issue is a difficult one. I'm not sure that equal distribution of oral reading parts is the answer, but it sure could help make the boys a part of the play. Sometimes using literature that is more African-American may also help them to feel a part of the classroom. Maybe spend some time on something like "Thank You Ma'am" by Langston Hughes, for example. Not as part of a Black History Month. Just by using works by and about African-Americans within each unit. Maybe Mrs. M. could show a clip of a Shakespeare video with African-American actors. That would be good for the young man that said Shakespeare isn't for black people.

Sincerely,
Laura

Dear Laura,

Literature (and I mean any Lit) should never be looked at as a black or white thing. In other words, it's our job to figure out our audience (the students) and where their interests lie. Therefore, the curriculum should be a true reflection of our desire to reach them (the students). It shouldn't just be a list of our favorite plays or novels or short stories or poems (although it helps to be enthusiastic about what we teach).

Obviously, this has its drawbacks when anthologies are all a teacher can access. Is *A Midsummer Night's Dream* in an anthology? If so, then forgive me, but the publishers screwed up. That's not to suggest that this particular play is lousy (I happen to really love it). But, obviously the play is having some serious problems connecting with certain students in this class (the boys in back). Compounded with that is their lack of participation and inclusion. They aren't "allowed" to read. So they feel even more alienated.

Of course, I'm going on and on about what you've already indicated in your earlier reflection. I'm just trying to give you plenty to think about for future use. (This class, of course, is Mrs. M.'s—not yours). However, Shakespeare can speak to most students when the themes are more universal. *Romeo and Juliet, Othello, Hamlet*, even *Julius Caesar* (which have all been anthologized for eons) are all classic choices because they deal with human themes of oppression, envy, and betrayal. And almost everyone on the planet can relate to that.

As for the oral component, it's been my experience as a teacher to utilize both audio and video tapes to "turn kids on to Shakespeare." As you pointed out, the students in the back feel left out when they aren't allowed to read. If Mrs. M. allowed everyone to read, and not just the good readers, would hearing the more challenged readers slowly stumble over the prose make the play live and breathe for the accelerated students? Probably not. (Go back and reread your musings about listening to them beat *Gulliver's Travels* to death.) There are great tapes from BBC radio broadcasts that are very lively and exciting to follow while the students silently read along in their texts. If videos are accessible, then having them watch the sequence for a particular act is a very effective way to iterate the action. Remember, plays are written for the stage, so seeing them acted out is essential. In many ways, it's better to watch the scenes first, then refer to excerpts from the text for clarity and emphasis.

Of course, this implies that the teacher should stop periodically to discuss what's up with an act, but writing down a review of what happened on the overhead may be a bit too specific. An even bigger danger with the overhead is if the interpretations of the play become too teacher directed. We should always try to refrain from interjecting and imposing too much of our own "correct" analyses on our students. We should strive to have the students discover the themes by truly writing and sharing their thoughts on the actions of the characters by giving the students some reader response prompts to write and share and discuss, leaving them plenty of room for interpretation. These are ways to include everyone.

Naturally, there will be times (and quite a few of them) when some students will not tune into almost anything we try to do (the slack factor is a reality). However, we should be concerned about the opportunity of inclusion for each and every student. After all, the students are our captive audience, and we (the teachers) are the masters of their cell blocks. So the key to keeping our little prisoners happy is to unlock their hearts by tapping and gently rapping into themes that will pitter-patter their way into their all-too-often hardened hearts. Therefore, I'm not too sure if a quiet and obedient classroom wherein the teacher demands silence and then writes down the interpretation of each act on an overhead for everyone to copy and take home to memorize is an indication of students really "getting" Shakespeare. It's probably more of an indication of the central power station in the classroom.

Respectfully,
Mike

Encouraging Silent Sustained Reading

Dear Mike,

   I've been thinking a lot about what you've been saying with regard to oral reading, and I must say I agree to a point. However, I am concerned if kids never have to actively read, they will get lazy and depend on the teacher or the audio tapes for entertainment. How can we motivate reluctant readers to actually read?

Laura

Dear Laura,

   Naturally, we must encourage our young people to read in a silent, sustained manner. That's why it's so important to supplement our literary classroom adventures with a free-reading workshop, wherein these reluctant readers can discover their readerly bliss without the restrictions of a certain number of books and pages, or a minimum amount of book reporting. All I require from my students is full participation during the half-hour sessions, a reader's log that tracks every literary piece they finish or abandon, and a biweekly personal letter to me, recounting their adventures. In these letters, they write about what they liked, loved, or hated in the stories, poems, plays, nonfiction narratives, or novels they've been reading. (They must read literature—no magazines, comic books, or newspapers.) They write about their personal connections with the characters and the plots. They write about their affinity or displeasure with the author's style. They write about what they're yearning to read next. And I write them each back a letter, sharing my own adventures and my enthusiasm for their adventures. We ask each other questions; we correspond. So far, this unencumbered discourse has proven to be one of the most productive aspects of my teaching career. It's an idea I stole from Nancie Atwell's terrific book, *In the Middle*. The teacherly objective? To get students hooked on books and to get them to respond like true readers. Nothing will improve their learning capabilities or their writing abilities more than if they read, read, read.

Respectfully,
Mike

The Importance of Variety

Dear Mike,

   Wednesday, the class was out of control. Mrs. M. said it had been as bad a day as she has ever had. Virtually everyone was rowdy and totally nuts. I really think Mrs. M. should be reading your e-mail. She needs some back-up plans or variations of activities. All the students did was copy off the overhead. They needed something where they could move around or talk or SOMETHING. Seems they could have had some kind of interactive game to review the play. Mrs. M. spent the entire hour just saying "Be quiet," "Sit down," and "You are driving me crazy!" The students don't care; they want to drive her crazy (one point for their side).

Ever since the Shakespeare play has begun, the class hasn't had much variety in activities. They take turns reading the play, then Mrs. M. goes over the different acts on the overhead. Any words of wisdom?

Laura

Dear Laura,

In this day and age, students thrive on stimuli and varied stimuli and enthusiasm and unpredictability. That's not to suggest that they don't need structure. Every lesson should have a well-defined form to its content. But when Shakespeare of all things is taught with overheads and blah, blah, blah, readings that go on and on every darned day, then the natives become restless, and an uprising swells into a tornado of anarchy. To quell such an insurgence of chaos, the teacher must be creative—not predictably mundane. That's why I liked your interactive game review idea. Figure out a way to make that happen. Your brainstorming ideas for activities show a lot of promise, too. Hang on to them and use them.

Which brings me to my biggest question: What's on those transparencies? The teacher's interpretation of the plot, theme, and character motivations? Just exactly what kind of information is shedding the light for these students who are literally sitting in the dark and blowing off the Bard?

It's also a bit disconcerting that your teacher keeps feeding these young adolescent students extended classic works without varying the stimuli. In the throes of a novel or play, a thematic mix of poetry, short stories, newspaper articles, songs, and nonfiction narratives is imperative. An occasional young adult novel wouldn't be a bad idea, either. There are plenty of high-interest adolescent reading materials that mirror the themes of classic Lit. And as teachers, we should utilize any and all avenues to peak our students' interest in the world of literary ideas and notions.

Respectfully,
Mike

Getting Responses That Count

Dear Mike,

Boy, am I getting frustrated. This teacher I'm working with is the head of the department and is supposedly "such a good teacher." BUT she does things so NOT the right way. She gave me their reading logs from the play to bring home and grade.

First, they didn't reflect on what they felt about the reading, but they wrote about what she TOLD them to write down off the overhead—word for word. To grade them, I had to give them five points for writing down the information and five points for responding. BUT the teacher said, "Don't read what they wrote in the response, just give them five points if there are any words written where the reflections go on the paper." *What*? That doesn't follow any of the reader response types of experiences I've learned about and how to use reflective logs.

Sincerely,

Laura

Dear Laura,

All too often overhead notes are specifically designed to spoon-feed critical information that a teacher expects his or her students to know and to learn so that they can regurgitate it. Isn't that ironic (or moronic)? It's a very bulimic concept. Teachers force-feed that which they want regurgitated. And how can one grow from that? Could this be the basis for a sound nutritional diet? Definitely not. Students need brain food chock full of heady thoughts. So, you're right!

Readers need to respond. Their journal topics should be reflective connections to the texts, to the characters' motivations, to the themes, to the conflicts, and to the issues as they relate to the world today. The brain is like a muscle. It needs exercise. As teachers, we need to require more mental fitness in our classrooms. We need to buff up our students' gray matter.

To do that, we must inspire and require our little darlings to actually think. To think critically. To think creatively. To ponder. To wax nostalgic. To analyze. To dissect. To express. To experience.

Thus, we must not be lazy teachers. We must work hard—not hardly work. I met an intern once at a conference who told me that her mentor's grading procedure on a five-paragraph essay consisted solely of counting to see if the students wrote five paragraphs. Talk about lame-o! We have an obligation to read and respond to what our students write. The content should be as much or more important than the form. Unfortunately, it sounds like your mentor is hardly working. I'm proud that you're so appalled. And my heart goes out to those little darlings. And to you, too.

Respectfully,

Mike

On Becoming a Democracy and Making a Play Sing

Dear Mike,

On Monday this week, Mrs. M. made me get up and lead the reading of the first act of *Pygmalion*. That was the extent of it, too. I read the narrator's parts. Students took roles and read. The parts were already assigned, and the assignment was supposed to take up the whole class period. Toward the end of the first act, I noticed that people were falling asleep. I made everyone stop and asked how they could be doing the play differently. Answers came flying out—the readers were boring, they didn't like to read plays out loud, and it was easier to follow if they read it to themselves. My solution was to reassign the parts to people who really wanted to read. I gave the actors the rest of the period to review their lines, then the next day I told them to get in front of the class and read with feeling. I was surprised at the results. The parts were played out with emotion, and the vocal inflection the students had was amazing. I don't think I will ever have my students read a play out loud from their chairs now. I will definitely assign parts beforehand, and be very upset if the students have not reviewed his or her part in the play.

Even worse, I had never read the play and was unable to lead any type of discussion. I felt very useless as an instructor. I took a book home and read parts of it before Tuesday's class. Therefore, I had a little better grip on the theme and plot for the reading.

The next day, I led the reading again, but included more discussion of language as a theme. I tried to relate it to contemporary life, focusing on the way people are stereotyped because of language usage, particularly Southern speech. For example, one girl pointed out that Southerners are considered to be stupid because of the slang and dialect that is used. In the play, the same type of stereotyping based on language is satirized. I asked a lot of questions and provided very little interpretation, but rather allowed the students to form their own ideas and interpretations, while guiding them with the items I wanted them to focus on. I asked students to back up their reflections with examples from the reading. This seemed to cause the students to pay closer attention to the plot and order of the play. Most of the students were responsive in both of the classes and one student, who claimed to have slept through the previous readings, was attentive and inserted opinions about the play.

I enjoyed today much better than Monday. I would rather be teaching than simply observing or doing the clerical work. I know that is a part of it, but the instructing is the icing on the cake. The students' participation and success are the decorative flowers that make teaching a beautiful art! I look forward to having a class of my own.

Sincerely,

Laura

Dear Laura,

If I were in your shoes, I'd be clicking my heels the same way. The stereotyping issue is key to understanding the conflict in the play. Down the road, the power of accumulating a mastery of language also plays heavily into the theme.

Most of all, I'm impressed with how you're interested in guiding them toward issues and themes, but you're allowing them to discover these things on their own terms (with a little kid glove pushing along). It's also noble that you stopped and changed courses when it appeared that the ship was sinking. Dozing mates is not a good way to keep a lesson afloat. You opened the class up into a democracy, and the students not only responded, but bought into the format. They felt like they were a part of something, and that makes a huge difference.

As you noted, the inflection of the readers' voices was also the key. Undoubtedly, assigning parts and having the students practice before they read in class helps make the literature come to life.

Most of all, I'm glad you had the experience of trying to wing it—as opposed to taking the text home and hunkering down with it and then coming up with a game plan. Without me belaboring the point, you've discovered the importance of being several steps ahead of the class and knowing how you want the text handled. You're cooking.

Respectfully,
Mike

FROM ANOTHER ANGLE

Like many of us, Laura is drawn to the teaching of English partly because she loves literature. She wants to pass along this passion to secondary-school students, and hopes to help them develop lifelong habits of reading and thinking about print texts. Yet Laura's initial observations and experiences in teaching literature have little relation to the ideal she has imagined. She is disturbed by literature classes that seem lifeless and inconsequential, by lessons that do not touch the students' lives. She wonders if the problem lies in her expectations, the texts being assigned students, the approaches used by her cooperating teacher, or a combination of these aspects of the experience. In Mike and Laura's conversations about the teaching and learning of literature, the pair address a variety of significant questions about the ways literature is presented and studied in secondary school.

Whose Interpretations Should Count?

The foundation that our English education program relies on (with regard to literature instruction and learning) is grounded in transactional theory and reader response-based approaches to literature. The theory has grown popular along with the emergence of constructivist theories of learning. Its most influential proponent is Louise Rosenblatt and her book *Literature as Exploration* (first published in 1938; published in 1996 in its 5th edition). According to Rosenblatt, we create "poems" out of printed texts when we bring our own experiences, knowledge, and expectations to bear on the text during reading. This view privileges the reader, even when the reader is a student. It also assigns the reader the responsibility for taking an active role as a meaning maker. In other words, transactional theory suggests that it is up to the reader, who uses the author's written text as the frame of reference for constructing an interpretation—not a critic, not the teacher—to determine what a text "means."

This view requires substantial change in the kind of role that teachers have traditionally played in the study of literature. In the past, teachers have told students what authors "mean." The traditional approach is tidy, because students learn what the teacher knows about a text, then merely have to remember and reiterate that knowledge on tests of literary understanding. In contrast, classrooms that are informed by transactional theory and that feature reader-response approaches are messier. They are characterized by sessions in which students engage in careful reading and study of texts, in which they work to connect texts to their lives and to determine for themselves what the texts "say." The teacher cannot decide, ahead of time, what a text will say to a particular reader, since the teacher cannot know what the reader brings to bear on his or her reading of the text. Yet because readers themselves breathe life into literature in these classrooms, it is these classrooms in which the teacher has a fine opportunity to show students how, in Mike' words, "the prose and the poetics sing and soar and lift the spirit." These are the classes that will allow Laura to work toward her goal of using literature as a place for "looking for similarities and symbolism to teach us something about ourselves . . . seeing ourselves . . ."

There is still a place for critics' and teachers' interpretations of texts, in reader response-based approaches, but only as examples of others' renderings, not as examples of privileged or necessarily "correct" readings. There are "wrong" interpretations when readers fail to notice clues and cues that the author gives them, or when he or she makes too much of insignificant details. Nevertheless, in classrooms based on reader response approaches, the literary event—and the construction of meaning of the text—belongs to the individual reader.

How Can Students Participate As Meaning Makers?

The preservice teachers with whom we work frequently participate in secondary classrooms in which teachers have not had experience using reader response-based approaches. In those situations, the preservice teachers feel off balance (Laura's frustration is an example). They want to develop lessons in which students are active participants, lessons that show respect for adolescents as thinkers, and help them explore the world—including their own lives—through the medium of literature. My colleagues and I feel that we need to continue to encourage the student teachers to introduce response-based approaches, and believe that there are ways to integrate such approaches even in more traditional settings.

In *Teaching Literature in the Secondary School* (1997), Richard Beach and James Marshall, who are literature theorists and pedagogical specialists, too, present a compelling description of various entry points through which readers can begin to explore written texts. They refer to the points as the "response strategies" that collectively "comprise a reader's full response to the text being read" (28). Student teachers have often reported that the response strategies have been useful to them as they begin to design, implement, and evaluate lessons for their secondary-school students. While Mrs. M. seems to believe that only experts can determine the meanings of literary texts, and that "knowing" a work of literature is the equivalent of "knowing" what an expert has said about it, Laura has learned to see literary events in a different way. She understands that readers who devote time and effort to literary transactions should be able to expect a reward that goes well beyond a good test grade. As Mike suggests, "The main objective should be for the novel to come to life." Although reading aloud is one way to ensure that students hear artistic language, and that they have at least heard the text, the strategy is often overused. Often, too, when unskilled or inexperienced readers are called upon to read aloud, students' enthusiasm for the text, and the momentum created by interest in the progress of the story, is lost for the entire class.

Laura's notes to Mike give us no evidence that Mrs. M.'s students are ever actually engaged with the texts, using any of the response strategies identified by Beach and Marshall. Instead, she reports that they seem interested in Shakespeare, since "They fight over getting to participate" in oral reading, and since "There is also very little goofing off while the reading in going on." Perhaps, though, what Laura interprets as students' interest could also be explained as their interest in gaining public attention and in passing the class hour quickly.

Mike's suggestions about using professional recordings of readings of literary texts, and his stated instructional preference, which is "to animate an author's prose with [his] own eloquence" are simple and effective strategies. They remove the problem of poor reading skills interfering with readers' ability to enter the world of the texts, even when the readers are ninth graders and the texts are by Shakespeare or Swift. Instead of treating literature as a problem to solve, Mike's approach to literature encourages student readers to see it as an art to be enjoyed.

We can only speculate about the reasons that Mrs. M. chooses to teach literature as though artistic texts are problems that can be solved only with precise, singular, expert answers, instead of being seen as organic entities. We can only speculate about why she views her interpretations, and those of critics, as more valuable than those generated by adolescent readers. Perhaps she is pushed for time, and knows that it will be easier to test students over a list of facts about a text that she presents to them, than to ask them to develop, articulate, and evaluate their own feelings about, and interpretations of, the texts. But we do know, with certainty, that there are other ways of viewing literature teaching and learning. Beach and Marshall remind us that with response strategies, the reader can be given the responsibility for making sense of the literary work. When readers are made responsible for constructing meaning, the teacher and students have the opportunity to be continually surprised by the variety of responses evoked by one text, and by the different interpretations of the text that emerge. In this way, literature instruction is a creative action; even when a teacher returns to a favorite text year after year, the text retains its wonder, because different readers, if given the freedom to deal with the text on their own terms, will come up with unexpected, new readings.

How Can We Select Texts and Create Engaging Activities?

One element of the conversations between Laura and Mike that caught my attention was the list of texts that Mrs. M. was having her groups of ninth graders read during one fifteen-week period: *Gulliver's Travels, Midsummer Night's Dream,* and *Pygmalion*. I would recommend that any teacher of ninth graders consider supplementing such classic fare with adolescent literature, books selected based on their thematic or topical appeal to the students in the class, books that will open up conversations about issues that are immediately significant in adolescents' lives. Adolescent literature holds appeal for secondary-school readers, particularly at the middle-school and early high school level, because it typically features teenage protagonists in situations that highlight problems that many teens face, including alienation, changing relationships with families and friends, pressures regarding sexual activity, peer pressure, decisions regarding their futures, and so on. Student readers see themselves in adolescent and young adult literature. They want to learn about how others, even fictitious characters, navigate the world they are traveling through, and therefore are drawn to adolescent and young adult books. We can take advantage of the appeal of these books in secondary classrooms.

As a preservice teacher who is only months away from her first paid teaching job, Laura has read many adolescent novels in her English education program. However, like many of her classmates, she may not recognize that some of those books, or others in the genre, could complement her literature instruction, even if Mrs. M. or the school insists that she include canonical texts such as *Pygmalion* and *Gulliver's Travels*. Yet, Joan Kaywell's *Adolescent Literature as a Complement to the Classics*, vol. I, II, III, IV (1993, 1995, 1997, 2000) is for teachers interested in adolescent or young adult literature. Every chapter in the series is written by an expert in adolescent literature who pairs a classic text or texts with adolescent books, and suggests teaching activities that engage readers of all abilities in the study of meaningful texts. Virginia Monseau and Gary Salvner's *Reading Their World: The Young Adult Novel in the Classroom* (2000) is a fine collection of essays by specialists in the young adult literature field, one that is worth keeping on the teacher's desk. These may help Laura find just the right books to balance the classics that Mrs. M. prefers.

Along with text selection, another troubling aspect of Laura's experience is the paucity of interesting, engaging literature activities introduced to the students with which she is working. There is a danger that students will leave Mrs. M.'s class with the opinion that reading literature is boring and frustrating, that they must rely on someone else to interpret texts for them, and that their own ideas are not good enough. However, when Laura writes, in exasperation, "These kids do very little writing. As a matter of fact, they do little other than listening. They don't do discussions and never group work," she is actually beginning to address these concerns. She recognizes that readers need to be encouraged to become involved with texts—to write and talk and wonder about them. With a list of response possibilities such as the one provided by Beach and Marshall (included above), she can continue to build a repertoire of ideas for getting students involved in literary events.

What Does It Mean to "Know" Literature, and How Do We Measure That Knowledge?

Yet another problem that Laura encountered was the implementation of seemingly punitive tests that followed each literature unit. Laura, like all preservice teachers, must develop a collection of methods for evaluating her students' growth in literary understanding. Further, the evaluation methods must reflect her goals as a teacher of literature. If she wants students to retain facts about the author, to reiterate minutiae of the texts, or feel how far from the insights presented by literary critics their own thinking is, perhaps traditional tests like those administered by Mrs. M. would seem appropriate. Yet Laura reports:

> I'm perplexed. The grades on the test over the novel were awful. It was an open book test. . . . The page numbers were given to them. I figured that after reading the material, having access to the book and notes and being given the page numbers to find the answers, they would have aced this one. They didn't! I don't understand why.

Further, she notes that "the students who seemed to be the most involved were the ones with the lowest grades," then hypothesizes that "Perhaps their attention was feigned, and they really didn't care. Perhaps their participation is another means of attention seeking. Perhaps grades are not a good enough reward." Part of Laura's confusion is created by the fact that she has learned that readers who are interested in a work of literature are more likely to "learn" that literature than readers who have no interest in it. If she had seen students' previous performances on Mrs. M.'s literature tests, Laura may not have been so surprised. I would add two hypotheses to Laura's list regarding the students' failure to do well on a test when so much information is provided: one possibility is that the test questions might not mirror the kinds of questions and instructional focal points that preceded the test. Another is that, since the students cannot read Mrs. M.'s mind, they fail when she asks them to interpret the text in the way that she interprets it.

If Laura wants to make the texts "come alive" for students, she will have to carefully consider what she will look for as evidence that students have experienced the texts as living entities. In literature study, perhaps even more than with other parts of the English curriculum, we can develop evaluations that continue the learning process, instead of ones that denote an end to it. In other words, literature learning can continue during the evaluation process.

Recently, I asked one class of preservice teachers to list alternatives for traditional multiple-choice and essay test methods for assessing and evaluating students' literature learning, and to explain the teaching goals that are compatible with the evaluative methods. Items on their collective list include these:

- Perform a role play in which characters from the story are put together, in a new time, place, or situation (particularly effective if the goal is for students to comprehend characters' motivations and relationships).

- Create tableaux of the most significant scenes in the story (particularly effective if the goal is for students to consider the impact of individual scenes on the development of plot and conflict, or to determine which scene is most important to an individual reader in his or her evocation of the literary work).

- Record a collection of popular songs that could be used as a soundtrack for a movie of the story (particularly effective if the goal is for students to consider the themes of the literary piece, and to make personal connections to the text).

- Create a newspaper that presents the main actions in the story, and that gives attention to the main characters (particularly effective if the goal is a general understanding of how different literary elements contribute to the overall sense of the piece).

- Hold a "Socratic seminar," or oral examination, in which each student answers thought-provoking questions about the ways he or she interprets and makes sense of the text (especially effective if the goal is for students to feel that they are responsible for their own interpretations of the text, and that those interpretations must combine attention to their reactions and to the text itself).

In each example on this short list, the learning of literature extends after the reading of the text is completed; each encourages readers to recognize the impact that literature can have on their thinking, and on their understanding of self and others. Each encourages teachers and students to view literature as an entity that has the potential to "come alive." Not one depends on a single "right answer" or holds one person's interpretation over another's. And each allows us to find "the heavenly space" that Mike believes that we inhabit as teachers during those special moments when connections connect, the musings muse, the fuses fuse.

I also recommend these sources of ideas for literature activities. Each features practical reader response-based strategies for activities that invite students to participate in learning.

Allen, Janet and Kyle Gonzalez. 1998. *There's Room for Me Here*. Portland, ME: Stenhouse.

Beach, Richard and James Marshall. 1997. *Teaching Literature in the Secondary School*. Belmont, CA: Wadsworth.

Golub, Jeffery N. 2000. *Making Learning Happen*. Portsmouth, NH: Boynton/Cook Heinemann.

Gregg, Gail P. and Pamela S. Carroll. 1998. *Books and Beyond: Thematic Approaches for Teaching Literature in High School*. Norwood, MA: Christopher-Gordon.

Jago, Carol. 2000. *With Rigor for All: Teaching Classics to Contemporary Students*. Portsmouth, NH: Boynton/Cook Heinemann.

Purves, Alan, Theresa Rogers, and Anna O. Soter. 1995. *How Porcupines Make Love, III*. White Plains, NY: Longman.

Rosenblatt, Louise M. 1996. *Literature as Exploration*. Modern Languages Assocation.

Rygiel, Mary Ann. 1992. *Shakespeare Among School Children*. NCTE.

Smith, Michael W. and Jeffrey D. Wilhelm. 2002. *Reading Don't Fix No Chevys*. Portsmouth, NH: Heinemann.

Tsujimoto, Joseph. 2001. *Lighting Fires: How the Passionate Teacher Engages Adolescent Writers*. Portsmouth, NH: Boynton/Cook Heinemann.

Wilhelm, Jeffrey D. and Brian Edmiston. 1998. *Imagining to Learn: Inquiry, Ethics, and Integration through Drama*. Portsmouth, NH: Heinemann.

5

Writing with Soul

Like a lot of passionate teachers, Paul believes that writing is the heart and soul of an English class. Throughout these exchanges, he attempts to shape his philosophy about journals, poetry assignments, peer editing workshops, effective essays, conferencing, and of course, evaluations and grades. More than anything, Paul begins to realize the recursive nature of working with young writers, as he mulls over his successes and failures in emboldening his young wordsmiths.

Journals—Encouraging Voice and Uniqueness

Dear Mike,

In our college classes, we have discussed the benefits of having students freewrite or respond through journals. How do you introduce students, who have never had to journal, to the idea? How do you explain it on the first day of class?

Paul

Dear Paul,

First of all, I'm a total proponent of focused journals that serve as follow-ups or preludes to discussions on literature (especially poetry), news articles, sociopolitical issues concerning school, the state, the nation, the planet, inner space—whatever. Hence, I only evaluate the students (gradewise) for HOW MUCH THEY THINK. And I assure them that I don't want them to THINK LIKE THEY THINK I WANT THEM TO THINK. In other words, it's critical that we offer our students a safe haven for their unique inner selves so they will sound their "barbaric yawps."

When I introduce the concept to my new students, I try to alleviate a lot of the stress factor by telling them that I don't grade for spelling, punctuation, or mechanics. That's why some teachers call journals "free-writes"—the writers are encouraged to become free-range thinkers and writers. And that's why it's paramount that we refrain from brandishing a blood red pen and circling all of the errors in their journals—it's equally important to encourage free thinking.

Therefore my objective for them is to think a whole lot with a bunch of details and tangents and wacky and insightful and humorous and personal stuff. This "personal stuff" needs to be addressed, however, in a manner that doesn't put you—the teacher—in a precarious position. No sex, drugs, or suicidal tendencies. Anything that may be illegal or immoral must be discouraged. If a student starts pouring out any personal issues that may be injurious to them or others, then you have a legal obligation to let your superiors know about it. Students need to know about these perimeters going into this forum. Consequently, it's best to stick to focused issues about characters, themes, and politics that don't gravitate toward exposés about their wild weekends at the Rainbow Gathering.

Journals are an essential part of my "writing is thinking" objective. They are a place for reflection, exploration, and experimentation. And while some teachers never grade or even read student journals (which is legally risky), I find this exchange a wonderful way to encourage voice and uniqueness. In the student journals, I write little comments and plenty of kudos; I also pose questions to encourage further exploration of an interesting idea. Overall, journals make up twenty percent of my grading policy and I have found them to be very rewarding for both my students and my relationship with them. Emerson called his journal his "Savings Bank" of ideas, and I agree with Sir Ralph, wholeheartedly.

Respectfully,

Mike

Letters That Empower

Dear Mike,

The theme we are discussing is discrimination, and this week we are focusing on class discrimination. Mrs. F. read them an article about the new county school being built on the northeast side of town, and yesterday they started writing letters/essays about how their school needs some of the $34 million just to bring it up to state standards. They are so aware of the fact that they don't have books to take home, and that they don't have the luxuries or even the basics in some cases that schools in more affluent areas have. It was very sad. But they were writing! This is the first major writing assignment I have witnessed since I started. The varying levels of writing abilities are amazing, but most of the students were very eager for advice on how to make their letter better or unique. I thoroughly enjoyed the day.

Paul

Dear Paul,

The new high-school letter is a grand idea. I hope the teacher mailed them to the Superintendent and the School Board. Some folks call this "workplace writing," but I call it real-world interaction. Letter writing is empowering; it gives the students a voice in the world around them. It also inspires the students take more pride in their work if someone besides the teacher is going to read their writing—especially in a real-world context. And we should always strive to expand the audience for the students' writing assignments. Plus, teaching activism should be an essential part of any communications course, especially in an underprivileged population. We need to teach students to passionately stand up for themselves by articulating sound logic and espousing high ideals. Letter writing also provides a super opportunity to teach persuasive writing, critical thinking, and sound logic.

In a case like this I would probably start by reading the article followed by an open-ended journal prompt. Then I would open the floor to a discussion which I would counter with the notion of using our expanded base of knowledge to compose a more formal letter to the Superintendent and the School Board. By using journals for self-examination, then opening the floor for a forum on the subject, the students have an opportunity to experience democracy at the apex of its vibrancy. They also have an opportunity to reexamine their positions and major points before engaging in the more formal aspects of persuasive letter writing. Overall, though, your teacher is on the "write" track.

Respectfully,
Mike

Directing Peer Editing

Dear Mike,

The students worked on their letters in a writing workshop atmosphere where they helped set their own goals, told the teacher what they would be working on, and held conferences with one another and the teacher. After a couple periods, it became apparent that there was too much play and not enough work going on, so the teacher did away with the privilege of conferencing with one another. In a way, it's a shame that the workshop format went away (not permanently—she's told them they can get it back—although I'm not exactly sure what they have to do to get it back), but I'm a big believer in dropping something if it doesn't work. So the loss is a shame in one way, but a good thing in another.

Maybe students at the middle-school maturity level need to be eased into something like the workshop. Perhaps a little structure is not a terrible thing?

Thanks,
Paul

Dear Paul,

Traditionally, students seem to have a real problem giving any kind of concrete feedback in a conference that is productive. Most of the time, they just offer innocuous platitudes, such as "It's really good" or "I kind of liked it." Then they'll redline a few misspellings, typos, and grammatical errors. In other words, their feedback isn't just useless, sometimes it can be downright misleading, unsubstantiated, and off base (which doesn't mean to suggest that they should just rip another student's paper, either—that's unproductive, as well).

Poet's Corner Editing Sheet

1. Look at the title for some clue as to what the poem's about.
2. Silently read the poem without stopping to analyze it.
3. Take a gut-check. How does the poem make you feel?

   What do you notice about the poem? What do you like?

   Write a sentence or two explaining.
4. Underline your favorite lines and write a sentence explaining why you like them.
5. Identify the narrator. How do you think the speaker feels? Write a sentence explaining.

Go around the circle and share your reflections...

6. Have someone in the group, other than the poet, read the poem aloud.
7. Mark the lines that contain sensory details and create concrete images in your mind. **Highlight and add a check mark (√).**
8. Mark your favorite line in the poem. **Highlight with a check mark (√).**
9. Mark any lines or phrases that **lack** flow, musicality, or clarity. **Highlight and place a question mark next to them (?).**
10. Mark any crucial moments in the poem where the action shifts, the direction changes, or the meaning alters. **Highlight and add a check mark (√).**

Also consider the language of the poem. Are there any words that seem stilted, too difficult, or too iffy? Are there any words or phrases that lack punch, resonance or poignancy? **Highlight them and place a question mark next to them (?).**

Any places where punctuation seems unnecessary or necessary? **Highlight these spots and put a question mark next to them (?).**

Write in your own words what you think the poem is saying.

Go around the circle again and share all of your marks, highlights, and reflections

Revision strategies—Write a short paragraph for the author clarifying this poem in its best possible form. For example:

In its best possible form, this poem would contain a lot more concrete images. It would eliminate many of the flowery adjectives and replace them with tougher power nouns and verbs. As for the flow, the poem would stick to the structure you created in the first stanza rather than abandoning it with a stream of short, pithy phrases. Some additional punctuation would also make the poem much more powerful. As it is now, there are very few places for the reader to breathe and contemplate. Finally, the poem could use a more poignant and intriguing title.

FIGURE 5–1

That's why I recommend that teachers spend time teaching their students about peer editing. Checklists are important, too. They provide structure and a road map to engage in the editing process. I actually make my peer editors write down their feedback, and I grade them for their insightfulness. I've enclosed a copy of a peer editing workshop that I recently used for a poetry workshop (Figure 5–1). Obviously, since each writing modality is unique, each workshop process should be tweaked to fit that style of writing. But remember that in all drafts, the first and foremost focus should be on content and voice. In other words, we should tune into what the writer is saying and how he or she is saying it. That's why it's so important to find those spots where the writing flows and the focus is sharpest. By pointing out the best in a piece of writing, we give the writer a glimpse and glimmer at the true potential for his or her overall composition.

An interesting, trendsetting book by Peter Elbow called *Writing Without Teachers* might help here. In this text, Elbow suggests some inventive ways for readers to give feedback that is more experiential and holistic—and less grammatical. Nancie Atwell's *In The Middle* also includes some great tips and lists for conferencing and peer editing.

As for the privilege thing, the adage, "If you abuse, you lose" seems most appropriate. When things get out of hand (after several warnings), a teacher may have to restrict the environment by taking away privileges. Most students comprehend this concept and learn that when the teachers say "Silencio," they mean it.

Respectfully,

Mike

Conferencing with Kid Gloves

Dear Mike,

On Friday, a student walked all the way across the room to ask me to "look over" her persuasive letter. Since it was two pages, I asked her if she had a specific question. "No!" She just wanted me to see if it was "okay." Again, I asked her if there was anything she thought she had had difficulty with. Again, "No, just read it and see how it is."

Well, it wasn't very good, frankly. It had so many problems I could take up an entire page writing them down for you. But most evident was the fact that it was unclear just what she was trying to persuade me to do or think. So, I asked her as gently as possible if a person who is unfamiliar with her subject would really understand what her topic was. She thought so (although it was OBVIOUSLY unclear). So, we asked a classmate. The classmate didn't understand it. So—what happened? The student got really upset and ended up resenting my one comment, despite the fact that I repeatedly told her to remember she had asked for my help. Revision is an important part of writing, and I also pointed out two good things about her essay. She obviously wanted me to say "Looks great!" When I didn't, she couldn't handle it. So how do you keep a student from getting mad and shutting down like that?

Paul

Dear Paul,

A key ingredient to a conference is its intimacy. In other words, bringing someone else into the mix (especially another student) circumvents your ability to build a trusting relationship with the student who's coming to you for help. I'm glad you threw in a couple of good comments; that's important. A positive discourse is the key to conferencing. Perhaps if you had quietly confided your own inability to understand her point, then you could have gotten the student to explain it to you orally. At that juncture, you could have easily proceeded. Once the communication lines are open, you can help guide students through their papers and show them where they need to accentuate their arguments so that it's clearer for the readers. You must understand that writing is a very sensitive process, and that students need to feel safe when they come to you asking for your approval of their work. As a result, you must create a safe comfort zone for them and always appear to be approachable. If you put the student on the spot and make her defend her premise, she will undoubtedly become extremely defensive. Looking back, you might see that your "one comment" may basically have been condescending. The student's paper didn't make sense to you and was unclear. That's a pretty scathing indictment of one's work. To back up your analysis, you upped the ante by allowing another student to iterate "your" point. If I were that kid given the same situation, I probably would have gotten on my high horse and ridden right out of there, too. No offense, amigo, but you need to overly sensitize yourself to the kiddos so they won't get mad, shut down, and shut you out.

Respectfully,
Mike

Objectively Grading Writing

Dear Mike,

I was allowed to look over the students' papers and write in notes for them. It was kind of fun, but my eyes started hurting after a while. Nobody did perfect, so I wrote little messages in the margins. The teacher did not tell me to do this, I just felt like it was a good idea. I felt very confident, but after looking at the teacher's notes I felt overcritical. It is an honors English class, and some of the papers were awful but were receiving Bs. Should I ask the teacher what her expectations are, or should I just write what I feel on the papers—as long as I am being helpful (my grade doesn't count anyway).

Thanks,
Paul

Dear Paul,

My main advice would be to ask about your supervising teacher's grading policy. Make sure you don't sound critical of her, just explain that grading is something you're feeling unsure about and you are having trouble figuring out how to properly evaluate the students' papers.

My personal take is that grading (especially of writing) can be very subjective work. Therefore, you must try to have clear objectives to facilitate evaluation. And different kinds of writing merit different objectives. In other words, if you're studying sensory details and that's what you want the students to accentuate—make that a key objective. If it's a persuasive essay—and logic and rational thinking and transitions are good guides—then make them your helpful objectives. If it is vocabulary work and you want all of the words used as their proper part of speech, and you want each vocabulary word clearly defined through the context of its usage—so be it. If you want anything else added to any evaluation of any assignment, such as overall spelling, punctuation, grammar, subject-verb agreement, varying sentence structures, or whatever else—design a system and make sure the students understand the evaluative process. In other words, you should be up front with each assignment and spell out "the terms of the deal" by telling them what you'll focus on when you read to grade before they actually begin to write. In the aftermath of any assignment, you may even want to give the students an opportunity to redo, resubmit, so you can reevaluate their revisions.

Eventually, you will have to come to grips with all of these decisions, so when you see things that you think need improvement in your mentor's system—store that information in your memory bank. For the time being, however, you won't be able to change any of the "systems" to which you are subjected. As an intern, you will probably have to adapt to your supervisor's evaluative process—so learn it, respect it, and follow it. When you become the master of your own domain, then you can reject it and perfect your own method of evaluation.

Overall, though, the more objective you can be, the less subjective your system becomes, and the easier it will be for you and your students to comprehend the evaluative process. For students to feel that a grade is justifiable, they need to know the terms for evaluation—right up front. Your little notes will help them understand, as well. I always think it's necessary to write comments on papers; it gives the students some guidance for improvement, and it also gives them some positive strokes for great passages and thoughts. In addition, it'll help you remember how and why the student got the grade he or she did. So kudos to you for doing it automatically.

Respectfully,
Mike

Recursive Teaching

Dear Mike,

For today's class, Mrs. F. had me design a lesson regarding creative writing. Of course, she had to be completely cliché and suggest haiku. I acquiesced and designed a lesson for expressive writing, using haiku. As I designed the lesson, I tried to keep in mind the different sizes of the two classes, and the classroom management required. For the small sixth-grade class, the lesson went wonderfully. They did free-writing for four minutes based on a work of art I displayed on the overhead, then we created haiku from our free-writing. The sixth graders seemed to be very interested in interpreting the art, and in writing poems based around the mood of the art.

The eighth graders, on the other hand, were more interested in writing silly poems about concrete things they saw in the painting. Isn't it supposed to be the other way around? I guess the eighth graders are just too cool to delve into the mood of a painting. For whatever reason, I was much more impressed with the poems that the sixth graders wrote.

I guess I shouldn't complain because at least everyone wrote. Once we finished sharing the haiku, everyone wanted to discuss the painting, so I allowed a few minutes for that. In this time period, almost all of the eighth graders were interested in talking about the painting and its meaning or mood. Maybe next time it would be a good idea to have a discussion about the painting between their free-writing and the writing of the poetry. This would give them all a chance to explore ideas about the painting, and formulate ideas for writing. I don't know how to get the eighth graders more interested though. I guess it might be a good idea next time to use something more relevant to them than an old painting. Perhaps they just didn't have anything to express about this painting.

Thanks,
Paul

Dear Paul,

Once again, I think you may have stumbled on to something critically important—and that's how we learn to do our most effective teaching—by thinking and rethinking what we've just done.

A discussion about the painting prior to writing probably would have inspired more poetics. The exchanging of ideas helps the writers visualize more than just the concrete imagery in the art. Hence, their writing might be a little more in depth and aesthetically insightful. So Paul, I'm just reaffirming your illumination, but I agree with your conclusion. Therefore, next time give that a try.

As for the eighth-grade "stick in the mud" syndrome, it's been my experience that all too often, upper classmen are "way too cool" for everything. Just wait until you get into the high-school arena. In other words, the fresh-faced freshmen are nowhere near as jaded as the tragically hip seniors.

Respectfully,
Mike

Connecting the Lessons and Objectives

Dear Mike,

As a follow-up to the haiku and a prelude to an autobiographical paper, I'm going to have the kids write a poem about themselves. Mrs. F. thinks it's a great idea, but she wants me to teach them some poetic literary devices and require them to use them in their poems. What do you think?

Paul

Dear Paul,

First of all, the tie-in between the haiku (poetic form) to more poetry is terrific. We should always try to connect our activities. That's why I like the fact that you're injecting a thematic tie-in with your autobiography paper that you're planning next. It's essential that we try to have a flow to our day-to-day activities, so the students feel the relevancy and impact of our English teaching magic.

As for the imposition of literary devices in their products—think of it in terms of using what they are required to learn. In other words, it's much better to give them a poetic tool belt they may need to write good poetry than to simply teach them the concepts and quiz them on their identification (underline and label the literary terms in the following poem). So I think Mrs. F. is on to something here. After all, similes, metaphors, imagery, and other literary devices are the tools of our trade. And even more important, is that these devices aren't limited to poetry—we use them in prose as well.

And finally, it's no more limiting than "making them" write a poem about themselves (your idea—and a great one at that). Hey, you're already teaching them thematics—another literary concept. So embrace the challenge: find good models, make up some of your own, then turn the little wordsmiths loose.

Respectfully,
Mike

A Poetic Safari

Dear Mike,

I am pretty impressed with the kids. They have been working on their poems which had to include two similes, one metaphor, and personification. Now that I am looking at their final copies, I am impressed. They have all managed to get the similes down. They even caught on to personification, but the metaphors were the challenge. I guess this illustrates how their minds work. Everything is so concrete. They have never been asked to think abstractly. Now that they are expected to, it is a challenge for them. Some of the things they write in their poems crack me up, too. They compare a necklace to a noose or a basketball shot to a nail in a coffin. It was a small success for me, but it gives me hope. Ahh, it can be done.

Adios!
Paul

Dear Paul,

SUCCESS! The poems were chock full o' chuckles and fun. They were entertaining. They reflected the objectives—similes, metaphors, and personification. They brought you smiles.

That is why teaching is such a wonderful service to provide for our planet's young people. It gives us a chance to help us open up our students, and poetry unlocks a lot of these mysteries with a literary flair. The students have fun playing around with language. On such a safari, they'll stalk the wild poetic image with reckless abandon. It's a joy to behold. And if you have them read their poems aloud, I guarantee you—you'll all get goose bumps.

Respectfully,
Mike

Assigning a Paper

Dear Mike,

On Thursday, I brought a ten-item questionnaire for each student to fill out as a "me getting to know more about you exercise." Mrs. F. let me distribute these, and I decided to let the questionnaire be an introduction into an autobiography paper. I instructed the students to fill out the form, then I would take them home to look at.

I asked them to begin a rough draft to bring in on Friday. For the autobiography paper, I have since made a handout listing the requirements. Students will do one more rough draft, which will go into peer editing, and then a final draft. I think we will make the final product equivalent to one test grade, but we might make it more, depending on how hard they work on their papers. I'll keep you updated.

Take It Easy,
Paul

Dear Paul,

The assignment sounds like it's going well. I'm glad you put it in writing for the students with clear objectives and requirements. This will make evaluating the papers easier. You have objective standards. That's good. I'm a little unclear about the prewriting activity. Did you discuss their questionnaires? Write feedback on them? Give them some direction based on what they indicated?

Let me know how the peer editing works, especially after Mrs. F.'s last catastrophe.

Oh yeah, I was wondering what aspect of their life they're covering in their papers? Please respond. I'm awfully inquisitive.

Respectfully,
Mike

Iterating Objectives

Hey there, Mike,

Hope you are having a nice day. Just to answer your questions about my questionnaire and the autobiography paper. The questionnaire was just something to get them thinking about themselves (as if they don't do enough of that already) and different aspects of their lives. The assignment for the paper is to choose four ways to approach the paper: write a narrative—tell about a single memorable event, write an obituary, write about a life in chronological order, or any other ideas they clear with us. No, I did not give any written feedback to the questions or to the ruff ruff drafts. I had considered it, then decided not to. Some of my students asked me why I didn't, and I felt bad. When I got your e-mail, I felt even worse. Thanks! No, I'm just kidding.

The cool thing is that I got everything done without any help. I could have been the substitute!

Paul

Dear Paul,

I'm so sorry that I added to your distress about the paper thing, but I think the students are right. They want to know what you think about what they're thinking. They need feedback, inspiration, and occasionally some direction. You needn't get heavy handed by intervening too much (unless they ask you to), but you probably should respond with genuine interest. The four options that you presented were great; students like having choices. It's empowering. I especially appreciated the fourth option—which was basically—design your own text (with prior permission).

Which brings me to my next annoying question, when you went over the autobiography requirements, did you clearly state "your" objectives? I'm really curious, not because I enjoy annoying you (although it is a little fun), but I've found that having some clear-cut objectives can help once the very subjective stage of evaluation begins. When you have to assign a grade to each paper, the more objective you can be, the more fair your evaluation will appear to both you and your students.

I'm really not as uptight and linear as I may appear at this point. I'm just a very annoying and curious sort of old battle-ax and warhorse.

I'll be patiently waiting.

Respectfully,
Mike

Accentuating Content

Hello again, Mike,

Mrs. F. helped me with the objectives for the paper. She insisted upon an intro, thesis statement, and conclusion. She also wanted clear transition sentences in each paragraph. Those are the main objectives—what we are looking for. I'm glad we have some sort of requirements, but I am so afraid of limiting them with the dreaded "five-paragraph essay."

Do you think we have? What else could I require instead, or as well?

I just wanted to have some way of getting to know them. I like this idea so far.

Paul

Dear Paul

Mrs. F. is right about having some set parameter for evaluation, but let's not overlook your main objective (CONTENT)—which was to have some way of getting to know them. So concentrate on having the thesis clarify something special about themselves then teach them how to develop that thesis with details. You might want to start by modeling a bit of your own "specialness" à la your own writing sample. Then you're teaching them a twofold lesson—you're modeling good writing with a clear thesis and a well developed product, and on a more personal level, you're allowing them to have the same experience with you as you want to have with them. They are learning something special about you, and in the process they're getting to know you better. It's a simple approach, but it should prove to be very effective. As teachers, it's important to provide our own selves as writing models, so the students can see us as works and writers in progress.

Respectfully,
Mike

Dealing with Rough Drafts

Dear Mike,

On Tuesday, I collected the students' rough drafts for their autobiography papers. I decided that since I had not yet given my students any response to their writing, that I would respond to their rough drafts. What I decided to do was instead of writing on each of their papers (because they will be doing peer-editing and I didn't want my opinions to get in the way), I would type my responses to each one up on the computer. Then after they do their peer editing in class, I will pass out my responses to each person. This way they will have two sets of feedback.

Mrs. F. warned me that this might be slightly time consuming—boy, she didn't know the half of it! This will be the last time I do this! Instead of going to class yesterday (I called and spoke to her about it) I spent the afternoon doing responses and I am still not finished. I will be watching *Friends* tonight with one eye on the computer. I told Mrs. F. that I would have the rough drafts back for Tuesday, and she told me we could do the peer editing then.

Paul

Dear Paul,

Once again, Mrs. F. proved correct-o. The typed response idea—although well intentioned—sounded exhausting. And in the real world of teaching, we can't postpone class or call in "sick and tired" just so we can stay home and catch up on our responses to papers. However, it was noble experience. Writing holistic notes or letters to the students concerning their works in progress is probably one of the most important steps a teacher can take in facilitating a student's progress as a writer. So don't abandon your intent with this approach—just tweak it.

As for the peer editing—have you given any thought for some constructs that the students will tune into? Remember the last fiasco Mrs. F. had with peer editing. You might want to check out the poetry workshop sheet I zipped you a while back. Maybe you could riff on that, and come up with your own process that will be relevant to this particular assignment.

Let me know how it goes . . .

Respectfully,
Mike

A Writing Workshop That Works

Dear Mike,

On Tuesday, I handed back the students' rough drafts with my IN-DEPTH comments on them. I thought I'd never see the end of the pile of papers. I was very pleased with the outcome, and so was Mrs. F. She was very impressed with how it all turned out.

First, I made sure I had everyone's attention. Then, I asked each of the students who hadn't turned in their assignments about their missing work. There were three in fifth period who did not have a paper, and they spent most of the period looking for theirs in piles of turned in work. We couldn't find the assignments anywhere, but it occupied them while I got to everyone else. Now I'm not saying this is a good thing. I don't think that I would have had this problem if it was my classroom, but I guess that is pretty easy to say. Once that was taken care of, I told everyone to get out his or her autobiography paper requirements, and then I handed out a peer-editing checklist (which was heavy on the content and clarity issues). Next, I began pairing up students randomly. This is where I was afraid it would get very hectic, but the entire switching of seats, putting desks together and assigning partners took about three minutes. I was pretty proud. Students then exchanged papers, and from their checklists they made suggestions and comments. A noisy classroom is a good classroom. When they were all beginning to finish up, I passed out my comments to each of them and let them see what I had to say compared to what their peers had said. Between the two sources, they have a good amount of suggestions for improvement.

Thanks much,
Paul

Dear Paul,

I really loved what you said today: "A good classroom is a noisy classroom." That's exactly why a lot of teachers have hang-ups about group work; they can't stand the madness. They have that old librarian kind of world view about learning: "Shhhhhhh, be quiet so we can learn something."

Vibrancy is often where the buzz and hum of electrical energy and brain synapses explode into the inner space of the heretofore dormant area we commonly refer to as—the high schooler's mind. I'm really proud of you. I'm so glad you're relaxing and having fun. And it's terrific that you included an editing checklist; I'm sure that's why your workshop worked better than Mrs. F.'s.

Respectfully,
Mike

Evaluating Writers in Personal Terms

Dear Mike,

I graded many, many papers this week, which I really liked. Until now, my experience with grading papers has been limited, so having the opportunity to actually read some papers and figure out who is who and where they are coming from was really helpful. I have experienced how difficult it is to determine grades, however. When you know one kid has a lower ability than another, and they both turn in the same quality of work, what do you do? Is it okay to give Susie a check minus because you know she spent the last ten minutes of class chatting and not finishing her work? It's so confusing.

Paul

Dear Paul,

Consider the PE coach's dilemma: Should the fastest runners and the buffest weightlifters be graded on the same scale as the proverbial ninety-eight-pound weakling? Go figure.

Each student needs to be challenged. The bright ones need to break just as much sweat as the ones waiting for the lights to come on. As teachers, we need to tend to their individual "light" fixtures by controlling the stage setting for the final act of grading. As directors, we call the shots. We make those decisions. Thus, grading must be objectively subjective.

Therefore, we must consider the individual student, and so, too, consider his or her progress. It's also paramount that we measure the extent of their labors— did he or she put out an A effort? While this may seem subjective, it's not. In Tom Romano's terrific book *Clearing the Way*, he calls this "participating in good faith." Hence, our evaluations are based on observable data—rough drafts, prewriting activities, improvement of texts. By the same token, we must respect the individual, and set realistic, but high standards for each one. No matter how hard we try to be objective based in our evaluations, we must be humanly subjective as well. It's our job to reach and teach each one. To do this, we must push the students with kid gloves and reward them for their efforts.

Respectfully,
Mike

FROM ANOTHER ANGLE

Paul seems able to use his intuition, as well as ideas that he has picked up from teacher preparation courses and classroom experiences, including his own development as a writer, when he reflects on issues related to writing instruction. Because he is willing to think critically about how students respond to instruction, and to adjust his instructional plans based on those responses, Paul is on his way to becoming an effective teacher of writing. Let's consider in greater detail three aspects of composition instruction about which Paul raises questions for Mike, since they are areas that are likely to be of interest to you, too: the use of journals, ways to respond to student writers, and the logistics of setting up a writing workshop.

Journals in Composition Instruction

Paul does recognize that keeping journals can help student writers develop their fluency. Mike helps Paul find ways to connect even free-writing activities directly to the content of lessons, particularly as a means of articulating initial responses to literature, when he recommends "focused journals." He notes that when teachers insist that the focus of journals remain related to class content, we eliminate most of the chances that our students will confuse class journals with diaries, too. I was a little surprised that Paul's mentor missed the opportunity to use focused journals when the class moved into a unit on discrimination. However, she did have students write from a personal perspective, and one that encouraged them to fine-tune their own stances, when she had her students craft letters about how their school needed more resources in order to be brought up to the county's standard.

Responding to Students' Writing

Paul states, early in his exchanges with Mike, that he enjoys writing "little messages in the margins" of students' writing assignments. Later in the exchanges, though, he runs into a problem: a student begs him to read her paper and give her feedback. He does give her feedback, but he tells her what she does not want to hear, including the fact that a reader might not be able to follow her main point. Her reaction includes "getting mad and shutting down." Still later, he finds that a decision to respond to each student autobiography with a complete letter is exhausting. With these three experiences, Paul has entered a territory that frequently causes concern for even the most experienced teachers among us. The questions that are raised might be stated this way:

How much time should we spend in responding to students' work (is there a point at which our efforts are overkill or wasted)?
What kinds of comments are the most helpful? Which produce negative effects? If we write too much on students' papers, do we in effect wrestle authorship—and authority—away from the student writers and shift it to ourselves?

Even subtler questions, such as where we place our marks and notes (over students' words? In the margins? At the end?), emerge as we carefully consider Paul's progress as a teacher who is learning to incorporate writing as a mode of thinking in an English class.

It seems, at first blush, that there would be research-based, solid, answers to these questions. And it seems, too, that we could safely assume that the more dedicated teachers are the ones who are willing to spend extra hours pouring over students' writing, adding their own comments, and, in Mike's term, awarding "kudos" to encourage student writers. Unfortunately, the situation is not nearly so clear-cut. Because writers are humans, our responses to them can never be based solely on what we know about good writing. Our responses to them must be based, too, on what we know about the student as a human being.

A recent incident reminded me of how inappropriate it is to rely exclusively on my own teaching instincts when I respond to students' writing. Here is what happened in an upper-division college class:

I am curious about how my students think and what they write, so I frequently collect their reading response journals. I read them and make comments on them. Students have spread the word that I am a prolific responder to student writing, so many are not surprised to see their papers returned with my handwriting all over them. I write questions to them, mostly—real inquiries that emerge for me as I read their texts. Most of the time, students appreciate the fact that I have spent a lot of time with their writing, even if the responses are to quick or informal writing assignments. It had never occurred to me that students would respond negatively to the amount of time that I take with their writing until one student, upon my returning a paper to her, looked at it with frustration, then exploded: "Why do you DO that? You TELL us that this is a tiny assignment, a little 'think-let,' something you are 'just curious about.' Then you write ALL OVER it, like you expected us to spend hours and hours preparing it. If you are going to treat it that seriously, the least you could do would be to warn us up front that it is going to COUNT that much!"

This episode surprised me. At first I was indignant; I wanted to ask her if she preferred that I treat her words as if they held no significance whatsoever by ignoring them. But then I thought about what had set her off. I believe it was simply a mismatch in expectations: I was treating her work as if I were talking with her about it and expected her to revise the piece based on what she thought of my comments. She was embarrassed that I seemed to treat a piece that she had spent little time composing as if it represented her full range of abilities as a writer and thinker. Neither of us was "wrong" in this scenario, but neither of us understood the other's intentions while we were in the middle of it, either. Had she not responded with such frustration, I would probably still be operating with the assumption that students prefer that I take all of their writing with equal seriousness and care.

Considerable research has been done on responding to students' writing, with results that indicate that those of us who write and write and write comments for students are wasting a lot of time. Richard Straub's *The Practice of Response* (2000) provides a careful look at this issue, and makes suggestions about what kinds of comments are actually useful and which we can learn to omit.

Questions About Establishing Writing Workshops That Function Effectively

Paul moves from questions about his own responses to students' work into questions about how to encourage students to respond in writing groups. The concerns he raises about how to make writing groups effective, in terms of enhancing students' writing and in terms of use of class time, reflect solid teacherly thinking on his part. Mike's advice, that Paul and his cooperating teacher work slowly toward a fully functioning writing workshop format, is right on target. We cannot expect to walk into a classroom and transform it from traditional to workshop-based in one easy step. Students have to learn how to react when they are given opportunities to think for themselves about which aspects of their writing they need to work on that day, what topic they will write about, what genre they will choose, which deadline they will work toward. Students have to learn how to edit their own and peers' work before they can be expected to make contributions to a peer-editing group. They will have to learn how to provide constructive criticism and encourage their peers if the workshop model is going to work. And they will have to recognize their own areas of strength and vulnerability, since their work will be more self-paced than in the traditional model for writing instruction.

Bigger Issues Beneath the Surface

Beneath the surface of his questions about assigning journals, responding to students' writing, and implementing a workshop format in the middle- or high-school classroom, Paul seems to be asking a single, and singly important, question:

How do we treat middle- and high-school students like writers, not like students who are merely impersonating "real" writers?

In *Room 109: The Promise of a Portfolio Classroom*, Richard Kent (1997) gives realistic and inspiring advice to all of us who struggle to make writing—and the desire to improve our writing—real. It is a book that I wholeheartedly recommend to Paul, and to you. In it, Kent describes how he welcomes high-school students to his classroom with a sincere letter about what they can expect in his room and in their thinking. Then he invites them, from the first day of class, to work as writers, beginning with a five-page autobiography. He responds to their autobiographies by writing personal letters. (Remember that Mr. Kent has been at this for years; responding to each student's work with a letter proved to be an unrealistic goal for Paul as a beginning teacher.) In his letters, Kent is unafraid to praise students for what they do well; he starts one by exclaiming to the student, "This is a brilliant autobiography! Expressive, honest, intelligent. You really know yourself and your life, don't you? Incredible" (Kent 1997, 17). Early in the year, he reads first drafts of writing because he prefers to hear the raw, "unfettered voices" of his new students, the "ingenuous and straightforward" writing that "comes from the gut" (Kent 1997, 14–15). Gradually, students learn that he intends for them to be writers and thinkers, and gradually, they live up to his expectation. While he admits that there are a few who refuse to try to rise to the challenges he poses, Kent's book provides evidence that we can expect remarkable work when students know that we are on their side, ready to support their growth as writers and thinkers. Kent offers a model that we are wise to consider: he sets clear and high expectations, and is not afraid to share his domain with students while he supports their growth. When we establish classroom environments and instructional formats in ways that treat our students as writers—giving and receiving input from many readers and audiences, working toward a variety of purposes, writing for diverse reasons—we also empower them as speakers, listeners, readers, and thinkers.

Another book that I would recommend to Paul, and to you, is Lawrence Baines and Anthony Kunkel's edited volume, *Going Bohemian: Activities that Engage Adolescents in the Art of Writing Well* (2000). This book is a collection of ideas contributed by a group of middle-school, high-school, and college teachers. Each of these ideas has been tried and proven in the classroom. You may find it especially useful once you have begun to develop a sense of your own philosophy of teaching and learning, because then you will be able to identify the activities that are a good fit. Some of my favorites include Baines' "The 120-Word Sentence" (17), Cara L. Turner and Irving Seidman's "The History of My Writing" (87), and Clarissa West-White's "Reflective Research: Portrait and Poem" (149).

There are many topics related to writing instruction that Paul has not addressed in his entries. Here are just a few of the questions that I had when I started teaching high-school English. I would like to hear Paul answer these at the end of a year of teaching high-school English. Maybe you have wondered about these, too.

ABOUT KINDS OF WRITING:

How will you decide on which kinds of writing you will have students focus as you are getting acquainted with them and their strengths and vulnerable spots?

How will you introduce students to different kinds of writing, and to different purposes for writing? Will they have opportunities to experience writing for purposes that extend beyond the classroom?

ABOUT EXAMPLES OF GOOD WRITING:

Will you encourage students to write in a wide variety of forms, or stick to standard classroom-type writing assignments?

How much importance will you place on "correctness," especially when your goals focus primarily on developing fluency in writing? What about when your goals include publication of polished writing?

ABOUT RESPONDING TO, ASSESSING, AND EVALUATING STUDENTS' WRITING:

What evidence of growth will you look for in the work of each student? How will you assign grades to students' writing?

What will you do to help student writers who are nonnative speakers of English, and those who use dialects that are different from standard English when they speak and write?

What kinds of questions might you use in a teacher-student writing conference?

How can you negotiate the role of writing coach and writing judge, since it is likely that, ultimately, you will have to be both?

These are questions that beginning teachers and experienced veterans still struggle to answer.

Other teacher-oriented books that focus on writing instruction include these; each is a book that we keep on our teaching shelves, in a place that we can get to quickly.

Golub, Jeff. 1994. *Activities for an Interactive Classroom*. National Council of Teachers of English and *Making Learning Happen*. 2000. Portsmouth, NH: Boynton/Cook Heinemann. Golub has a quirky sense of humor, and he does not try to hide it beneath stuffy academic language in these practical, useful books, each of which is filled with ideas that will help you encourage adolescents to become engaged with writing.

Jago, Carol. 2002. *Cohesive Writing: Why Concept Is Not Enough*. Portsmouth, NH: Heinemann. Jago is a veteran teacher of high-school English and director of the California Reading and Literature Project at UCLA. In this short text, Jago acknowledges the influence of writing theorists James Britton, Donald Graves, Peter Elbow, Dixie Goswami, and James Gray, leaders who are in part responsible for shifting instructional attention away from the product of writing to the process. This shift from product to process has had a tremendous influence on the way that writing instruction is carried out in the twenty-first century. She then addresses writing instruction with a dual aim: to discuss the kinds of assignments that high-school students need to be able to do in order to graduate (persuasive and narrative essays and writing about literature, for example), and to promote the kinds of writing that high-school students can be encouraged to do in order to better know themselves as thinkers and as humans. Her advice is practical, direct, and well grounded in theory.

Tsujimoto, Joseph. 2001. *Lighting Fires: How the Passionate Teacher Engages Adolescent Writers*. Portsmouth, NH: Boynton/Cook Heinemann. Not every teacher can be as openly passionate about writing instruction as is Tsujimoto, a teacher of middle-school students who is also a poet. Yet we can all learn about the possibilities that emerge when teachers interact with their students, when all are treated as growing writers, by reading this inspiring text. Tsujimoto's notion of the "function paper" is a particularly welcome take on the idea of having students write about topics on which they conduct research.

Strickland, Kathleen and James Strickland. 2002. *Engaged in Learning: Teaching English 6–12*. Portsmouth, NH: Heinemann. This book has a particularly useful chapter on the writing workshop (Chapter four). The chapter addresses topics ranging from the teacher as a writer, to the use of minilessons to develop editing skills. They extend the focus on real-classroom writing scenarios into a chapter on using computers, the Web, and other technologies (Chapter five) for enhancing instruction in writing and the other language arts.

6

Doing the Two-Step: Using Writing to Teach Literature

For his internship, Antonio is working in one of the oldest and most well-respected high schools in town. His students are predominantly middle class, and they are a blend of Caucasians and African-Americans. Antonio has a positive way of relating to his students so that they see him as an approachable authority; he also suspects that they are a little intrigued by the Hispanic undertones of his dialect, and he uses his voice and dialect to his advantage by speaking with and reading aloud to students often. The concerns Antonio expresses focus on his desire to get students fully involved in literature study. He has a sense that using writing to teach literature is a powerful combination, and Mike's suggestions reinforce his instincts.

Eliminating the Multiple-Choice Mentality

Dear Mike,

The honors students are already halfway through with *Huck Finn*, and I have a pretty good feeling that they are bored to tears. Mrs. F. has such a great rapport with her students and I think the students who are actually reading are learning a lot, but she runs her class very differently than how I would. It is very teacher-centered, very structured—which has its benefits.

Anyway, I got to give an oral reading quiz on a few of the chapters in *The Adventures of Huckleberry Finn* that Mrs. F. had created. I liked the questions because they weren't too hard. In grading them, you could tell very easily who had read and who hadn't. That brings up the subject of testing. This was a short-answer quiz. I think I like that test format the best. I think literature lends itself to essay and short-answer tests because it is so open to interpretation. Having kids write about what they've read forces them to think harder about it, rather than just having them regurgitate events or the teacher's ideas about the story on a multiple-choice test.

Your pal,
Antonio

Dear Antonio,

Personally, I abhor multiple-choice tests. They belittle both subjects we teach: students and literature. By nature, these quizzes rely on nitpicky, simplistic answers to surface structure questions especially designed to trick our students into "careful" readings of the text. A student teacher of mine last year complained that when she was in high school, she always felt like these quizzes penalized her for reading ahead because she would forget the minute details such as the proper name of Aunt Polly's kitty cat. Bah, humbug. Therefore, I believe in written responses that inspire the students to react and reflect on what they have read. After all, isn't that what these honors kids will be doing in college? Believe me, essays are harder to grade (they take more time and you can't use a Scantron bubble sheet or a student aide), but these types of responses are much more thought provoking for teachers. They give you a glimpse and glimmer into the students and their musings on the art. Plus, it beats the heck out of redlining A, B, C, or D, or even the tedium that short-answer exams elicit. *What was the name of Aunt Polly's cat?* In Carol Jago's book *With Rigor for All*, she encourages teachers to give "tests that teach." She has the students react and reflect on their readings in a number of interesting ways, such as poems, graphs, art work, role-playing essays, and journals. It's a terrific blend of creativity and critical thinking. And remember—writing is thinking, so it stands to reason that we would choose to have our students think and write about what they have read.

Respectfully,
Mike

Getting Young Readers to Respond

Dear Mike

Mrs. F. lectures on some very interesting things about Mark Twain and his novel. That is, it's interesting to an aspiring English teacher like me. But, I see a lot of the students tuning her out or reading something else during her lectures because they aren't really encouraged to participate that much. She asks yes-or-no questions every now and then. A couple of times she asked an open-ended question, but just went on to answer it herself. I saw the chance for a great (but somewhat tangential) discussion come up while Mrs. F. was talking about the character Emmaline Granger from the novel, who was apparently obsessed with death. One student tried to make a comment about whether or not Emmaline spent a lot of time thinking about her own suicide, but Mrs. F. had already moved on to reading a poem Emmaline had written. Instead of asking the class what they thought of the poem, she went on to tell them that it was really bad, trite poetry. Don't get me wrong, I really do have a lot of respect for Mrs. F., but I think she feels a lot of pressure to cover a lot of material in a little time. She wants to expose them to as much American literature as she can, while at the same time prepare them for the SATs and all kinds of other stuff. I also know that the pressure is not imaginary. But I really believe that by just glossing over or rushing through a whole bunch of stuff, students won't be as interested or focused, and therefore they won't learn as much as if the pace were slower and they were truly given a chance to contemplate what they are reading, and to discuss it. What do you think?

Antonio

Dear Antonio,

An intriguing school of thought is based on depth of knowledge rather than breadth. Instead of being so curriculum driven, we should be more interested in getting our students engaged by really examining our objectives—whatever they may be. Hopefully, the primary objective is to get them to think.

Which brings us to your critique of Mrs. F's "sit-and-get-it" lecture style. In actuality, any class will get pretty darned boring if the teacher tends to yammer on all the time (college classes, too). But this is especially true in English classes. Literature should become the springboard for discourse. To ensure this, I utilize Louise Rosenblatt's reader response journals as a model, which I've attached (see Figure 6–1). By getting the students to find relevant quotes, copy them, respond to them in writing, and then call on them in class—the teacher affords the students the opportunity to open up the communication channels into the directions that are relevant to them. *Huck Finn* would, could, and should be a stimulating vehicle. It deals with child abuse, racism, coming of age, rebellion, and unyielding friendship. These themes, issues, ideas, notions, and aesthetics need to be shared and reflected on by everyone in the classroom in their own terms. That's what makes the study of literature so exciting. But it's the teacher's obligation to get the students into it. And that's where focused journal prompts can help as well. Take for instance your example of Emmaline Granger—phrase that student-generated gem into a journal prompt, then start calling them to the plate. Better yet, have them respond in a "Write Down and Share," then get them out of their seats. Put the "Yes, she thinks about suicide" respondents on one side of the room, and the "No, she doesn't" ones on the other side, hustle the wafflers into the center of the room, and then monitor the ensuing debate. Encourage the students to contemplate what's been said and being said—encourage them to switch sides physically and mentally by drifting to the other side of the issue and the room. But make them accountable for their actions. Have the ones who change, explain their thinking regarding their evolving sense of right or wrong.

I do this with literature and writing quite often, and it's lively and insightful almost every time.

Respectfully,
Mike

FIGURE 6–1

© 2003 by Mike "Wiggs" Rychlik and Pamela Sissi Carroll from *13 Ways of Looking at Student Teaching*. Portsmouth, NH: Heinemann.

Providing Creative Assignments with Gradable Objectives

Hey, Mike,

Listen to this: my teacher, Mrs. F. passed me the reigns of the class. After they finished reading *Huck Finn*, I gave four assignments for them to choose from. It was really interesting because Mrs. F. wanted me to have at least one assignment that also brought in social studies (geography). Well here they are:

1. Create a new book cover for the book. Include images which represent what you think the book is all about.

2. Compose an interview script. Pretend you are working for the local newspaper and you were asked to interview Huck.

3. Use magazines and media-center materials to create a collage (similar to the book cover). Be able to explain why you chose certain pictures, and what they represent in the book.

4. Using maps of the Mississippi River—map out Huck's journey. Also, choose five specific areas (cities, rivers, lakes), and show longitude and latitude.

I knew none of the students wanted to do the last one. I guessed that the collage would be the most popular project they would want to do, but I didn't expect how much. I provided a model for each of the assignments, showing one example of how they could be done, and that I had fun doing each one. I think that was well appreciated by them. It made them feel like I wasn't just telling them what to do, but that we were going to have fun together.

In the first class, about twenty-five out of thirty students chose to do the collage. Since I had said they would have the choice, I didn't want to go back on our word and assign them projects. The media center provided them with poster board, and I told the kids that there could be no empty spaces on their final product.

Before the next class came in, though, I cut up index cards with either one, two, three or four on them. I put the numbers in an empty tissue box. After explaining the projects, the students were more excited about who they could have as a partner, rather than which project they'd get. It was really great because these kids are "kind kids." Rather than whining about who they had to pair up with, some more outgoing students chose the more shy ones. It was really interesting to watch. They also could opt to do the project by themselves if they would like.

Next step: Each student presented their projects to the class, and they were also videotaped, like a speech. Some students who chose to do the interview did the presentation using their own video camera and brought those tapes in. Some students did the interview as a talk show, or on a journalist level. All of them were creative, witty, and hilarious. We also have some really great artists in the class who came up with some great book covers. Students working on the map were provided with maps of the areas, and I really tried my best to help these students, because it seemed to be really time consuming. There were also globes in the class and large pull-down maps which they could use.

We used one class period to present the assignments, to divide up the class, and to get them talking about what exactly they wanted to do. A second class time was for working on the projects. And finally, a third class was used for presenting the projects. Mrs. F. asked me to grade these projects. I'm just a little nervous about that.

I'm just excited, because I think they really like me. I know now I'm writing too much, but this was neat.

Write you later,
Antonio

Dear Antonio,

Bravo! Bravo! Bravo!

Aside from the inventiveness of your lessons and the inclusion of choice, what I really appreciated was your incorporation of so many types of learning styles that students could access to demonstrate their connection to the text. I was also impressed (as were your students) that you took the time to come up with your own examples to demonstrate the various activities. Teacher models are always a plus. The most awesome aspect, however, of your incredible journey was how you adapted your lesson for the next class after you saw how most of the kids were gravitating to the collage activity. This was sheer teacher genius on your part. The group aspect lessened the tension of "having to do" a certain activity, and it spiced up the presentations by having the gamut of activities being demonstrated. The videotaping was awesome (students can be such hams), and I just can't believe what an amazing job you've done.

As for the grading part—simply revisit your objectives as stated in the explanation of the assignment. By focusing on how well the kids demonstrated your stated objectives, it makes your job less stressful and less subjective. In other words, how well did they do what you asked them to do?

In reviewing your assignment, I see that options three and four have very specific objectives or perimeters for you to consider: "Be able to explain why you chose certain pictures, and what they represent in the book." And: "Map out Huck's journey. Also, choose five specific areas (cities, rivers, lakes), and show longitude and latitude."

On your first two choices, however, the guidelines for your objectives are a little less clear: "Include images which represent what you think the book is all about," or "Compose an interview script. Pretend you are working for the newspaper and you were asked to interview Huck." In both instances, the assignments lack specificity. It's a little less clear what you expect. How will they demonstrate the connection of their image to the book?

By stating (like you did in option three) that they should be able to explain that connection, you've stated your objective. Of course, Jim Burke in his classic book *English Teacher's Companion* suggests students who present artwork or graphs or other visuals for a literary response should also be required to write an explanation interpreting their work. I totally agree, and encourage teachers to always have students prepare a script for any speech or presentation. There's nothing worse than a student stammering an ill-conceived speech à la "Well, like, uh, you know, uhhhh, this just sorta reminded me of, uh, like Huck, or something."

With regard to the interview script, were they just coming up with questions, or were they imagining Huck's answers, too? How many questions did you expect? And did they have to be written in a journalistic manner—who, what, when, where, why, and how?

Don't get me wrong, Antonio. You've done an incredible job here. Grading, however, is such an integral part of what we have to do; it also can be the most daunting. More than anything, students want to know why and how they got their grade. By going into our activities with clearly stated objectives, it clarifies this process for them and us.

Respectfully,
Mike

Hello, Mike, it's me again.

First of all I wanted to thank you for all of the compliments and words of encouragement. Also, I wanted to clarify some of the expectations I left out on my last note. The collage activity was probably the most vague. Along with cutting out pictures, words, or phrases which were associated with the book, the students were also asked to write out a one-minute speech explanation regarding their collage. While they were working on it, I supervised them closely. I went around asking them "Why did you include this picture," and so on. If they weren't really clear on it, I asked them to take it off, and find something else to replace it.

With the interview, I explained that no question they created could be answered by just a yes/no or short answer. They were asked to use eight model questions, or use them as a guide to construct their own. Again, like the collage guidance, I checked up on these students and asked them to tell me a few of the questions when they considered their project to be over and done with. The questions were originally supposed to be directed toward Huck, but some students wanted to include other characters in the interview as well. They seemed to be very enthusiastic about it, so Mrs. F. and I just "went with it," and they all did an exceptional job.

Antonio

Dear Antonio,

Wonderful job with your objectives—so thorough and well thought-out. Bravo, again! So when you grade the projects, refer to your objectives, then make your call (it'll still be somewhat subjective). Remember, you're the ump, the judge, and jury—you're a keen, lean, and not so mean grading machine.

Respectfully,
Mike

Ditching the Film Version

Hello Mike,

Well, today is the day of truth. The students are taking a complete test on *Huck Finn*. I hope it's fair. The kids have expressed a liking of the book—at least the ones who finished it. I told the rascals to rent the movie if they weren't done yet. I want them to pass.

Antonio

Dear Antonio,

The movie? The movie is never the same. Plus, the only good version I've ever seen of Huck was on PBS about twenty years ago. It was about an eight-episode version that might be hard to locate.

No offense, BUT standards and procedures should dictate that the prose of Twain be honored. (Can you feel the ire of ye olde' English taskmaster?)

While "passing the test" may be nice, the students shouldn't pass "Go" and collect their payoff (à la Monopoly) if they haven't read the text. Naughty, Naughty.

Respectfully,
Mike

Hello Mike,

I got your e-mail and you are right about the movie. I guess I just wanted the students to do well. I was so excited when one of the students ran into class to tell me how much he loved the book. He said he couldn't put it down near the end and finished 100 pages the night before the test. This made me so happy. He truly enjoyed it.

I graded their tests as soon as it was over. Some were happy; some mad. But I know it's not my or Mrs. F.'s fault that they were too lazy to read. I gave them a creative extra-credit assignment today. I am sure most of them will do it. I like artistic things, so I gave them an opportunity to create a book cover or a CD with songs for the book and characters. Of course my directions were more detailed. I think it should help them, since it's getting close to the end of nine weeks.

Once again, I dorked it about the movie. Thanks for calling me on it.

Antonio

Dear Antonio,

Congratulations! The student read 100 pages to finish the book at the finish line, and he loved it. That's what makes a cool school happen. So when and if any students get behind next time—forget the movie. Tell them to burn the midnight oil and hunker down. And who knows? Maybe they'll learn something like "that Mark Twain cat can really write a great American novel."

Of course, movies do help ESL students who are struggling with the text. For that reason, you may want to talk to the ESL support teacher in your school, and set up a time and place for the struggling students to view a representative movie of the novel you're studying. The problem therein, however, is that most movies pale in comparison to the books. In addition, they often stray from the text.

Respectfully,
Mike

Prepping for the Tests

Hello again, Mike,

This week was pretty laid back—the kids watched *Huck Finn*, which they just finished reading. (You were right; the movie was awful—it was a really sappy musical version.)

They also got their unit exam back on the novel. The scores were terrible, mainly in the sixties. Mrs. F. wasn't all that upset with the grades, but I was. I spoke with a couple of the girls in the class, ones who I thought were bright enough to make more than a sixty-three or sixty-five. I asked them what happened. I know by their journal entries and quiz scores that they read the book. They told me that it was really difficult to remember the quotes from the beginning of the book and to put them in context.

If that were my class, I would have discussed the test with the class and done some serious soul searching about whether or not it was an accurate measure of the students' abilities—especially since even the brighter students flunked, but Mrs. F. did not. She hinted at the fact that there would be ways to make up for the poor score before the semester was over. It was killing me because I wanted them to understand the novel, not just pass the class. I would have loved to do a minilesson on how to study or read for understanding. I kind of alluded to the fact that many of the students may not know exactly how to study for an exam of a novel, but Mrs. F. did not pick up on it or was not interested, so I backed off. I didn't want to step on any toes.

One method I think could be helpful is for the students to use index cards to write down important quotes, information, or issues and their significance to the novel as we discuss them in class. By clipping the index cards to the page where the issue is addressed, it gives the students a place to start in their studying. Mrs. F. just didn't seem interested. She had already moved on to the next unit—short stories. Oh well, live and learn.

Antonio

Dear Antonio,

With regard to novels or any other literature, I don't like to spoonfeed the students as to what everything means. It's critical that we require them to think; hence, the term "critical thinking." Of course, we do have to teach the kids the process, and we also have to provide a safe environment for them where they feel comfortable enough to "go out on a limb" and express their ideas. I agree that a review would be beneficiary and a preview before the test about themes, quotes, characters, etc., would help, too.

Requiring the students to keep reader response logs along the way also helps to keep them in tune with a novel. With this approach, the teacher requires the student to pick several quotes from each section of the book as the class peruses through it. Occasionally, you could even include a couple of required quotes for them to ponder. This is a great way to get the students to really think about what they're reading while they're plowing through a book. At the end of the novel, the students have then cultivated a homegrown study guide.

Where I would tend to be careful is in the review process. If we prep the students too comprehensively, then the process reeks of leading the students by the nose into the direction of what is going to be covered on the test, and how they should interpret it when they study for it. Of course, we shouldn't have tricks up our sleeves when we test the students anyway. Heck, I give them the questions ahead of time and put them in study circles. I want them to know what's coming, but I refrain from telling them what to think, only what to think about. That's why I give the students essay tests when we study novels. For me, this method has proven to be the most effective way for students to truly express in their own terms what they've gotten from such a lengthy text.

I also like to give the students a menu of topic choices on which to chow down. I want them to showcase their most insightful analyses, so I give them a plethora of thought-provoking prompts. Another key is to make the menu à la carte, with each essay choice derived from each section of the novel. Then they've got their appetizer, their soup or salad, their main course, their side dishes, and of course, their delectable dessert. By giving them a full-course meal with a full menu, they can really pig out on the Lit.

Respectfully,
Mike

Playing with Literary Concepts

Dear Mike,

I'm finally going to do another full lesson. At first, I was excited until I found out that I am to take the literary terms that Mrs. F. has highlighted in her book and devise a way to test the students on the fifty or so terms—allusions, metaphors, illustrations, etc. Not the creative path I would have chosen. Mrs. F. says that her colleagues are amazed at how well her students do on the literary meanings of terms. The students seem pretty clueless to me, judging from grading their last test. Aren't there a lot more important parts and issues in this book to address than—*does this line include a metaphor or a simile*? I really wish I could do something else with this book and my lesson. Oh well. Any ideas on how to make literary terms exciting and interesting?

Sincerely,
Antonio

Dear Antonio,

Once again, we run into the depth and breadth issue. Since this isn't your domain, though, you must make due. Under these circumstances, I would probably put the students into small groups, give each group a few terms to tackle, and tell them that they are responsible for learning the concepts well enough to teach the class. Of course, the groups should compose original written examples of each term to illustrate their points. If you have access to blank overhead transparencies, get the groups to write their examples on the overheads to show the class and allow them to add artwork to illustrate their point. You may even want to compose your own examples to iterate each point.

By getting students to use the terms, it heightens their awareness of the importance of such devices. After all, these aren't really terms to identify in a piece of literature—they are literary tools that writers use from their toolbox to create effects in their storytelling and poetry.

Hence, we should always include a writing component when we are studying these terms. It iterates the importance of the toolbox theory. For homework you might have them write a silly free verse poem that uses several different devices, then get each student to read their "monsterpiece" to the class. As a follow-up, have the students guess which terms their fellow colleagues use by specifying where and when and how. You could even put them back in their groups during these presentations, and keep score.

When you become your own boss, though, I would encourage you not to overwhelm your students by barraging them with such a massive list of terms. I'm afraid that the impact of regurgitating such important writerly information in such a small frame of time will interfere with the true beauty of these literary devices. Naturally, we should integrate our study of such concepts within the context of the storytelling and poetry we read and study.

For instance, when my students tackle "The Lottery" by Shirley Jackson, I use the story to "show" them the impact of point of view. As a follow-up, the students rewrite a first-person account of the lottery "celebration" from the viewpoint of one of the characters in the story. As objectives, they must stick to the facts in the story, but they are free to interject their own thoughts regarding the brutality and fear that would naturally be associated with such an intense day (which is the essence of the first-person POV). Then they read their stories to the class, which gives their writing an expanded forum. By hearing the various viewpoints, however, the students begin to see the wisdom in Shirley Jackson's third-person (not omniscient) POV choice. Undoubtedly, "The Lottery" would lose its horrific surprise ending if it were told from a more intimate point of view. Hence, the students vicariously learn the importance of such writerly decisions by rewriting the story themselves. Obviously, this coupling of literature with writing makes the literary devices not only come to life, but it gives them a more meaningful context.

Respectfully,
Mike

Creating Effective Literary Follow-Ups

Dear Mike,

I teach a lesson next week on Edgar Allen Poe. I want to make it a lesson to remember—exciting, fun, and above all interesting! Whoa, so much to try to do.

Antonio

Dear Antonio,

Don't sweat it! Poe is a kid icon. The students love him, so that's already in your favor.

Just don't just give them a comprehension quiz to see if they were awake. The worst thing you can do is have them read the story, then answer the questions at the end of the selection in complete sentences:

1. Who is the author of the story?

The name of the author of the story is Edgar Allen Poe.

Your follow-up is critical. Find an interesting objective that you can tie to the story. Personally, I like to focus on some outstanding aspect about a story, essay, or poem, and then get the students to somehow reflect, respond, and mimic that aspect. It could be the theme, the tone, the imagery, the character motivation—something that strikes you as relevant and important and fun. Therein lies the key to your follow-up.

In "Tell-Tale Heart," for instance, I have the kids tune into the sensory details—especially sounds. I give each student a printout of the story and a highlighter, and let them have at it—highlighting every sensory detail they can find. It almost becomes a game of sorts.

Hence, my objective for studying the story is to learn how sensory details can create tension. To iterate my point, I show a couple clips from Hitchcock flicks (*The Birds* and *Psycho*), and have the students write down the sounds they hear as a scene intensifies. The students also write about the director's usage of music.

As a final follow-up, I have them write a poem or short narrative creating tension with acute usage of sensory details (especially sound). Of course, the students have to polish their monsterpieces, and eventually read them to the class by candlelight in the dark. Yikes—such freaky fun.

Hence, the literature becomes a springboard for writing.

Respectfully,
Mike

Making Your Overall Objectives Clearer, or Why Am I Having Them Do This?

Dear Mike,

My lesson on Edgar Allen Poe went pretty well. Based on our discussion, the students seemed to like reading the story. But I was very disappointed with their follow-ups. They were supposed to write a "what happens next?" ending, but most of them just summarized the story. I suppose I should have been clearer with my instructions.

The nice thing was that a lot of the kids asked me if I was going to continue teaching them, and they seemed genuinely enthused when I said that I was.

Antonio

Dear Antonio,

It sounds like a good idea, but you probably did need to clarify your objectives better (especially with yourself). Why did you have them read this story? What did you want them to glean from it? And what did you want them to do as an exercise reflecting this knowledge? (Remember "The Lottery" assignment?)

One of my favorite wrinkles on the "what happens next?" writing prompt is a group composition of a script. For instance, after my students read John Updike's classic coming of age story—"A&P," I put them into small groups then have them write a short vignette in the form of a script wherein they role-play different characters from the story reacting to the tumultuous decision of Sammy—the main

After reading Updike's "A&P," write a three- to four-page script involving the characters from the story recounting their reactions to the incident regarding Sammy and Queenie and Lengel.

To receive a most excellent grade, student scripts should:

1. remain true to the characters and their situations in the story.
2. reflect and ruminate on the dynamics of Sammy's actions and decisions.
3. be performed for the class with all group members taking an active role.
4. be scripted in play form replete with stage directions and a cast of characters.

FIGURE 6–2

character who impulsively quits his dead-end job at the A&P after the truculent manager insults three teenaged girls who saunter into the store wearing bathing suits. The exercise (see Figure 6–2) works on a lot of levels. But most importantly, the students empathize with the differences in the adult and adolescent worlds by role-playing different generations. And empathy is always an important teacherly objective.

By far, the most impressive aspect of your e-mail was the enthusiasm a lot of the students already have about your teaching style. Hey, maybe they didn't quite get the creative aspects of your "what happens next?" assignment. With their multiple-choice, short-answer regimen so engrained in their brains, it may take time and patience for them to tune into their creative channels. Keep challenging them, though, and pushing them with kid gloves by combining tasty Lit and spicy writing in your English classroom gumbo.

Respectfully,
Mike

FROM ANOTHER ANGLE

Antonio is already far ahead of where I was when I began teaching; he recognizes that students can use writing, visual art, and drama to enhance their study of literature. I was not confident enough to try to engage in "integrated instruction" during my early months as a teacher of English. My early literature lessons involved asking students to write expository pieces about the literary elements of texts, so I asked them to use writing in order to allow me to assess their literature learning. But I did not know how to incorporate writing, speaking, visual art, and performing into their learning of literature. Rarely did I ask the students to use writing to explore their own responses to texts, to write a poem in response to a story, or to find a song that could represent a character's feelings in a novel. I can't remember asking students to dramatize a scene in order to more closely analyze its components and its impact. I don't think that I gave students an opportunity to take on the role of a character and role-play a scene that could have happened outside of the text, as a means of exploring characters' motives and attitudes, during my entire first year of teaching. I did not understand what Antonio already knows: that literature instruction is enhanced when it is supported by use of the other language arts.

In desperation, I made another huge mistake when I first started teaching a literature-heavy curriculum, one which I was reminded of by Antonio's questions about how to use films and videos to complement literature instruction. Here is what sparked my error: I found, quickly, that reading and evaluating students' expository essays about the literary elements and effects of "The Raven" was extremely time consuming. Instead of throwing up my hands and claiming, "Nevermore!" in regard to assigning essays, I took a decidedly different route: I decided that each Friday, I would show students a movie that was related, in terms of theme, topic, or author, to the literature we had studied earlier in the week. This would mean, I reasoned, that I could spend almost all day on Friday reading students' expository essays while students enjoyed the "day off" from our normal classroom routines.

This scheme worked well for a while. Students watched a cartoon version of "The Raven," and intelligently discussed how its tone differed from the tone established in Poe's original text, as we had read it in class. After reading a few stories by James Thurber, we watched a long film clip from one of his stories, *The Incredible Mr. Limpet*. As they had done during our reading of Thurber, students were able to discuss Thurber's use of exaggerated character traits and humor and his challenging vocabulary after watching the film.

Then one Thursday afternoon after school hours, I ran into a problem: instead of the biography of Robert Frost that I had ordered for "film day," I received, by mistake, a film about the hibernation habits of black bears. I would like to say that I was able to re-direct my plans for Friday. I could have chosen to allow students an opportunity to write poems modeling those they had read by Robert Frost. I could have arranged for them to read the works of other poets of his generation and recite their favorites. I could have asked them to work in groups to prepare dramatic choral renderings of a Frost favorite, and to present it to the class. But I did none of these. I have to admit the truth: I decided to go with the film. While students watched the film on black bears, I read and evaluated their essays about the four Frost poems we'd studied that week. I got their essays graded that day, but I thought about my own failings, and students' reactions to my decision, all weekend. What was perhaps most surprising was that none of the students challenged my choice; although the film had absolutely nothing to do with the current focus of the class, they did not complain or question. After a lot of honest reflection, I understood why: my students had learned to define "film day" as "free day" or "fun day." The movie about black bears fit the bill—it gave them freedom to watch or not, to think or not, to sleep or not, while I hid at my desk, grading papers. They had uncovered the truth: I had been trying to use film as an extension of literature instruction, but I was not successfully integrating films into literature instruction in a meaningful way.

These two issues: the use of all of the language arts to support, broaden, and deepen literature teaching and learning, and the place of film in the English classroom, are two interesting focal points in the exchange between Antonio and Mike.

Inviting Students to Enter Texts and Wander Around in Them: Moving Toward Critical Literacies

Antonio articulates a struggle to balance two schools of thought on literature instruction. One school of thought holds that, especially for students who may never read after high school, it is more important to read widely than deeply, to nibble on a variety of literary hors d'oeuvres even if there is no time to consume a main course. Teachers in this school typically strive to "cover the curriculum" during the year. They are likely to move through literature anthologies like their counterparts in social studies classes move through U.S. history textbooks, sometimes having to rush the last few decades if they are still in the early twentieth century by spring break. The other school suggests that significant literary experiences require the reader to spend a significant amount of time with a single text before moving on to the next. These teachers strive to "uncover the curriculum." They may not require that students read a great number of texts, but that they spend a lot of time with the few texts that they do read. The first approach is not inherently wrong, but the latter tends to do more to encourage students to engage in literary experiences, because it provides time for students to not only enter texts, but to wander around inside them, using writing, speaking, listening, and media-related activities that promote students' connections with texts.

Antonio has learned, or instinctively knows, that literature learning can be enhanced through the integration of other language skills and expressive outlets during literature study. He designs a lesson in which students can choose to respond to the teacher-chosen text from a variety of graphic and verbal response possibilities. It seems that he wants to begin to see himself not only as a teacher of literature, or even of English, but also as a teacher of critical, focused, clear, powerful thinking.

You might be ready for that kind of more expansive thinking, too. If so, I encourage you to begin now to think of ways that you can learn to connect literature with your students' lives. Next, set goals for helping them transfer skills and habits of thought that they draw on in the study of literature to other situations that require multiple literacies. For example, have students work in groups to explore the theme of a short story and examine the author's intentions. From there, have students use writing, speaking, or drawing to explore the theme and intentions of a television advertisement, or to critically analyze the lyrics of a popular song. After students have written about how a novel reflects the values of a time period, ask students to use their analytic writing skills to participate in community conversations, through the local newspaper, about social issues that are important in their town.

Reading and Writing: Meaning-Making Cognitive Activities

In *The Reading/Writing Connection: Strategies for Teaching and Learning in the Secondary Classroom* (2003), Carol Booth Olson draws on years of experience as a classroom teacher and National Writing Project chapter director, as well as experience working with preservice teachers, to recommend practical, engaging activities to integrate instruction in literature, reading skills, writing, speaking, and listening. Olson first establishes the need for a teaching perspective in which reading and writing are viewed as meaning-making activities. She notes that the processes are similar in that both readers and writers are actively engaged in constructing meaning from and with texts; they go back and go forward in a recursive process; they interact and negotiate with each other (i.e., the reader keeps the writer in mind, and the writer keeps the reader in mind); they access a common tool kit of cognitive strategies, including planning and setting goals, tapping prior knowledge, asking questions and making connections, constructing the gist, monitoring, revising meaning, reflecting and relating, and evaluating; they use skills automatically; and they are motivated and self-confident (Olson 2003, 17). She acknowledges that there are differences, too, in that readers are concerned with finding meaning, while writers are constrained with communicating their information or ideas or feelings with a reader (Olson 2003, 15).

Then she explains how Howard Gardner's theory regarding multiple intelligences (1983) can guide teachers as we seek ways to reach students, including English language learners, who have linguistic, musical, logical or mathematical, spatial, bodily or kinesthetic, intrapersonal, and interpersonal orientations to learning and knowing (Olson 2003, 73–79). When Antonio gave students options that included drawing book covers, writing an interview script, creating a collage, and mapping Huck's journey as ways to respond to *Huck Finn*, he provided students with various learning modalities to fully participate as respondents to the text. Yes, his evaluation and grading of students' efforts would be more problematic than had he given students a multiple-choice test, or a single essay topic. Yet the payoff was worth the extra effort. Through their creative efforts, Antonio had the opportunity to watch as students did an "exceptional job" expressing their understanding of the novel.

One aspect of the lessons that Antonio may not have been able to observe, since he had not been in Mrs. F.'s classroom when they began studying the novel, was what she did to help students "enter" the world of the text. When we walk into a brand new building, one that looks different from any we've ever seen or been inside before, we appreciate having a guide nearby. We count on the guide to tell us about some of the things we might find there, and then we hope the guide will open the door for us, and stay nearby as we cross the threshold and begin to wander down the corridors. Teachers are guides, in this sense, when we bring students face to face with works of literature. Although the format of a new assignment, like four brick walls of a building, may be familiar—one novel looks pretty much like another novel, for example—the interior is sure to be different from the other novels that our students have explored. When students enter a new text world, they can easily be overwhelmed by the unfamiliar vocabulary, narrative structure, temporal and geographic settings, characters, tone, and so on. In order to alleviate potential problems caused by the newness of new texts, we can engage in prereading activities that prepare students to enter the text world with confidence, and with enthusiasm about what they might find there. Jeff Wilhelm, with Tanya N. Baker and Julie Dube, in *Strategic Reading: Guiding Students to Lifelong Literacy 6–12* (2001), refer to this kind of guiding as "frontloading." They define the concept this way:

> Frontloading is a way to prepare, protect, and support students into the acquisition of new content and new ways of doing things. Frontloading is the use of any prereading strategy that prepares students for success—and in

Vygotsky's view, students must be able to be successful with challenging tasks if they are going to truly learn something and cultivate a continuing impulse to learn (92).

We can only speculate about what kinds of frontloading Mrs. F. did before students began reading *Huck Finn*. Which textual, cultural, social, and personal issues might you prepare twenty-first-century high-school students for before walking with them into the door of *Huck Finn*? Would you focus on Twain's rhetorical structures and vocabulary, or the point of view employed by the novel? Would you introduce concepts related to racial attitudes in the mid 1800s? Might you introduce criticism of the novel from Twain's day and in the present? Would you have students consider the geography and significance of the Mississippi River? Would you want them to think, before reading, about the qualities they look for in a friend, or consider injustices they have suffered based on others' bad assumptions about them? Regardless of your personal teaching goals, and thus your choices at the prereading stage, the features that you choose to highlight during frontloading should be ones that are important to students' experience with the literary text. Trivial information that does not contribute to readers' abilities to enter the world of the text are better ignored during the prereading period, so that they do not interfere with the students' enthusiasm for walking into the text world and wandering its corridors.

The fact that these same students had test scores that Antonio calls "terrible" suggests that there was a mismatch between instruction and evaluation, and perhaps that the goals for instruction did not inform the method of evaluation. While Antonio and Mrs. F. emphasized that students' renderings of the text were paramount when the class read and studied *Huck Finn*, that focus on response was apparently shifted when the test, which included a section for the student to match the quote to the speaker and explain its significance, was given. This situation sends up a red flag for experienced and beginning teachers: our instructional goals and teaching and learning activities must be reflected in the kinds of evaluations of student learning that we make. To teach one aspect of a novel, yet test on another one is not fair to students; the test, in that case, does not provide students with a continuation of learning, but with an exercise in frustration.

Movies and Print Texts: Are They Enemies in the English Classroom?

Antonio has probably been in classes like those that I confessed to teaching in my early years—ones in which films are used as a way for the teacher to buy some needed time. He has probably been in ones, too, in which the teacher relies on a film version of a book or story as a vehicle for reviewing the contents of the literary work. It is not surprising when he mentions to Mike that he recommended that students who had not finished reading the book rent the movie, since he "want[s] them to pass" their *Huck Finn* test.

With this statement, Antonio shows us an example of a caring, enthusiastic beginning teacher who, unfortunately, fails to consider his overarching goals when making instructional decisions.

Like the mismatch between the literature lessons and the test, Antonio is using the film, not for its abilities to enrich students' experience of the novel, but as a quick substitute for that experience. If Antonio wants students to read *Huck Finn* only to remember specifics of story content (what is Emmaline's middle name? How long did Huck and Jim hide?), the use of the film as a substitute for the book might be an appropriate strategy (and then, only if the movie is a reliable, complete version of the book). However, Antonio has been, to that point, concerned with getting students engaged in the pleasures of reading. It is evident that his goal is more closely aligned with helping students learn to approach literature from an aesthetic stance, one in which they read for the pleasure of reading, with an eye toward enjoying the transaction with the text. With that as his goal, the movie-as-substitute idea is inappropriate; it does not work toward his goal.

Later in his exchange with Antonio, Mike suggests using films that reinforce the theme of literary texts. He gives the example of showing cuts from *The Birds* and *Psycho* when his objective, for teaching Poe's "The Tell-Tale Heart," is to focus on "how sensory details create tension." This is an excellent idea, one that not only allows deeper thought about the literary text, but one that also encourages students to think of the ways that film and television makers manipulate viewers through their choices of music, motion, camera angles, lighting, dialogue, and so on. It supports the goal of promoting critical thinking while allowing time for students to live through an aesthetic literary experience.

The question then becomes, "Is there a place for movies in the literature classroom?"

In *Reading in the Dark* (2001), an exciting book on incorporating film study into the English classroom, John Golden describes how he teaches students about films from the perspective of insiders. Golden explains, for example, how he has them roll up a sheet of paper to create a crude "camera," then gets them involved in a series of activities with those cameras. The camera play includes having students try different camera angles (low, high, eye, and Dutch), various framing techniques (long, close-up, and medium shots), several camera movements (pan, tilt, zoom, tracking), and specific lighting techniques (low-key, high-key, neutral, and bottom/side). And Golden doesn't stop there. He has students critically analyze the effects of each of the different camera actions. Students begin to see how viewers are intentionally guided and manipulated by those who make films. Here, he is teaching and promoting a habit of critical thinking among his students, one which they can apply to their out-of-school viewing of television shows, advertisements, movies, videos, and so on. Golden then goes on to explain similarities between reading of texts and reading of films, drawing on a response-based pedagogy. Golden's classes extend beyond the traditional definition of English classes to promote the kind of critical literacies that our students need in order to participate fully as citizens in twenty-first-century society.

The e-mail exchanges between Antonio and Mike raise significant questions about the role of the English teacher in this century. Each of us, as experienced and novice teachers, needs to consider how we will define and develop our goals in order to meet the literacy needs of our students. Given the limited amount of time that we are allowed to spend with our students, as their language, literature, writing, speaking, listening, media guides, we need to develop efficient and effective methods of integrating instruction. The reasonable place to begin is with having them read and write texts—including nonprint texts—about subjects and themes that matter to them, and help them make connections across texts, from one subject to another, and from academic lessons to their lives.

I encourage all first-time English teachers to keep copies of these useful books on their teaching desks.

Golden, John. 2001. *Reading in the Dark*. Urbana, IL: National Council of Teachers of English.

Teasley, Alan B. and Ann Wilder. 1997. *Reel Conversations*. Portsmouth, NH: Boynton/Cook.

7 *Search and Research*

In these heartfelt exchanges, Marcus finds himself in the middle of one of the toughest writing exercises teachers and students attempt to negotiate—the research project. As a young intern, Marcus identifies with the struggles this group of general English sophomores encounter as they try to select a topic from a menu of rather limited choices. Then he plods along with them as they amass materials in a perfunctory fashion, and as they lumber to the final draft finish line.

Providing Choices and Setting Objectives

Dear Mike,

The class is starting on a research paper, which Mrs. J. usually does with a literary figure. Seems pretty typical. I would love to try a research paper on Tallahassee history or family genealogy or something that would add a personal interest to the students. Any suggestions of things that have worked for you? My cooperating teacher tells me that they are pretty much restricted because of the depletion of material in the library. What are some things that would be permissible? Can we ask that they go to the public library or use the Internet—even if it means working on it off of campus?

Thanks,
Marcus

Dear Marcus,

This research assignment does seem kind of limiting—students need choices—especially if it's on such an extended project. If you have to stick to the literary figure idea, maybe make a list of authors, writers according to personality types. Then the students could match up according to their own self-image. That might be kind of interesting. Or try including different genres that might encompass the contemporary front, such as screenwriters, songwriters, and journalists. Of course, your supervising teacher would have to go along with this plan. It's her class.

When you have your own domain, you will have to ask yourself, "What is my objective?" Is it to force the students to write about something they don't care about or something they already know a lot about, or is it to teach them how to research and get jazzed about it?

If research is your goal, open the channels, make the accessing, recording, reporting, summarizing, and conceptualizing the information they amass your primary objective, which brings up another roadblock regarding your mentor's situation. It sounds as if the school library is it. Therefore, you might talk to her about coordinating a field trip to the state, university, or public library. If that's not possible, give the students extra credit for going on their accord.

Since I teach eleventh grade (most of the students can drive themselves to the library), I require the students to use different sources of information, such as microfiche, microfilm, web documents, videos, public documents, narratives, periodicals, newspapers, books, along with primary sources. Consequently, the students learn the real deal about research: how and where to find information. To make sure they access these different sources, I limit the amount of Internet sources they may use (two data bases). I purposely steer them away from the cyberhighway because I want them to learn about other ways to seek information.

That's why I really like your idea about local history or family genealogy. Primary research is a terrific component to include in almost any research project. With my students, it's the primary objective (no pun intended). The students have to interview someone over thirty-five to help put a focus and voice on a historical, cultural, or sociological phenomenon. Then they use their additional research to enrich and support their interviews. I use the age limit to force the kids to break out of their boxes and explore another generation's experience. Initially, a few moan and groan, but it always amazes me how jazzed the majority of them get by the experience. Topics are wide open. Students have written about Beatlemania, World War II, the disco era, Viet Nam, hiking the Appalachian Trail, the women's movement, the civil rights movement, conscientious objectors, Elvis Presley, hitchhiking cross country, vegetarianism, Buddhism, life in hobo camps, Watergate, the depression, hula hoops, and the big band era.

Of course, the assignment inspires a lot of the students to use family members as primary sources—which is really terrific because it brings them closer to someone they should already be close to. One student interviewed his grandfather about playing minor league baseball in the Chicago Cubs organization when Ernie Banks was breaking the color line for that club; another student interviewed her German-born grandmother about being brainwashed by the Hitler Youth Movement, and yet another interviewed his dad about the harassment he endured as an Iranian-American during the Iran hostage crisis. In these cases, and many more, students learned invaluable lessons about family members and the human experience. More importantly, they began to realize that incredible stories are all around us—in our families, friends, neighborhoods, counties, countries, and planet. And that's a pretty cool lesson to learn.

Respectfully,
Mike

Greasing the Wheels with Prewriting Time

Dear Mike,

Thanks for the heads up about research. Back in the trenches, things are good. I conferred with the students about their outlines. I found this to be a much easier task than their thesis statements because the students already had their thoughts together, and I did not have to do all the work. With the thesis statements, a lot of the kids didn't have a clue what to write about, and they didn't seemed to buy into many of my ideas. Consequently, helping with the outlines seemed fairly simple. The teacher had already gone over different outline strategies, and we had been to the library a few times, so they had begun finding some sources and some information to map out in outline form. It was a good week, and I am looking forward to reading some of the students' finished papers.

Marcus

Dear Marcus,

The thesis statement is always a toughie. Students tend to whimper and snivel with the hackneyed, "I can't think of anything to write about." So you rack your brain trying to help a student come up with something, and he or she reciprocates by mumbling the inevitable, "I don't like that; it sounds boring."

Wah, Wah, Wah.

Remember—school shouldn't be a place where students come to watch teachers work, so they really need to figure out their own focus and thesis.

As an avid wordsmith, I firmly believe writers need time to think about what they are going to write before they actually can write. (Seems pretty obvious, huh?) My students get a little wigged when I tell them that I do my best writing when I go for walks or when I'm driving alone in my car or when I'm doing yard work. Seriously, the solitude inspires thoughtful thoughts and helps me figure out where my prose is flowing (unless the traffic's bad or the weeds too high). Consequently, I rarely suffer from writer's block because I rarely sit down to write until I know what I'm going to write about.

That's why I think one of the worst things a teacher can do is say "Today I want you to write a theme about blah, blah, blah. Now get out your paper and pen or pencil. On your mark, get set, go. And get those creative juices flowing. Hut, two, three, four. Hop to it! Move, move, move! You've got fifteen more minutes 'til the bell rings. Why aren't you through yet?"

Of course, that's what we do for standardized writing tests, but that's another beef/subject.

Yuck.

In other words, I think it's paramount to plant the seeds of any big assignment way ahead of time. Give the students journal prompts and writer models to ponder, then brainstorm ideas with them. Then give them plenty of time to think about the assignment before they actually have to formally state a topic, a written thesis or a commitment. Once they get the hang of this prewriting routine, it usually eliminates the thesis stress for you and for your students.

Respectfully,
Mike

Staying the Course

Mike,

We finished the outline phase of the research paper. I helped a lot of students with it, but quite a few of them had trouble getting organized. I enjoyed getting the time to interact, though. Today was kind of lazy. The outlines were due, so we spent a great deal of the time just talking. It was like the perk of this job. The students were interactive, and it was okay to laugh with them. Along the way, we spoke about shootings in schools, and we wound up having a great talk about it. Students amaze me. As much as they have to learn, they still remain very aware of the world today, and have some really great opinions. I almost wished I was teaching a unit on choices because this talk could have been a great stimulus. Instead, it was just a time for a great chance to know the real students I try to educate. Food for thought, huh?

Learning more each day.

Marcus

Dear Marcus,

Not to burst your bubble, but if the students are having trouble organizing themselves, why not use the downtime to bridge the next step in the process and go from outline to rough draft? Often, this is a troubling step. Perhaps your cooperative teacher should have picked up the pace during this lazy day. It's been my experience that research papers often drag along, and then whammo—final drafts are due, and the students go spinning off into plagiarism land because they haven't spent quality time getting down the basics, such as summarizing and paraphrasing and making someone else's ideas a synthesis of their own presentation or argument (critical thinking skills and sound support).

Don't get me wrong, I love interactive yammering with students about issues that really do matter (such as violence in schools). But, thematic units need to stay the course. If the focus becomes too blurred and cluttered with the easy going passage of time, I'm afraid that some of these final products may turn out on the slack side. (Not a slam—I'm speaking from my own experience as a student and a teacher.)

Nonetheless, kudos to you for finding the students amazingly interesting. Believe me, teachers need passion for the subject they teach—their students.

Just remember—when students who make such an arduous task as a research paper seem so simple—simplicity is what they may end up eventually producing.

Respectfully,
Mike

Supporting the Student's Voice and Perspective

Mike,

I've been helping students work on their final drafts. It was good, because I can finally see some of their papers coming together, and some of my ideas are incorporated in them. I got a lot of satisfaction out of one girl's efforts, because I ended up tutoring her on the whole writing process. Her analysis of Amy Tan was outstanding. Go me!

Marcus

Dear Marcus,

It is such a treat when you work with a student on a paper, and the final product is so succulent and sweet. Congrats! I know that felt good. Just make sure it's her analysis of Amy Tan. We must be careful to coach the "writing process" not the thought and content process. In other words, we do not want to suggest too heavily to our students what to actually think. After all, students have traditionally been taught to think like the teachers want them to think—which suggests that teachers always have the best answers and directions for everything. Yikes!

Respectfully,
Mike

Jazzing Up the Projects

Hello Mike,

After grading some of the research papers, I realize that most of the students simply wrote a biographical report on their literary figure. Go figure. If the teacher hadn't given them such a narrow focus for their papers, maybe the kids would've been more creative and passionate with their papers.

Again, I would not do it this way. I think that if at all possible the students should be allowed to select the direction of their papers, themselves. Of course, guidelines must be set in place, but letting the students make the decisions only enhances their eagerness to do it.

When you assign a biography, what is your method for getting the kids to tackle a project like this?

Marcus

Dear Marcus,

Funny you should ask. I just completed a historical poem assignment (see Figure 7–1) with my ninth graders in conjunction with a hero/shero thematic unit that tied into the theme of "Overcoming Oppression" as an extension of Black History Month. Basically, the students learned about heroism in the classic socialistic sense. For models, we used Frederick Douglass, Paul Laurence Dunbar, Jackie Robinson, Satchel Paige, Rosa Parks, The Freedom Riders, Martin Luther

Historical Heroic Poetry Assignment

Write a poem, lyric, or song about a heroic historical figure or group of figures.

The hero/shero or group of heroes you select must embody the qualities of goodness that we have identified in this unit:

> Standing up for the good of all humanity
> Sacrificing their own well-being for the good of all society
> Confronting and overcoming forces of evil in the society
> Leading noble movements to overcome adversity
> Doing good deeds for the betterment of all society

Poetic examples we've studied—Frederick Douglass, Martin Luther King Jr., Paul Laurence Dunbar, Satchel Paige, and Rosa Parks

Preferred length—two to three stanzas or 18–24 lines
> (Add a chorus if it's a song or lyric.)

Poems must include a minimum of ten facts about the hero/shero/heroes
For full credit, students will read, recite, or sing their poems to the class
> (They may also show a home-made video or play a recording.)

Students also must include a two-page, typed, expository essay justifying how their hero/shero/heroes fit the criteria for such a heroic classification.

FIGURE 7–1

King, Ralph Ellison, and Nate McCall. Using that rubric and those models, the students had to research and find their own hero/shero. For final products, they had to write a justification/persuasive paper explaining how their person fit the criteria, then they wrote a free verse poem extolling the virtues of their hero/shero which they ultimately read in class. Overall, it's a very interesting coupling of critical thinking with creativity, and it works rather well.

So you're right! Empowering students with choices is critical for motivational purposes, but you still must set criteria and certain limits. In other words, give them a playground with boundaries so they can frolic and revel within its perimeters.

Respectfully,

Mike

FROM ANOTHER ANGLE

If anyone were to do research into my early career as a teacher, the topics "Teaching the research paper," and "Teaching students to be researchers," would be one of the dark, gloomy ugly chapters. I did a terrible job of trying to teach students to write research papers. The first time I tried, I was teaching eleventh graders. It was spring, and those who were going to pass the class and move on to become seniors had already been assured of their status, thanks to an odd and incomprehensible grading and promotion policy that was popular in some school systems in the early 1980s.

First Set of Mistakes: When I announced that our last push for the year would be toward writing research papers, I was met with challenges:

Research paper? What do you mean?
I don't want to waste time in the library now!
Why would I want to look up a bunch of information on something I don't care about, anyway?

I should have taken at least one of these exclamations as a hint, and worked with students until they identified topics in which they had interest, but I was impatient and a little anxious: I distributed a set of topics that I created, based on the topics of essays they had written during the expository writing unit earlier in the year. Each student was to choose a topic from the list to expand into a research paper. My intention was good—to allow students some choice, and to provide topic choices based on areas in which they had shown some interest. What I didn't realize was that they had consumed all of their interest for the "expository essay" topics during the expository writing unit. Unable to demonstrate any flexibility at that point, I plowed ahead. One student chose legalization of marijuana, one chose changes in the Olympic Games, another chose civil rights. None was particularly interested in his or her topic. I could imagine the bland prose that they would produce, and later, my expectations were met.

Second Set of Mistakes: I assumed that these students understood that writing a research paper requires a few different steps. What I found, instead, was that the eleventh graders were overwhelmed at the thought of producing a twenty-page, typed paper. I found, too, that they needed information not only on the stages they could go through in order to write the paper one step at a time, but that they needed instruction in some of those steps. Unfortunately, I learned that too late. The extent of my instruction, that first round, was to announce, "Your thesis statement and outline are due in one week, and your first draft is due in two weeks. Be sure to have at least five sources of information, and include your note cards when you turn in your draft. Use MLA format in your bibliography. Now let's all go to the media center together, so that you can get started." The assignment sounded about right to me (I had been out of college for less than a year, and was used to being given few details for major papers). When the few who tried the assignment brought in their drafts two weeks later, I realized that I had violated a crucial rule of writing instruction: I had *told* them to write, but I had not *helped* them in the process of writing. Their papers were collections of long quotes pulled out of encyclopedias and almanacs, articles from the vertical files and some old books. (This was pre-Web days for most high-school students and high schools; I am sure that, had I repeated my mistakes in 2003, students would have responded by turning in unexpurgated copies of texts that they had downloaded from the Internet.)

Third Set of Mistakes: I did collect drafts, and wrote extensive comments on each, then returned them during a teacher-student writing conference. During the conferences, I gained some sense of the frustration that students had felt with the assignment, but I attributed their frustration to laziness, not to my lack of clarity. I followed this informal formative evaluation of their progress with a round of grading the final papers, rubric at my side, red pen in hand. I got through only a few of the papers before I began feeling slightly sick; I had caused students to waste a lot of time on a poorly designed project, and was paying the price of having to take hours and hours to grade each product. The final straw came the day after I returned the papers. A student named James came to see me after school, furious that he had been given a D on his paper. He literally yelled at me, "My paper is perfect. I know it is, I checked it on my spell checker and grammar checker. There are no mistakes!" The problem, I tried to tell him, was that his paper, though technically sound, said absolutely nothing.

I wish I'd known then what I know now. Like Mike, I would encourage teachers to open up the possibilities for topics, including items of immediate and real interest to their students. One method of coming up with a list of topics is to conduct a few class brainstorming sessions; students can grab ideas that appeal to them from the class-generated lists, and might even meet with a small group of classmates to discuss ways to approach the topic. I would also encourage students to experiment with several methods for generating ideas that might be included in their papers. The traditional topic outline is useful, once ideas have been collected and written down, as a means of checking organization, but it does little to stimulate the production of ideas. As Mike says, we must allow students time to think. Writing specialist Tom Romano draws from the work of John Mayher, Nancy Lester, and Gordon Pradl (1983) when he recommends that we provide plenty of time for "percolating" ideas (Romano 1987, 55). During percolating, writers prepare to write: they might talk, doodle, run, wander the halls, or put their heads on their desks, and close their eyes. One or two might even create an outline, draw a web of related ideas, or make a list. The point is that the student writers need time, and they need the freedom to use generative prewriting activities that work best for them.

I wish I had been aware of Ken Macrorie's now famous "I-Search" strategy, too (*The I-Search Paper: Revised Edition of Searching Writing* 1988), since it calls for students to conduct research as real researchers, not just as collectors of others' ideas. In I-Search papers, students use the first person to discuss what they know about a topic, and what they have learned about it as a result of their research. I wish, too, that I had been one of Mike's colleagues, close enough to steal the hero/shero idea for my students.

It is encouraging for me to see that Marcus has so many concerns about the nature of the research project that he was involved with as a student teacher. I feel confident that he will not make mistakes like those that I made the first time I taught a research paper. I am glad he won't have the problems that I did the second time I tried to teach the research paper, too. That year, I overcompensated for the lack of structure that I provided the first time around. I demanded that students turn in a small part of the research paper assignment every single day for three weeks, and gave daily grades on items such as "completion of five bibliographic note cards" and "thesis statement that is clear and concise" to "turned in first draft on time" and "turned in comments on classmate's first draft on time." I was an incredibly slow learner when it came to managing long-term writing assignments.

I am encouraged, too, that Marcus notices the link between a writer's interest in the topic and the quality of what is written. Further, he understands that grading research papers requires us, as teachers, to reflect on the nature of the assignment itself, to think carefully about what our goals for the assignment are, and how we assisted students in achieving those goals. If we conclude that we did nothing more than give an assignment and step out of the way, then perhaps we should create a column in our grade books in which we assign ourselves a (low) grade.

Finally, I am encouraged that Marcus is interested in getting to know students as people, in exploring their interests and concerns. The better he knows them, the more likely he will be to design lessons, even long-term writing assignments, that will allow them to address their interests, to bring their worlds into the classroom for a closer look.

Some books you might turn to for ideas that add to the list of possibilities for alternative research papers include these:

Tsujimoto, Joseph. 2001. *Lighting Fires: How the Passionate Teacher Engages Adolescent Writers*. Portsmouth, NH: Boynton/Cook Heinemann. See especially his description of the "Function Paper," Chapter seven, pages 144–167.

Burke, Jim. 2003. *The English Teacher's Companion*, 2nd edition. Portsmouth, NH: Heinemann. See especially not only his chapter on teaching writing (Chapter 7), but also his chapters on digital literacy (Chapter 12) and media literacy (Chapter 13); each of these will provide you with realistic yet out-of-the ordinary ways to conceive of the possibilities for taking the traditional research paper assignment into the twenty-first century.

Baines, Lawrence and Anthony Kunkel. 2003. *Teaching Adolescents to Write: The Unsubtle Art of Naked Teaching*. Allyn & Bacon. See especially Chapter 3, "AP Aliens: An Interdisciplinary Unit Involving Poetry, Persuasion, Myths, Heroes, Language, Government, Peace, War, and Apologies," pages 43–65.

Baines, Lawrence and Anthony J. Kunkel. (Eds.) 2000. *Going Bohemian: Activities that Engage Adolescents in the Art of Writing Well*. International Reading Association. See especially Clarissa West-White's "Reflective Research: Portrait and Poem," pages 149–152.

Dornan, Reade W., Lois Matz Rosen, and Marilyn Wilson. 2003. *Within and Beyond the Writing Process in the Secondary English Classroom*. Allyn & Bacon. See especially Chapter 5, "The Essay and Other Write-to-Learn Assignments," pages 119–148.

Soven, Margot Iris. 1999. *Teaching Writing in Middle and Secondary Schools: Theory, Research and Practice*. Allyn & Bacon. See especially her advice about sequencing assignments and setting deadlines (Chapter 6), as well as her description as the teacher, as a researcher, and a writer (Chapter 9).

8 — Special Care for Special Needs

Over the course of his middle-school internship, Freddie bemuses the plight of his General Ed classes wherein unmotivated students, reluctant readers, ESL (English as a Second Language) and ESE (Exceptional Student Education) kids struggle side by side. For a novice, Freddie exhibits a lot of maturity; he questions the motives and effectiveness of this labeling system, as he ventures outside of his domain to check out the Special Ed classes. Freddie also spends a lot of time thinking about the needs of each and every student, along with the mission of compulsory education—qualities that Mike not only applauds, but equates as essential ingredients for a truly effective teacher.

Remembering the Subject We Teach

Dear Mike,

I did some research on the mainstreaming issue, and most of what I found were unsupported political diatribes about how it "isn't fair" to isolate students who are SLD [Specific Learning Disabilities] or ADHD [Attention Deficit Hyperactivity Disorder]. But, I did run across what was apparently the first clinical study of how teachers are reacting to the problems of mainstreamed SLD kids, and the conclusions were not surprising:

1. Teachers don't plan anything special for SLD kids.
2. Covering content was far superior to comprehension.
3. Teachers have little if any contact with a Special Ed teacher.

So! In order to not hurt anyone's feelings, the "powers that be" have created an impossible situation. We are reading and talking about how important it is to plan so well that you seem flexible, and that it is equally critical to manage the time so that you squeeze the last drop from the class period. But the situation I see here is untenable under those criteria.

This kid, Alex, a hyperactive space cadet, is constantly distracting what is an already easily distracted class. He is just one of six troublemakers! I am teaching a prereading activity (a really simple poem) tomorrow. Because of the SLD kids, my activity is so chopped up and slow that it has to be insulting to some of the other kids.

What I wonder is how in the hell do you plan for so much diversity? It seems to me that the ends get chopped off, and the teacher has to aim for the middle.

Freddie

Dear Freddie,

What it boils down to is this—you're dealt a hand—a class full of students. Then you play it. You can either fold or gamble, bluff yourself or call their bluff.

Personally, I like to keep them guessing. I like to play. I like to play with students and their curiosity about life. I am wildly fascinated by what I can learn from them. I consider them individuals. I try to find out what's amazing about each of them. It is an ongoing process that lasts at least a semester. Most often, a school year. Sometimes, a school career. And occasionally, a lifetime. I still hear via e-mail and get periodic visits from former students. Some of them even seek me out to help them with collegiate papers in progress. I tell them, "Once you are a student of mine—you're a student for life" (but only if they want to be—it's not a life sentence).

As for the research article, consider it for what it is—someone else's opinion. Of course, there is a lot of truth in it. And that means that you will have to deal with the labels and the labeled kids—who, unfortunately, have become victimized by the system. Too often they are put into "special classes" with loads of worksheets and uninspiring pedagogues—who don't plan in a creative way for their kids. That's why it is important for these students to be mainstreamed. But, it can be trying.

Of course, most general classes are very trying. Basically, they're packed with unmotivated and disgruntled malcontents, sprinkled with a couple ESL kids, along with a smattering of ESE students (naturally, there are some bright gems in these General Ed trenches as well). But, the classes are usually quite large. The AP [Advanced Placement], honors, and Special Ed classes tend to be much smaller. Once again—welcome to the real world of teaching.

And in the face of such absurdity, it is ironic (and somewhat moronic) that the "regular" classroom teachers don't seek out the Special Ed teachers for help. Most ESE students take an academic support class which is the equivalent of a very intimate and structured study hall. Personally, I've found it very helpful to use the ESE teachers as homework and project buddies for my ESE students. It proves invaluable for these support teachers to be in the loop and know what's going on in my arena. Ditto for ESL support classes.

So for you, Freddie, the choice is to play or fold. Remember your environment is their domain. Your task is to elevate their expectations of themselves. To tackle such a daunting endeavor, you must embrace the youngsters. Pique their interest in themselves. Get them to truly reflect on the madness that surrounds us all. Teaching is a wildly fascinating art form. The medium, though, is not some "set-in-stone" curriculum that the state or your principal or any educational design instructors have mandated that you must do. To be a brilliant sculptor of young minds, you must first get your hands into that clay, and feel the energy force that you want to shape into some viable work of art. The student is your medium. The true teacher rolls up his or her sleeves, and gets down and dirty with the elements bestowed upon him or her in that class. The system throws down the gauntlet; the knight in shining armor accepts the challenge and makes beauty from chaos. Am I a madman? Close, but not quite. I am a teacher, a redeemer, a seer . . .

You, too, may be—if you truly accept your mission.

Respectfully,
Mike

Stimulating the Unstimulated

Dear Mike,

I have been doing some real thinking about what you said in your last reply, and I am beginning to see the light. From that perspective, everything comes to a peaceful synthesis. It seems that the "It's about the kids" bit is the sort of revelation that only comes to the mystics after a lifetime of sacrifice and meditation. I feel like I've been given one of the last true nuggets of wisdom left in the world. It is just so hard to stay focused, and not discouraged, and not so consumed by the details that one misses the big picture.

This week I observed two different classes besides my own. I observed an eighth-grade Special Ed and a seventh-grade class of gifted kids. The two classrooms were very different, although some of the students did not seem all that different.

In the Special Ed class, there were only eight students—two girls and six boys. All but two of the students were black. I noticed this, but it really didn't draw my attention until the teacher commented to me that she really thought that this certain boy (the only white child in the class) ought to be moved to a mainstream classroom. Then she said that she thought this other boy (Hispanic) probably ought to be moved up as well. I wasn't sure what to think. Was she unconsciously making value judgments based on ethnicity? Or was it only a coincidence that the two who needed to be moved up happened to be the only two nonblack students in the room? I don't know.

During class, most of the students watched a movie. Apparently, they earn points during the week, and watch a movie on Friday if they earn enough points. The students who did not earn the points sat in a different side of the room and grumbled. The teacher did not provide an activity for these students to do, and so most of them got in trouble. One boy walked out of the classroom, and the teacher had to call the office. Another girl sat in her desk and yelled at the teacher, using fluent profanity. Some of the students actually sat quietly and earned the ability to go over and watch the movie with the other students. While they were watching the movie, one girl kept alternately yelling and moping. Meanwhile, the teacher told me about each of the students. She had been working with Special Ed students for over ten years. She pointed out which students had which deficiency that qualified them for the class. There were a few LD [Learning Disabled], a few "behavior problems," and at least one EMH [Educably Mentally Handicapped].

I think most of the students must have had a mixture of problems. For instance, the yelling girl was pointed out as LD, but she obviously had many other problems. She would not look at either the teacher or me, and she only smiled whenever she told us to *&#@ off and leave her alone. She almost acted autistic in her absolute refusal to look at us or relate to us as people. I guess it's just toward teachers, though, because I saw her relating to other students in the hall, and she seemed pretty normal. Really strange. I really don't know how I would handle a student with her type of behavior.

Some of the other students seemed to fit their labels better (I guess that's how I can describe it). The student who had been identified as EMH was eager to please and easily guided. He had something wrong with his eyes and kept looking amazed. All in all, I was a bit overwhelmed at the serious problems and behavior issues. I don't know how they ought to be handled.

Were they aggravated by their recognition and isolation? Would they do better if they were not singled out? I think that they might be singled out more in a mainstream class, though, because the teacher would constantly have to reprimand them or assist them. How does a regular teacher handle students like that when they're in their regular heterogeneous classrooms?

The gifted science class had twenty-three students. They split into groups and worked together well. A few (one in particular) were loud and disruptive, but the others kept them under control and worked quietly. They all seemed more cheerful and optimistic and eager to please the teacher. The teacher told me that in their eagerness to please, they sometimes ended up in the psychiatric ward. I guess from the pressure they would put on themselves. This group seemed relaxed, though, and seemed to be enjoying themselves. Is this because they were expected to do well and behave? Were the problems in the other class caused by negative expectations? What do you say about it all? I'd like to hear your thoughts.

Thanks,
Freddie

Dear Freddie,

Big question—what were the racial dynamics of the gifted classes?

My guess? Not quite so minority based. Obviously, you've hit a nerve, so I'll climb back on the soapbox.

Basically, the EH [Emotionally Handicapped] and EMH labels are used by the system to weed out the behaviorally unacceptable kids. The minority bias comes from the style shifting that goes down with the territory. In other words, a street attitude doesn't bode too well in the school community. So we give the troublemakers an arcane label, stick them in a stigmatized Special Ed class, dumb down our expectations of them, baby-sit them, expect little or nothing, house them until they can bust out and wreak havoc on the streets of America.

Consequently, some Special Ed teachers don't bring much hope or enthusiasm to these classes. Quite often, they try to keep the kids busy with busywork à la the worksheets and the workbooks and other unimaginative distractions. Then they bribe them with candy, cookies, games, or other treats such as movies. By the way, what was the flick of the week, *The Terminator* or *Liar Liar*? Probably something of little or no educational value.

It saddens me to no end. These are the students who need us the most. These are the ones into whom we need to be pouring more of our time and energy. If we were to use the gifted classroom model (interactive, hands-on activities) with these students, then maybe we could stimulate a better climate in the classroom and get them more excited about "learning" something.

When you refuse to teach students something valuable, they often respond with profanity and profane behavior. So we sit on them, and "busywork" their senseless days away. Meanwhile, the gifted students (usually white and upper-middle class with computers and books and parents who offer them the world at their fingertips in their comfy homes) get more educationally stimulated at an added price tag for the system. Thus, the fat get fatter, and the lean get meaner.

Sorry for such rantings, but you asked.

Meanwhile, don't fall into this trap. All students are worth teaching. But, to teach any of them, you've got to reach out to each and every one of them.

Respectfully,
Mike

Embracing the Challenge of Challenged Readers

Mike,

Today, the students got "Troll" book order forms. I watched them when Mrs. N. gave the students ten minutes to look at them. Some threw the order sheets on the ground and either sat there, bored and quiet, or tried to whisper to one another. Some were eagerly picking out exactly what books they wanted. This class is heterogeneously mixed, and so the students' feelings on reading vary drastically. Now I'm trying to figure out how I'm going to deal with that. I don't know how to interest those students who are ESE or ESL. For them, reading is an extremely grueling activity. As a teacher, though, I must also allow room for those accelerated students, so they don't feel bored or slowed down. One girl in this class of seventh graders is reading Theodore Drieser! I haven't reconciled this yet; I am not sure if I can. I'm trying to think of ways to get their interest.

On Wednesday, several kids were sleeping in class, even though the lesson was interesting. When I was in middle school, the English lessons consisted of opening our *Warriners* grammar book and diagramming sentences or reading boring short stories and answering the questions at the end. These kids are reading some good stuff—Richard Wright! so if the motivation isn't going to come from the material, at least not at first, and since they are so tired (well it is fifth period), I'm thinking about bringing in candy. I can get them to try for the candy through answering questions, and maybe the sugar will do them some good.

Wednesday, one of the students had to leave early to go to court for committing some crime, and has not returned as of today. How am I supposed to get them to give a crap about passing state mandated tests of achievement, like the FCAT [Florida Comprehensive Assessment Test], when they are facing juvenile detention? They don't do their homework; they fail their tests. And it isn't that the material is boring or unmotivating, because the homework assignment was to make up a resume (either for a fictional character or for themselves), which I thought was pretty decent. It gave them choices and allowed for creativity.

Plus, it didn't have to be perfect—just a rough draft. Only three turned theirs in today. I think there are some problems at home. One girl wrote a dialogue which was about her mother beating her. I guess the best thing I can do is to try and make the time in my class as interesting and pleasant as possible. I was supposed to go to a teacher-parent conference today, we waited twenty minutes or so, and the parent never showed up. That's a more powerful lesson that the parent is giving to the child than I can give.

Freddie

Dear Freddie,

Bless your heart, and believe me I understand your dilemma. I taught in a juvenile prison for three years, where almost every child was a walking horror story. Most had been abused emotionally, many physically, and some sexually. They were a totally twisted bunch, but the one thing I soon realized was that they thrived on positive vibes. So I became a cheerleader for educational values. I not only cherished the Lit we read, but I cherished the writings they produced. We made books and newsletters. We role-played, writing letters for characters in stories we read, or we wrote screenplay adaptations and videotaped scenes (the little hambones loved to see themselves on TV). Interactive activities proved especially effective for the disenfranchised, the ESE, the ESL, and every other student in the joint (including the really bright ones—and there were plenty of them, too).

Mind you, these were middle-school kids with rap sheets a mile long. Some of them were reading on a second- or third-grade level. So by golly, I had to bust my tail to reach them. We were reading Langston Hughes and Richard Wright. We were reading S. E. Hinton and Mark Twain. We were reading newspapers and the back of baseball cards. We were reading wrestling magazines and stock car periodicals. Whatever it took, we read. I also elicited the support of the county's reading specialist. She started coming out three times a week and working one on one with students. Whenever you end up with students with severe reading difficulties in your classes, make sure you seek out and utilize any and all of the resources your county provides.

It also helps to do some reciprocal reading with the students—one on one. Back then, I used to schedule meetings with kids during my planning period. We would find high-interest/low-skills books to read together. I would read a passage aloud, then the student would repeat the same passage. Then we would switch roles—the student would read and I would follow (or reciprocate). After a while (the warm-up), we'd abandon the repetition and just take turns reading passages. At the end of the session, the student would recap in a journal what we read for the day (usually a chapter or two). This is a terrific strategy to use to help a student's reading improve. It also helps the teacher connect to the reluctant readers and vice versa. Unfortunately, it takes up planning time, but small doses work wonders.

In class I found it really important to read the more complex Lit aloud for the students to follow. And despite the misgivings that some teachers may have about this process (obviously, most English teachers were good readers, so as students they had hated to have teachers read aloud), the students got jazzed by the literature because I read dramatically with pizzazz. As a rule, this simple strategy works especially well with heterogeneously mixed, general ed groups. These same strategies are also very effective with the ESL kids. During my stint at the center, I had two Haitian students, one Vietnamese boy, and a couple of Cuban kids from Miami, and all of them became better readers and thinkers by hearing and seeing the language. Even the more advanced enjoyed this approach, but the key is in the delivery. You must practice reading the text aloud, so it becomes animated and lively.

Of course, it's also important to stop periodically during a reading to discuss and clarify what's up with the Lit. In doing so, you must become the catalyst to the connections between the text and the inner souls of the little darlings. Don't spoonfeed them, but dream up schemes for literary analyses and follow-ups that involve skills, issues, and themes that you (as their guiding light) realize are key for them to grapple with. Hence, the key is—knowing your students. Find their interests, tap into them, and then mine their little nuggets of brilliance with plenty of jazzy, interactive adventures. As you've noted in your previous tirades about ESE classes and skills kids, work books and busywork won't get these students (or any others for that matter) excited about learning. So maximize your creativity, and weave a tapestry of interactive magic to make the reading and writing come alive.

Group work is also helpful; it's amazing how much the students can help each other learn and understand. But it is important for the teacher to carefully stay involved with the groups. Think carefully about whom you put with whom. For groups to truly be productive, you need a balanced mix. Don't just let the students work with their buddies. All too often, the work turns into play. That's why it's also important to circulate and observe and occasionally interact with the groups to make certain they stay on task. A lot of teachers use group work time as an excuse to hunker down behind their desks and get some paperwork done. While relieving the desk of its paper load is a necessary part of our jobs, group work isn't the time or occasion to become disengaged with the class's activities. Circulate, stimulate, and motivate.

Candy as a reward? Forget about it. We're not training circus bears here. Believe me the sugar thing has an undesirable effect. They'll be literally climbing the walls, while you figuratively follow suit. Instead, give books and magazines and art supplies as rewards. Have essay contests and offer rewards for outside reading achievement. (A lot of times bookstores will donate out-of-date materials for such a cause, or you can write a grant, or use monies from your school budget for such costs.) It works. At least it did for me at the juvenile prison. By the time most students were released from our program, their reading level had increased and their attitude toward school had improved.

For me, the payoff came in providing a glimmer of light in these young fellows' otherwise rather dull landscapes of life. Being a beacon of illumination is obviously an enlightening experience (hee, hee). It gives your life meaning and purpose. And I hope that's why you want to teach.

So reach out and grab the students' imaginations. Find out about *them*. Get them to write about their lives, their cultures, their experiences (this is vital for the ESL kids and all students, for that matter). Give them class time to write drafts. Put them in groups. Embrace liveliness. You seem to have the sensitivity and enthusiasm needed to really do it. And they all need someone like you. Whatever you do, don't give up.

Respectfully,
Mike

Getting Past the Institution of Education

Dear Mike,

My lesson went better than I expected. Mrs. N. really turned me loose. I had to deal with everything! At first I was only thinking about the lesson—the content—but I had to deal with one student, who kept asking me to write him a pass for the clinic. He was dying! Oh, the melodrama! I asked him to sit down until we were finished discussing the story, and he moaned throughout the period until I finally gave in and let him go.

Mrs. N. said afterwards that I shouldn't have let him out—that he's a con artist. But I just wished I had let him leave at the beginning of class, so he wouldn't continue to bother everyone. I guess that's a poor attitude, but I feel like if a kid doesn't want to be there, we shouldn't have to put forth so much effort in forcing them to stay. That time, money, and energy would be better spent in the classroom for those students who do want to be there. Education is a privilege, yet we treat it in the U.S. as a punishment, and force kids to go.

Anyway, my plan was more successful than I thought it would be. They hated the story, but I got them to talk about it, and to think about it, instead of just going to sleep in the back of the room. One girl has done nothing but give me nasty looks, and I got her talking, because she absolutely could not stand the story—so she had something to say—and I was listening to her. It was pretty awesome to see a student actually start to relate to me, simply because I was listening.

So now I'm looking back on my lesson and trying to figure out what I could have done differently. I got what I wanted out of it. They read, discussed, and wrote. But they hated the story. They wrote me and told me to please never subject another class to the story—it was boring and it didn't have a happy ending. I used Toni Cade Bambara's "Happy Birthday." So I guess I need to look for more action-packed stories. Any suggestions? And they have to have a happy ending!

Freddie

Dear Freddie,

There are three institutions in America where people are committed without consent. The prison system, the psychiatric hospitals, and the public school system. Pretty sicko, huh? As jail keepers, we must peacefully keep the institution from becoming chaos. We must keep the little inmates in the class. We cannot give them an early release, until they're sixteen.

Consequently, we have to put up with a great deal of abuse. I'm afraid there is a lot of truth in what your supervising teacher is saying. If we sent every student who was a nuisance out of the room and to the office or to the media center or to the school nurse or the parking lot or the gym or home, the administration would begin to get suspicious about our abilities to control our classrooms. I know this sounds totally party line, but I'm afraid for reasons of job security—it's the gospel.

On the other hand, I totally agree with what you're saying. I really can't stand keeping them under lock and key. But, it's my job.

So the key to our success is unbridled enthusiasm. Which brings me to my next step on the soapbox: Don't let the weenies and whiners and wimps get to you. They're going to tell you everything sucks and is boring. So when they complain about the abilities of Toni Cade Bambara as a storyteller, make them back up their analyses. Get them to think critically. In other words, just saying something "sucks" or is "boring" or is "okay" or even "kind'a good" is a total cop-out. Make the complainers stand behind their convictions. Heck, if they want a happy ending, put them in groups of two or three and have them write a more uplifting ending to the story, then have them read them to the class. By holding them accountable for their thoughts and opinions, we require them to ponder and to think. My bet is upon closer examination, they'll begin to appreciate the immensity of Ms. Bambara's talent. And after reading their own "cheesy" happily-ever-after, uplifting twaddle, they might even begin to realize that happy endings are for fairy tales, and that an essential ingredient of quality literary fiction is conflict. With conflict comes pain.

Hence, I feel your pain. I've experienced the same "sucks" and "boring" blanket indictment about literature for nineteen years. Nonetheless, your job is to overwhelm them with your belief in the beauty and the art and the relevance and the awesomeness of the wonderful prose and poetry that you are sharing. Then have the activities to back it up. Get them involved in the process.

Respectfully,
Mike

Staying Misty-Eyed and Connected

Dear Mike,

About all I have done this week is go over a pretest for a story the class read together. I was struck by how complicated the kids could make something as simple as an answer sheet. You have to go section by section, line by line to keep them from getting lost. Understand, I don't mean to convey a snotty tone here. I am just remarking that I would have taken it for granted how simple an answer sheet is. Every day, it seems I am presented with material that has to be broken down into its simplest, tiniest steps in order to be efficient. I take too much for granted.

I have also done some thinking about how innocent a sixth grader really is. I did some comparing between all I have experienced in twenty-eight years versus the kids in Mrs. N.'s class, and I am filled with hope. It seems that I have always been this very cynical, pessimistic old grouch. Being around them reminds me that I haven't always been this way.

These kids have an entire universe of stuff to do and see and understand. When I think how much my experiences can help them to be better people and to fashion a better world, I almost get misty-eyed. That, it seems, is what I need to be focusing on. So the key is for me to focus on how much help I can be to these veritable babies, to ease them into the very indifferent, if not downright cruel world of the adult.

If you haven't noticed, I am very concerned with not just "getting the job done," but to be the best English teacher in the whole confounded world. I sometimes feel so unprepared and overwhelmed by all the details that I wonder what in the hell I am doing this for. I think I have come to some conclusions on my own, but any tips you could give on managing these feelings would certainly be appreciated.

Freddie

Dear Freddie,

Listen, pal, stay misty-eyed and you won't have any problems. The students are the reason we're there. You have realized that, and that is the ultimate lesson. If you want to be "the best confounded English teacher in the world," just find out where they're at—skill wise, head wise, interest wise—then reach out and grab them with your unbridled passion and enthusiasm. This is what makes for great teaching. You figure out your audience—then you create a playlist for them that'll make you their hit maker. Be creative, my friend.

As for the tedium of instruction, remember: "Never assume they know anything." Even if they do know whatever it is you're doing or discussing, quite often they'll act like they don't. Consequently, you'll continually have to remind them about class procedures, school rules, supply demands (paper, pencils, etc.), homework, codes of conduct, morals, virtues, beatitudes, attitudes, and almost anything else under the sun, the moon, and the fluorescent lights of your classroom. So stay patient, and remember that the tug o' your heart you feel for the students is what makes teaching so important.

Respectfully,
Mike

FROM ANOTHER ANGLE

In 1990, I was working with a student teacher in a rural high school in a small town in northern Kentucky, near where the Toyota company had recently built a huge new factory. The student teacher's assignment was to work alongside an eleventh-grade English teacher for the semester, and she was diligently implementing literature and composition lessons with attention to grammar and mechanics added to both. But she had one female student who never said a word. Over the course of a few weeks, this student seemed to shrink from the classroom. She literally slid further and further down into her desk until she was hardly visible at all. The student was Japanese, and she spoke no English when she arrived at the school. No one at the school knew how to address her needs as a nonnative speaker of English. Consequently, the student tried her best to disappear from the scene. Who could blame her?

Sadly, none of the teachers at that school had learned enough about TESOL (teaching English to speakers of other languages) strategies, at that time, to intervene. A few of her teachers assumed that she must have been "slow" and "unintelligent," since she "didn't even try" to participate in their classes. Even those of us who were able to separate notions of her innate intelligence from her failure to use English had no real way to gauge her potential as a thinker; we were unable to break the linguistic barrier that kept her locked away from us. Despite our good intentions and our caring attitudes, we failed her completely.

Eventually, she was moved to a school in which an ESL (English as a second language) program had been initiated. Yet the student teacher, cooperating teacher, and I were left to deal with an ugly reality: we had proven completely unable to help that Japanese student; we could succeed as teachers of English only when the students came to us equipped to play our game as speakers of our language.

Freddie's situation reminds me of that Kentucky classroom, of that Japanese student, in many ways. When he asks, "What I wonder is how the hell do you plan for so much diversity?" he reminds me of the difficulties and opportunities that we face as teachers in a multicultural, democratic nation. But when he follows his question with the statement, "It seems to me that the ends get chopped off, and the teacher has to aim for the middle," he reminds me that there are aspects of education in which we have made little progress. Even in our multicultural world, even in public education, we are left with this equation: students who are different are, in some settings, doomed to be left out of learning.

Recognizing the Differences Among Differences

While it is admirable that Freddie has tried to uncover some information about teaching Exceptional Students (ESE) and English Language Learners (ELL), his own words bespeak two damaging yet common misconceptions about these two student populations. First, he lumps together exceptional education students (those with ESE labels who receive special education programs) and students who are English Language Learners (ELLs). He fails to distinguish between the kinds of issues that cause concern for ESE students and their teachers (the students with specific learning disabilities or SLD who demand two minutes of attention from their teacher just to get them to sit in their desks, for example), and for ELL students and their teachers. It is possible that Freddie, despite his good intentions, assumes that all in-school learning barriers—whether they are caused by a disability or by the student's use of another first language—spring from a common source: inferior or underdeveloped intelligence.

This perception is problematic in several ways. It implies, for example, that a learning disability necessarily limits all aspects of a student's ability to learn, but it ignores the fact that a student with a particular learning disorder or disability is likely to have average or above average intelligence. Have you ever thought, like Freddie might have thought, that a student with a learning disability could do better if she only tried harder? Have you focused on the student's limitations but bypassed your responsibility to use instructional methods that teach the ESE student alternative ways to receive, organize, remember, envision, or articulate ideas? I don't ask these questions in order to create guilt; instead, I hope that they encourage you, as a beginning teacher, to look for the gaps in your own education, and to begin to try to fill them.

The perception that all learning differences are limitations is also problematic for the English Language Learner. Many of the ELL students whom you will teach may in fact have superior literacy in their home languages, yet they will be prevented from articulating their ideas in class—not because they don't have ideas, but because they don't yet know the language that is used in the classroom. They will be barred from class participation, not because of an inability to think, but because they speak a language that is not used in the classroom. Unless an ELL student is also a special education student, his teacher should be prepared to address his needs as someone who needs to learn English, but not misinterpret it as a learning disorder or as an intelligence deficiency.

Debunking the Deficiency Myth

This first misconception, that ESE and ELL students should be lumped together in the classroom, goes hand in hand with a second common misconception: school children who are different from the norm are, necessarily, deficient in some way. Freddie refers, early in his conversations with Mike, to the "problem of" teaching ESE and ESL students. Like many teachers, Freddie apparently (though unconsciously) operates on the "deficit" model. According to the deficit theory, children who are outside of the mainstream are considered to be deficient "in language, social development, and intelligence" (Nieto 2000, 231). Teachers then see their roles as filling the gaps that exist in the experiences of these children, as writing on the (supposedly) blank slates that these children bring to school with them.

This perspective is limiting to ESE and ESL students alike, since it ignores the special talents, skills, and learning that they might bring with them to the classroom. Taken to its extension, the deficit model would suggest that a student's use of a non-English home language must be eradicated through school lessons. Further, it would require that the home language be replaced with English, and only English, in all situations, since English is the language of the classroom, and standard English is the language of social and cultural power in our society. But do we, as teachers, really want to send the message that our students' home languages are inferior to English, that the language that their parents, grandparents, and others in their neighborhoods use to communicate effectively is deficient? I doubt that any of us want to see that kind of message sent to our students. We realize that the deficit model is outdated and undemocratic. It ignores the linguistic and life experiences of more than 6.3 million children and adolescents, or one of every seven students in our public schools today, who are speakers of non-English languages (Hernandez 1997, 19).

Expectations Regarding Special Students

When Freddie's comments are focused exclusively on the ESE students whom he observes, he brings attention to another common reality: special education classes seem chaotic and the expectations regarding student behavior and academic performance appear to be low, while gifted classes seem to be orderly and the expectations regarding student behavior and academic performance appear to be set at a high level. (As a preservice teacher, he was surprised to learn that both special and gifted students are classified under the ESE umbrella, and thus both qualify for Individualized Education Programs, or IEPs, that must be written by a team that includes their teachers, counselor, and parents.) Freddie raises appropriate and compelling questions when he asks why a disproportionate percentage of African-American students are in the "special education" section that he observes. Mike notes that the racial makeup of the gifted classes is probably more white than racially mixed. Hernandez (1997) points to research by Lee and Slaughter-DeFoe (1995) that demonstrates that African-Americans have, since the mid-1980s, shown "disproportionate retention, drop-out and suspension rates; disproportionate and inappropriate representation in special education programs; and inequitable resource allocations" (in Hernandez 1997, 25).

Freddie believes that the students who are in the special education class need more attention from their teacher, more structure, more organization, and clearer expectations. He concludes that these features of a successful classroom would be more beneficial to the special education students than specific curricular interventions that are designed to meet their particular disorders. While Freddie's conclusion is premature, since he is only observing these classes a few times and he has no background information regarding these students and their particular conditions, he does raise an important concern, which might be paraphrased in these questions:

What kinds of expectations can we set for students who are labeled as needing "special education," and who are English Language Learners? (Can we accept the fact that ESE and ELL students bring different kinds of challenges and strengths, yet find and implement strategies that assist both groups—and the others in the classroom, as well—as learners in our classrooms?)

What kind of classroom environment can we establish in order to help these students take themselves seriously as learners?

How can we best support these students as they work toward meeting expectations?

Collaboration and Scaffolding

Freddie and Mike point toward at least one potential answer for these questions when they note that purposeful, collaborative (or cooperative) group work has potential for getting all students involved in classroom instruction. This instructional format can be combined with scaffolded instruction to help level the playing field, without requiring that low- and high-performing students be "chopped off," sacrificed for the satisfaction of students who are in the middle range of performance as readers, writers, and thinkers. (See more about collaboration in Chapter 13, "Interactive Jazz.")

In addition to collaborative grouping, ESE and ELL students can benefit from the sequenced instructional approach that is referred to as scaffolded instruction. The reciprocal reading that Mike advocates is a form of scaffolded instruction. In *Language and Reflection* (1992), "scaffolded instruction" is described as a strategy that is used by teachers who adopt a stance that views language teaching and learning as a series of development stages. This perspective complements the approach taken by special education teachers, because it allows students to "build upon previously learned skills" as they move toward "more advanced skills" (Gere et al. 1992, 116). Within the language-as-development perspective, learning is goal oriented. In scaffolded instruction, four steps are included: modeling, guided practice, independent practice, and feedback (Gere et al. 1992, 120). First, the teacher models a task. She might read a poem silently, for example, but as she reads, she comments on what she is thinking, and jots down the questions that she asks herself while she reads. This process shows students, through modeling, how they can use metacognitive thinking to aid in their comprehension of a poem. Second, she guides students as they practice the task as a group. She might give the class a poem and read it aloud to them, so that they can focus on making comments about ideas that emerge as they read along with her. She might also ask the class to compile a list of all of the (metacognitive) questions that they used to check their comprehension as they silently read the poem along with the teacher's oral reading. Third, she observes and assists while students practice the task independently. The students would read a poem independently, and employ the method of writing down questions that helped them check their comprehension during the silent reading. Fourth, the teacher provides feedback to students regarding their independent attempts to complete the task. After leading a discussion of the poem itself, she might ask students to discuss the ways that the metacognitive questions helped them make sense of the poem; she might have students turn in the lists of the questions that they used to help them with their comprehension. In either case, she would provide students with comments that encourage their further development of a repertoire of metacognitive questions.

Collaborative grouping and scaffolded instruction are examples of two instructional models that teachers can incorporate to try to provide comprehensible and useful instruction to all students. But they are not an answer to the question, "What does an English teacher need to know in order to work effectively with ESE and ELL students, while keeping the kinds of learning challenges and strengths that they bring into the classroom separate in our minds and planning?" Clearly, we all must learn, even as mainstream teachers of English, everything that we can about the characteristics of different learning disorders and disabilities. As a starting place, we must learn to recognize and address the following kinds of disorders and disabilities: those related to reading, mathematics, and written expression; language disorders, including phonological, expressive, and receptive disorders; emotional and behavioral disorders; and other handicapping conditions such as visual impairment and hearing impairment. We must learn, too, how to separate assumptions about a student's intelligence from information we gather regarding that student's use of English, especially if standard English is not the student's home language or first dialect. We need to find out what we can about our ELL students' literacy in their home languages, so that we can know how many concepts about reading and writing the students understand, for example, since they will be able to apply those concepts to the acquisition of the English language.

An Underdeveloped Area of Teacher Education

In the past, ESE and ELL students would be sent to special classes where they were isolated and treated as different. Our hope is that, through inclusion and mainstreaming of these students, the special students and the teachers with whom they work will learn to take advantage of learners' strengths, wherever they lie and whatever language they use most confidently, and build on them.

Teacher education programs in all subject areas should prepare prospective teachers to work with students who have various learning disorders, disabilities, handicapping conditions, and who are English Language Learners. But the reality is that many do not. There are so many content-related issues to teach that we often push aside issues related to students with special learning or linguistic needs. It is no surprise that Freddie, and other preservice teachers who are beginning to work in classrooms with diverse student populations, wonder why they have not been prepared to teach all kinds of students. This is one area in which traditional, subject-oriented teacher education programs must expand their perspective in order to meet the needs of the public school populations of the twenty-first century. Preservice teachers such as Freddie, who are raising legitimate questions about what they have not been taught regarding working with special student populations, will help nudge the field toward change.

You might start with the following books in order to learn more about issues related to ESE and ELL students:

Suarez-Orozco, Carola and Marcelo M. Suarez-Orozco. 2001. *Children of Immigration*. Cambridge, MA: Harvard University Press. Implications of the findings of the most thorough longitudinal research on the children of immigrants in the United States ever conducted are presented in a highly readable format in Harvard researchers Carola Suarez-Orozco and Marcelo M. Suarez-Orozco's *Children of Immigration*. The authors present insights into the experiences of immigrant children as they grow up in the United States. The attention they pay to the ways that learning English can separate the children from their non-English speaking families and neighbors encourages teachers to remember the crucial role that language use has in family and social settings, and encourages us to treat our students—and the languages that they speak—with dignity. As teachers, we might be especially interested in their comments on the "fields of opportunity" (133) that characterize schools where signs are written in several languages, student art and writing are displayed, and computers and software are up to date and accessible to students. Schools that present "fields of opportunities," even when they are in low-income areas, are contrasted with those that present immigrant students with "fields of endangerment" (133). In the latter, students might have to walk through neighborhoods infested with drugs, gangs, and prostitution just to enter a dilapidated school building. In these schools, "concerns with survival, not learning, prevail" (133).

Nieto, Sonia. 2000. *Affirming Diversity: The Sociopolitical Context of Multicultural Education*. New York: Longman. Sonia Nieto presents teachers with a series of case studies through which we can examine what we know, the stereotypes on which we rely, and the changes that we can make to be sure that our classrooms are welcoming educational places for all of our students. Nieto encourages us to find ways to take advantage of the richness that multicultural students bring to our classrooms. She also presents realistic information about how stereotypes have short-changed students from ethnic and language minorities in U.S. schools. This book, like *Children of Immigration*, is one that we, as teachers of English, will want to share with our colleagues in other subject areas. Especially useful for English teachers, however, is a list of multicultural literature that Nieto recommends for classroom bookshelves (381).

Delpit, Lisa. 1995. *Other People's Children*. New York: The New Press. A powerful book that urges teachers to look for the strengths that all of our students, regardless of their backgrounds, bring to the classroom. This is a book that effectively debunks the notion that children who live in minority neighborhoods and homes, and children who live in poverty, should be treated as deficient.

Hernandez, Hilda. 1997. *Teaching in Multilingual Classrooms*. Upper Saddle River, NJ: Prentice Hall. Hilda Hernandez presents an overview of the social, cultural, and linguistic processes that characterize multilingual classrooms in this text. She gives direct advice to teachers of English in terms of language and literacy development, academic language development, and assessment and evaluation of students who are English Language Learners. This is a useful guide, a book that you will want to keep on your teaching desk.

Chamot, Anna Uhl and J. Michael O'Malley. 1994. *The CALLA Handbook: Implementing the Cognitive Academic Language Learning Approach*. Reading, MA: Addison-Wesley/Longman. In this book, Chamot and O'Malley, both English as a second language specialists, present a framework, which they call the CALLA approach, for teaching English Language Learners (ELLs) across the disciplines. The approach relies heavily on teachers' instruction in metacognitive learning strategies; the strategies support learning of ELL students and all students.

Davidman, Leonard and Patricia T. Davidman. 2001. *Teaching with a Multicultural Perspective: A Practical Guide,* 3rd edition. New York: Longman. This book is helpful for all teachers, beginning and veteran, because it brings our attention to definitions of multicultural education, as well as related issues including equity in education. It then presents specific strategies for teaching complete interdisciplinary units and individual lessons in ways that recognize the multicultural nature of our classroom populations.

Venn, John J. 2000. *Assessing Students with Special Needs*, 2nd edition. Prentice Hall. This book provides an overview of specials needs, and of methods to assess and address them.

Cummings, Rhoda and Gary Fisher. 1993. *The Survival Guide for Teenagers with LD*. Minneapolis, MN: Free Spirit. This book is useful as an introduction to learning disabilities, and offers the unusual perspective of being written for teens who have the disabilities, in an effort to help them better understand their conditions.

9

Grades and Standardized Testing

In this discourse, Elizabeth enters a middle-school classroom after winter break, and her timing couldn't be worse. She's teaching eighth grade in a state that places strong emphasis on standardized tests. In Florida, eighth graders are held accountable for their success on the FCAT and Florida Writes Upon Request tests. If the students don't pass, they don't move into high school. As a young teacher, Elizabeth questions not only the validity of these tests, but their influence on the way we teach English. Like many of us, she also grapples with grading processes and policies in general.

Rethinking, Redoing, Resubmitting, and Reevaluating

Dear Mike,

This middle school doesn't give failing grades. From what I understand, the system runs as follows:

4 = A
3 = B
2 = C
Below a 2 = Incomplete

When a student receives an "I" he or she has the option to do remedial work to improve the grade. The student can receive no higher than a 2 on any remedial work.

Why am I upset? Basically, a student can fail a test, complete a remedial assignment, fail that, then the cycle goes on until he finally passes. It seems to me that kids won't benefit from this program. When a student fails within this system, we lower our standards for the sake of school image. For instance, Ms. Mc. gave an assignment where students were to read a story and write a paragraph describing the events that went on. Some students did fail the assignment. Their remedial assignment was a list of questions they had to answer about the story. If a student failed that part (one did), he or she was asked to just draw a picture of what occurred. The particular student who failed twice, finally passed the picture assignment. Now, how is that language arts and how is this kid learning? I guess my fear is that these kids are just going to keep being passed on and will come out of high school illiterate. I know it is happening because my classroom is an "eighth-grade advanced class." Funny how some of them are on a third- or fourth-grade reading level.

Elizabeth

Dear Elizabeth,

I have a policy that I use called "rethink, redo, resubmit, and I'll reevaluate." There are no guarantees, however, that the grade will automatically improve. Naturally, if the student and I work together (I make myself available during lunch and after school for conferences), then things have a better chance of changing for the better. But I don't deviate from my original standards or expectations to accommodate any failure rates. Students need to be held to high standards. They also need to be given the opportunity to occasionally fail. Success is relative and if they're given a grade or passed on to the next level because they can't fail again, it's not doing them or our society much good. I do, however, believe that English (and writing in particular) is a recursive and imperfect discipline—if a kid doesn't get it the first time, I encourage them to retry and get it "more correct" the second or third time.

Respectfully,
Mike

Enforcing Deadlines

Dear Mike,

After reading your e-mail, I see the benefits for those students who maybe had a bad day or want to improve, but there comes a time when utilitarianism has got to be looked at. Late work runs rampant in these classrooms because there is no motivation for turning things in on time. In other words, if a student does not pass an assignment because he never turned it in, the grade book is always open to change the "I" to a grade. I don't see how a teacher can realistically deal with that.

Elizabeth

Dear Elizabeth,

The deadline thing is important. Back in my slacker days, I accepted work whenever I got it (I was just happy to get something). All that did was breed weakness. The students would wait until the last minute (the end of the grading period), then burden me with humongous stacks of mediocrity. Finally, I realized that I was doing all of us a disservice. Students need to be held accountable for their actions and their inactions (blowing off assignments).

Besides, Fs are powerful. They send a message. I agree with you that "incompletes" breed complacency. There is no need for a student to embrace any kind of work ethic when there's no such thing as a deadline. I used to take off ten points every day an assignment was late. Then I toughened up my standards and began to give them half-credit for any late work (and it had to be turned in the next day). The results have been amazing. The students take their work more seriously, and I'm not burdened with stacks and stacks of mediocrity.

Respectfully,

Mike

Teaching the Testing Measurements

Dear Mike,

Today the students were busy practicing the Florida Writes Upon Request Test. I'm concerned about the grading of that test. The actual test will be given in February, so Ms. Mc. wants to make sure that her students are prepared. Last year, no one at the middle school received a 6, which is the highest score. One student scored a 5.5, and eight students received 5s. This is usually a timed test, so Ms. Mc. tried to teach the students the best way to approach timed writing when it's based on a forty-five minute limit. The state sent out examples of what was expected of the students, so I was fortunate enough to review it. The students are responsible to write a five-paragraph essay, and they also had to do an outline (which they hated). The students had an option to do this outline, so Ms. Mc. awarded them with ten extra points for doing the outline. All the students did the outline!

I spent most of the period grading their essays. The writing prompt was on whether they preferred television or books. Most students preferred reading books because it was more educational, but others thought that television was more entertaining. Overall, they all did a wonderful job comparing the advantages and disadvantages of television and books. I was kind of curious about how should I grade the papers, because I had to remind myself that they are eighth graders, so I had to be a bit more lenient. I ended up giving check pluses to the more detailed papers, and check minuses to the less detailed ones. In-between essays received a check.

Elizabeth

Dear Elizabeth,

If you're using the essays to gear up for the state test, check out the rubrics for evaluating it. That will you give you a more objective way to evaluate their papers and to teach the students the test (as weird as it sounds, "teaching the test" is a reality).

So check out the testing material, then explain to the students how the test is graded. Show them what the evaluators look for and tie those rubrics into some future lessons on essay writing techniques. Look at the sample essays the state includes in their promotional materials. I've found that having students grade with the state's six-point scale really helps them better understand not only the grading process but the writing process as well. (The practice testing materials usually come with several examples of student essays.)

Respectfully,

Mike

Tackling Standardized Testing

Dear Mike,

Now the school is preparing for FCAT testing; it is interesting how intense the students and teachers have become. I can remember when we were administered the California Achievement Tests some years ago. I was complacent about the test and did not really care about the scores. I am glad it was not weighted as heavily as the FCAT is for the students of today. March seems like a bad time of year to administer this test. The students are already getting spring fever, and the teachers are in need of a break and the temperature outside makes me want to just run and play.

Elizabeth

Dear Elizabeth,

Standardized testing has really become a barometer for school and student success (especially in Florida). Of course, I'm not suggesting that this is a good thing—it's just a sad reality wherein bubble sheets and multiple-choice thinking are the standards by which we are all judged. As English-teaching people, we are naturally more impressed with creative and critical thought. Therefore, this processed information-type, cognitive associative, highly homogenized, cattle-herding mentality is quite offensive. Nonetheless, we must do our best to prepare our students for the cattle drive—even if it is compounded by the beauty of budding spring.

Remember—students and schools are judged by the results of these tests, so administrators take the results very seriously. The local paper prints the results on the front page, as if it were a high-school football jamboree. Even worse, the state of Florida uses the results to "grade" schools. Our funding is linked to these results, and job security also depends on stellar results. So don't blow it off. It's one of those "teach the test" kind of "professional obligations."

Of course, many legislative leaders would disagree with me, concerning this "teaching the test" advice. According to them, these state-mandated tests simply measure and mirror the state standards for communication. Naturally, this is yet another area where I take serious issue with the state's "standard" view of education. As a lover of literature and writing, I maintain that the true beauty of expression stems from the individual. Hence, there should be little or no room in our literary explorations for ditto sheets and multiple-choice exploitations regurgitating petty details or "right" answers. Literature and writing are much more important and personal than a state-mandated teacher's manual would lead us to believe. Nonetheless, we remained strapped to having to take this task very seriously.

Respectfully,
Mike

Breaking Away from the Ditto Sheets

Hello Mike,

As you know—not much really happened this week because it was FCAT testing week, so Ms. Mc. was showing the movie *To Kill a Mockingbird*. If I am not mistaken, she isn't even having them read the book. They have seventy-five surface questions they have to answer while they watch the film, which totally flies in the face of what your last e-mail said. As a budding teacher, I see so many more possibilities that the film provides for students to explore. They could write and react to the racism in the film or the nobility of Atticus or the kindness of Scout. They could write letters from one character to another. They could even do a movie review. But another A, B, C, or D multiple-choice test after FCAT! Yikes!

Hopefully, this next week I will have the courage to ask if there are any creative writing classes I could observe. I can't wait for the chance to be in an environment where I can address literature and language on my level. I want to have a class dig in the metaphors and pull out the meaning as it applies to their lives. I want the students to write, write, and write some more. Only through active creation can one truly gain a better understanding of the power of words. I can only hope that my karma starts flowing better for next semester. I hope to have a better opportunity to experience teaching as I see it should be done.

Elizabeth

Dear Elizabeth,

Bravo, and hang tough. Just one troubling "slip of your tongue" in this e-mail.

"I can't wait for the chance to have an environment where I can address literature and language on *my level*."

To teach them, you must reach them—so level your sights on "them."

That's why your other comment *rings more true* to the course, "I want a class to pull out the meaning as it applies to *their lives.*"

And kudos on the incredibly enthusiastic, unlimited writing quotient you aspire to utilize in your future idyllic domain! Your quote—"Only through active creation can one truly gain a better understanding of the power of words"— is unforgettable and inspiring. Keep that notion at the heart of your teaching philosophy, and eventually your teacherly karma will indeed start flowing. Take it from another writing intensive-type teacher—*self-expression will indeed strengthen the pulses of your students' critical and creative heartbeats.*

Respectfully,
Mike

Keeping Grades Aboveboard

Dear Mike,

Today was progress report day. The grades were terrible overall, and there was a general sense of sadness and disappointment among the students and the teacher (and, consequently, me). I don't think the teacher really knew how much they had been goofing off until she plugged grades in and checked to see which goals had been met (pretty much none, for the vast majority of the class).

Elizabeth

Dear Elizabeth,

I'm shocked that the grades were such a surprise to everyone (teacher included). One of the most important aspects of teaching secondary school is making this vital information (grades) available to all parties at all times. Personally, I use a triweekly checkpoint system wherein each student is given a computerized update as to their progress or lack thereof in my class (learn to use the electronic grade book—it's terrific for spitting out precise information on individual and group grade status). These periodic updates also give the students an opportunity to check up on my record keeping. Therefore, grades never come as a surprise to anyone—not even parents—which is why I call home if one of my students is in danger of failing at the midterm, progress report point. Too often the students don't take the reports home, or they intercept the mail to keep their parents clueless about their lack of progress. Hence, I actively solicit parental support. I let the parental units know my concerns, and most of the time they are very supportive and glad to hear from a teacher who cares. While this system is not 100 percent effective (a few students still fail), I feel very fair minded and at peace with my role in the process.

Respectfully,
Mike

FROM ANOTHER ANGLE

Another View of Standardized Tests

I suspect that Tallahassee, Florida, is a lot like the town in which you will be teaching: the residential property values are highest in the neighborhoods that have the best schools. And the "best schools," these days, are often defined as those in which students earn the highest scores in the vicinity on the state tests. In Florida, schools now receive grades; an A grade is an indicator that the majority of the school's students have scored well on the state's standardized test (and the cynics among us suspect that an A also indicates that many of the teachers in the school are spending as much time preparing students for the test itself as they are teaching their subject). There are other variables in addition to standardized test scores, including a low incidence of absenteeism, and few suspensions for misbehavior (prompting some schools to underreport problem behavior in order to protect their grades), but as Mike states, it is the test scores that make newspaper headlines.

Standardized testing, regardless of whether you believe it is the right way to measure students' educational progress, is a reality, at least for now. And I believe that beginning teachers are not in the best position to buck that system—yet. Despite your desire to shelve the test-preparation manual and activities in order to delve into *Flowers for Algernon* or Edgar Allan Poe, you need to find ways to prepare students for the standardized tests they are required to take. Take heart, though: If you are teaching according to the standards of your state and our profession, you can be confident that you are preparing your students for the subject matter content of the standardized tests. Your primary job, as it is related to standardized test preparation, in that case, then becomes taking time to familiarize students with the kinds of questions they will be asked and the kinds of answers from which they will choose. Standardized test preparation should be, for the most part, a matter of emphasizing reading comprehension skills and test format awareness (including the kinds of writing that will be scored well if a writing sample is included on the test), not subject area knowledge itself. And you should not be left alone as a faculty member in this endeavor; your colleagues across the disciplines should be available to help with reading comprehension and other test-savvy skills, too. The biggest mistakes you can make, in my opinion, are (1) to pretend that these tests don't matter, or (2) to use your philosophical opposition to standardized tests as a reason to ignore the tests and thus fail to prepare your students for them.

In the English/language arts classroom, "tests" have personalities that are very different from that of standardized tests. *Tests* should be only one way that you assess, evaluate, and produce grades for the students in your classroom. And although you might be tempted to use the terms "assessment," "evaluation," and "grading" synonymously, you might find that your job is clearer when you use distinct definitions for each of the four. Let's see if you agree.

"Assessment" is the ongoing collection of data that you will gather regarding your students. Assessment should help you answer questions such as these: "What do these students know already about X?" and "What kind of evidence will I seek to show me that my students are learning Y?" Notice that you need not give a test in order to produce answers to those kinds of questions. Instead, you can observe students as they engage in learning processes and make anecdotal notes about what you notice. You can also talk with your students about their learning, survey them about their attitudes and background experience with a topic, incorporate self-evaluations and peer evaluations, look at the kinds of work that they produce as a result of their learning, and so on. Your goal in assessing students' learning, as James and Kathleen Strickland note (2002, 142) is "to collect data or evidence, not to make judgments."

"Evaluation" follows assessment. When you consider the data that you collect and begin to make sense of it, in terms of what it reveals about your students' learning, you will be involved in making informed judgments, or "evaluation." As Strickland and Strickland (2002, 143) point out, evaluation "is most useful if it is for the student, if it helps the student along a path to further learning." Often, evaluations are reported to students in the symbolic form of letter or number grades.

"Grading" should help students understand where their strengths and weaknesses are. If the letter grades or numbers that you assign offer too few details about a student's performance or learning, you will need to explain the criteria you used to arrive at the grade. Grading is particularly tricky in the English/language arts classroom. Could you explain the difference between an essay that earned an A– and one that earned a B+? Could you explain why one student's speech deserves a B while another's earns a C? Grading is subjective, at best, even if you use the most detailed rubric for grading essays, or have a complicated score sheet for students' speeches, and so on. All English teachers have to be careful when assigning grades. We must be vigilant that we do not rely on one source of data, such as tests, to generate the set of grades that are added and averaged together to become the students' final grades in any one marking period or year.

But how can you avoid using tests as the final means of measuring students' learning? In the English class, there are many alternatives. A few examples include these: the use of dramatic performances to evaluate comprehension of a short story; the writing of a poem as a means of evaluating the rendering of a novel; participation in an "arranged conversation" with two classmates (conversations in which students have to use a number of their new vocabulary words in appropriate contexts). Probably the most popular alternative to testing in the English/language arts classroom is one that you may have been required to use yourself: the portfolio.

Portfolios come in many variations, and you will want to decide which format best fits your needs. One format involves having students include virtually all of the work that they do in your class (all drafts of writing assignments, vocabulary work, quizzes, usage exercises, and so on). You might then develop a rubric for evaluating and grading the portfolio that is based on evidence of growth in each of the content areas that is represented in the portfolio. For some teachers, this kind of portfolio includes work that has already been graded, and allows for revision of work before the portfolio is turned in for final evaluation and grading. If this collection of work seems unwieldy (it does to me), you might opt for the more focused "polished portfolio" format. To create a polished portfolio, students collect their work throughout the grading period, but before they turn in the portfolio, they select the works that best represent their learning, polish those, and submit them. Students add to the polished portfolio a letter or essay that explains what the selected samples demonstrate about their growth.

For an invigorating look at testing, grading, and standards in education that pushes readers to think about the goals and directions of American education, see these books by education and social critic Alfie Kohn:

Punished By Rewards: The Trouble with Gold Stars, Incentive Plans, A's, Praise, & Other Bribes (1993)
The Schools Our Children Deserve: Moving Beyond Traditional Classrooms and 'Tougher Standards' (1999)
The Case Against Standardized Testing (2000)

See, too, former teacher Susan Ohanian's provocative *One Size Fits Few: The Folly of Educational Standards* (1999).

For a variety of perspectives on grading, ones that might help you crystallize your own ideas on the subject, I recommend Libby Allison, Lizbeth Bryant, and Maureen Hourigan's readable *Grading in the Post-Process Classroom: From Theory to Practice* (1997).

10

Time Managment, Classroom Management

For students fresh out of the university setting, time management in secondary schools is often perplexing and unnerving. In other words, the civility and professionalism in their college classrooms has made it easy to forget the chaos that corralling a room full of high-school students can undoubtedly breed. In these exchanges, Randy continually frets about maintaining an effective flow in his classes while he ponders strategies to properly gauge and monitor his activities, equipment, and materials. With Mike's encouragement, Randy begins to plan accordingly by coupling behavior components into his lessons.

Displaying Makeup Work

Dear Mike,

Mrs. P. has one of the most efficient classrooms I have ever seen. There is very little I would change about it. Her desk is against the west wall of the room with her computer on it. Her more important objects, such as her bookshelf and file cabinet are right behind it so that you have to go by her to get to anything. Less important stuff, like crayons, tape, a hole-puncher, and scissors, are against the back wall by the door for the students to use when needed. The students sit at tables that are parallel to each other, extending down the center of the room. Mrs. P. can see everything from either the front of the class when she is teaching or at her desk. It's very effective. The only thing I would change is to move one of the tables away from the overhead TV. The students who sit there seem to have a hard time keeping out from behind it, or playing with the wires that plug in. Not quite as bad as sniffing glue, but it could cause a problem. The pencil sharpeners are located by the boards so that students from one desk don't have to invade the area of the other table.

The students' responsibilities are all posted on the wall with the task of the day on a display board that Mrs. P. has put on the front door. I like this because students have no excuses for not knowing the procedure. Any questions that they have can be answered by directing them to the display board. Overall, I picked up a few new techniques in classroom management, and I'm beginning to feel a lot more comfortable.

Thanks,
Randy

Dear Randy,

I don't know about you, but the "less important stuff like the crayons, tape, a hole-puncher, and scissors" are the things that tend to walk off. Granted, the file cabinet is important—especially if it contains graded and ungraded work. And books are essential, but what tends to disappear from my classroom is the "less important stuff." And believe me, that stuff is annoying and expensive to replace (it adds up). So keep your eye on it—all of it.

On a more upbeat note, posting "work due" and "work in progress" notices around the room is a wonderful strategy. The real key is to always make sure you have your assignments in written form. Having students rely totally on taking notes is insane. Invariably the notes will get misconstrued, then you will be left to explain the assignment over and over again. In addition, there's the makeup work issue for the ones who are absent. Having the assignments written out, complete with objectives, makes it easier to get the absentees back up to speed.

It's also incredibly important to have the teacher's desk prominently placed, so everyone can be seen from that command center. Overall, it sounds like Mrs. P. has her house in order.

Respectfully,
Mike

Managing Time and Bouncing Back

Hi, Mike,

Each student started writing a first draft of a personal narrative. Mrs. P. has seven computers, and the principal at the middle school wants the teachers to incorporate them into the classroom. These computers are ANCIENT and since there are only seven, some of the students rushed so they could be the first ones on them. Because of time, those seven kids were the only ones who really got to use them, and since their papers were already on disc, they were the ones to use them the next day.

I could see Mrs. P.'s frustration with the whole process (lack of computers, ancient equipment, and disruption in the classroom). I worked with the students as they were working on their writing. And a lot of them seemed to want my help—they were lined up to show me what they had written.

The second day went much better. Mrs. P. talked about different types of introductions and she gave examples of each type by reading from different stories in the literature books she has available. She then had them either rewrite or write an introduction for their stories. Again, she and I worked with all of the students, making suggestions, brainstorming ideas, etc.

The students did a good job on the narratives—and I have to admire Mrs. P. for handling a bad situation. It was a little crazy the first day, but on the second day, she was prepared after seeing what had happened the day before and she had them on task the entire period. That's what I like about her—she realizes when something has gone wrong—thinks about it—makes corrections the next day—and lets the bad day go off into history. I know she was frustrated with the computer situation (because she said, "I know the principal wants the students using the computer, but I don't think I'll ever do this again"), but the next day, you would never had known that the day before had been out of control. I guess that's what we have to do—just regroup and go on and do the best we can do. I really admire her.

Randy

Dear Randy,

That computer and editing thing sounded crazy. What I try to do with those types (no pun intended) of situations is monitor the amount of time each group gets on the equipment. Divide the time equally and stick to it. Fifteen minutes on. Blow the whistle. Holler for the next group. That should diffuse that racing to the computer and holding on for dear life kind of turf wars stuff.

As for the bouncing-back-ability of your mentor—good teaching is a recursive process. Mrs. P. saw some trouble spots with their narratives, so the next day she had a minilesson on introductions. Kudos, Mrs. P.

Respectfully,
Mike

Switching Gears Regularly

Dear Mike,

Today, Mrs. P. gave me some exercises to go over in class. When the class came in, I called roll, then began leading the students in correcting the exercises. I felt like this went very well for about fifteen minutes, then the students' attention began to wander. At that point, Mrs. P. suggested that the students work silently for a while on some other exercises. This change of pace was exactly what was needed. She reminded me later that the teacher should change activities every fifteen or so minutes. I had known this, but when it came to actually doing it, I was lost (yet another lesson).

Randy

Dear Randy,

Mrs. P. was totally bingo on her advice. Switching gears keeps them from grinding, burning up, and self-destructing. The key, however, is to thematically interconnect the activities, so there is a cohesiveness to your game plan. In other words, the progression of activities is most effective when it is heading in some kind of sensible direction that is clear to both you and your students. And while grammar exercises may appear interconnected, I wouldn't encourage them as a recurring theme.

Respectfully,

Mike

Running a Smooth Discourse

Dear Mike,

Do you use the "call out" method or the "raise your hand" method for classroom discussions? So far, I feel that I like the "call out" because it keeps the discussion centered more on the kids, but it may intimidate the shyer ones. As a contrast, the "raise your hand" way keeps me in the spotlight, but it does allow me to keep a better control over who gets a chance to speak (and even to get those who are not participating to participate). I was just curious if you had any additional comments or ideas.

Randy

Dear Randy,

I prefer to use both. In other words, allowing someone to spontaneously add a counterpoint or comment to a discussion (as long as it's appropriate) is a healthy way to keep a discourse lively. Of course, the teacher's role is to maintain some sort of order, so if you let the kids just blab and blurt whatever, whenever, it can get way out of hand real fast. Your class will get as wacky as a Ricki Lake or Jerry Springer shouting match.

Thus, you have to become a benevolent dictator to really keep any class discussion in check and on task. Obviously, encouraging kids to raise their hands is a healthy way for them to show respect for those around them. It keeps them from interrupting one another, and it forces them to listen a bit more closely. If you have a lot of hands up, try to eventually get to each one. Tell the students to "hold their thoughts," maybe even jot down a note or two, so they won't forget. But, try to get them all involved if possible. Another critical aspect is you don't want the same kids dominating every class discussion. You'll always have pushy ones who frantically wave their hands and feel like they have the most valuable comments about everything and anything. Don't dwarf their enthusiasm, but don't fall into a pattern wherein you rely on them to always keep the discussions going. This doesn't lend itself to a very thorough or complete interaction with the classroom community.

Therefore, I also prefer to use the "call on" method. I don't look at "calling on" students as a way to embarrass them (unless, of course, they're "off task" and I want to reel them in by making them blush a little and 'fess up to their transgressions). To facilitate this process, I often use what I call a "write down and share" prompt. I give the students something to think about, have them write a three- or four-line response then call on each student to sound off.

In order for any fruitful discourse to regularly occur, however, the essential key is class climate. At the beginning of each year, I make it well known that I am going to require all of them to actively participate in our safe learning community. As educators, it is essential that we push our youngsters (with kid gloves, of course) to voice their opinions and stand up for their beliefs. And what better place to encourage this encounter with ourselves and our emotions than in a wonderfully warm English class wherein put-downs are strictly forbidden and where hearing each other out is held in such high regard.

Respectfully,
Mike

Using the Overhead Effectively

Dear Mike,

Monday Mrs. P. had the students copy notes off the overhead while she explained point of view. This got me curious about how much a student can understand as they write down the notes and listen to the teacher at the same time. I never really had a problem with this as a student. But I'm an audiovisual learner. I think if I use this approach, I'll definitely cover up the notes and reveal them as I go along, rather than having the students two or three Roman numerals ahead.

Randy

Dear Randy,

Your observation about the overhead is interesting. By covering up manually what is to be covered next mentally, it keeps the students focused on the single task at hand. Asking questions and checking comprehension along the way helps, too. It reasserts the audio aspect of learning.

Respectfully,
Mike

Managing That Idle Time After a Test

Dear Mike,

During the first class today, I didn't really get an opportunity to do much.

The class was taking a test on the parts of the sentence, so I just basically sat in the back and watched. I did notice that it was a good idea to put handouts at the front of class for students to pick up and read after they finished their tests. This way, they all had something to do when they were finished. Most times teachers tell students to sit silently or read something of their choice after a test, but this usually leads to students goofing off or distracting test takers.

Thanks,
Randy

Dear Randy,

Having handouts for students to read after they finish a test is a pretty nifty idea. A posttest "chill time" where students may quietly read something of their own, or rest, or do other homework, or doodle still isn't a bad option, though, if the class proves it can handle that downtime well. A lot of times after an examination, students kind of do deserve a quiet break.

The key to making sure that the imposition of your library quiet zone works is to circulate and assert your body language so that the kids don't "try you" by whispering, pestering each other, goofing off, or cutting the fool. In other words, you can't sit at your desk grading papers and expect your students to be little angels.

Respectfully,
Mike

Making Film Time Meaningful

Dear Mike,

The eighth graders watched a movie version of *Something Wicked This Way Comes*. While watching the movie, the students were very disruptive. Mrs. P. threatened to stop the movie several times, but she did not. She just got tired of having to get on to them about their behavior so she finally just continued to watch the movie herself. After class, she talked to me about their behavior. Instead of talking to me about it, she should have been talking to the students about how she felt about their behavior.

Randy

Dear Randy,

The behavioral chaos that your cooperating teacher is experiencing apparently stems from her unwillingness to confront the insanity spinning around her. In other words, the flick should have been turned off, the behavior addressed and an alternative assignment given—so that the message that "Films are to be taken seriously" was delivered. Obviously, idle threats have no impact on bad behavior. You have to add some bite to your bark, or you'll spend most of your time growling and snapping to yourself.

Another thing to remember with regard to films is to keep them interactive. In other words, have designated spots where you stop the flick and get the students to reflect on what's going on. This helps the class keep an educational spin on what's being shown; it also keeps the students involved. For a lot of kids, once the lights go out in the classroom, the lights go off in their sleepy little heads. Hence, movie time becomes snooze time, or even worse—party time.

Respectfully,
Mike

Giving Each Student Special Attention

Hello Mike,

Last week, I wound up working one on one with a student from each of the first two periods. Mrs. P. had alienated both students for behavior reasons and seemed to have given up on them. I found if you give them attention they'll do wonders. It's easy to give attention to students when there is more than one adult in the room. My question is how do you adopt more one-on-one attention into your classroom? I know for a fact kids hate to come after school for help.

Randy

Dear Randy,

First of all, your observation proves that students respond to positive attention (even tough ones). Having a good attitude toward every student and treating them with respect usually brings out the best in them. Of course, everyone occasionally drifts over to the dark side of life and acts a little devilish (even teachers). However, positive attitudes usually produce positive results.

As for the one-on-one issue—it does create management problems. When you're so engrossed with one kid, won't the others just goof off? What has usually worked for me is a miniskill session. I usually engage in this activity after the students have written a draft of sorts, and I've had time to evaluate it. Procedurally, I give the class their rough drafts back and explain to them that they need to reread their drafts and examine my comments. They also are required to write down three to five questions about my comments and their paper in general, so when I visit their desks, they have refamiliarized themselves with their text. After they finish, they have free, silent reading time or a study hall of sorts for makeup work. In a positive classroom community, the students realize the importance of this opportunity, so they usually will stay on task. I also make sure I announce this upcoming activity well in advance, so the students come prepared to engage in silent individual work.

Once I've gotten everyone settled in, I circulate and quietly go over their papers with them individually. Since I've already assessed their work and made notations, I explain ways to improve trouble spots and answer their questions. I set the timer on my watch and divide the time accordingly. Of course, the system works better at my school since we are on a block schedule, which affords me class periods that last an hour and forty minutes. In that amount of time, I have enough space to accommodate everyone. In the standard forty-five minute period, it would probably take two days to accomplish such a task. If you use your imagination, I'm sure you could come up with a two-day quiet activity that would accommodate this need. Just make sure that you've announced it ahead of time, so that your learning community can come prepared with books and plenty of pensive work in tow. One-on-one work is a key for promoting success.

As for more informal ways to engage the perplexed ones—if you just circulate and offer assistance when they're working on assignments, the students who are having trouble picking up the concepts can be accommodated. This also ensures that the playful ones will stay the course. The key is to make it a top priority and to sell the idea to your students by showing them how wonderful the experience can be for them. Once they value this special connection with you, your community of learners will respond with proper behavior. Naturally, you'll run into a few bumps and stumps, but overall the opportunity to really connect must be nurtured and protected.

Respectfully,
Mike

Making Each Day Count

Dear Mike,

This week has been kind of frightening. The students are writing book reports on books of their own choice. I can understand that some of the students haven't finished their books and that some continue to leave their books at home or in their locker, but I can't figure out why over half of the class doesn't take advantage of the opportunity to get the report done in class. Only one student seems interested in making sure all of her thoughts and ideas are right. I want to shake her hand and congratulate her on taking advantage of the situation. Sure, there are some students who are done with the report already. One student even read two books, but this worries me because Monday the show becomes mine.

I've discussed my lesson with Mrs. P., and we both feel confident about it. It's a creative writing assignment involving pictures on the overhead. Taking Mrs. P.'s advice, I model the first picture for the students. After we talk about the picture, I will show them my writing model, and then give them a picture of their own to tell a story about. My apprehension comes from watching them wander and goof off when they are given the chance to write on their own like the last two classes I observed. I think the opportunity for them to be at the controls of what they are writing may help, but who knows.

Randy

Dear Randy,

When only one student is using the valuable class time to actually work, then it's time to change gears. A teacher should always be armed and dangerous with plenty of lesson plans, just in case the "plan in progress" isn't working. If the class breaks down and splinters into gale force winds of hot air and aimlessness, forge ahead. Move into new territory, turf, and other vibrant activities.

There is too much to do and too much to learn for anyone to waste time by wasting space. Every class is precious. Share your value of education. Set high standards. Set sail into uncharted waters. And by all means, don't give any scalawags the time or space to shipwreck your mission.

Of course, Captain Randy, you're preparing for your maiden voyage, and you've charted a wonderful passageway. Your art/writing model is awesome. You've done what you're asking them to do. You've modeled for them. And you're planning to share. So stick to your course. Don't let the storms you've seen brewing or the troubled waters get you off course. Set very strict perimeters.

If it's a journal or free-write activity, require that it be completed during the period. Explain that grammar, spelling, and mechanics won't be the evaluative measure, but that creative thought in conjunction with the art work will be.

Or if it's going to be an extended assignment, have them list images, cluster nuggets of images, freewrite impressions, or come up with three or four directions that their stories might take with sketches of character or setting. And then have them turn them in at the end of the period, so you can give them some informal feedback the next time you set sail.

Or you could even pair them off or put them in groups of three and have them write a collective poem or children's story that they would choral read to the class. That might be kind of wild, but it might get them going. You assign the groups, though. Don't just let them buddy up!

Whatever you do, require them to turn in something of quality by the end of the period. Set perimeters that they can't stretch, bend, fold, spindle, break, or otherwise mutilate.

Be clear with your objectives up front, and you'll find that the sailing will flow smoother. You'll have fun, and believe me, any "would be" pirates will, too!

Keep me posted, Captain.

Respectfully,
Mike

Holding Their Feet to the Fire

Dear Mike,

I took your advice on my lesson. The kids had to turn in a brainstorming journal at the end of the period, and they really came up with some wonderful ideas. They were so creative and really funny. I gave them back the next day with a ton of comments for further exploration, and then gave them some more writing time in class to work on a rough draft of their stories. I walked around the room and talked to the ones who were having trouble deciphering my notes. The class stayed on task the entire period. I made them hand in their drafts at the end of the period and only two kids didn't finish. They were working, though, and they promised to bring their papers in the next day. Thanks for the heads up,

Randy.

Dear Randy,

No problem. Deadlines and circulating the room does wonders.

Respectfully,
Mike

Pacing the Grading

Dear Mike,

Yesterday was an evaluation day (what they used to call teacher planning day). I expected to go to the campus and find a lot of interaction among the faculty. I expected they would consult each other about "stuff," get together for lunch, and enjoy adult companionship while they did grades. Wrong. The campus was ridiculously quiet, except for occasional interruptions via the PA system.

Randy

Dear Randy,

Grade deadline days are the busiest times of the school year, especially for English teachers. If you're not careful with the paper chase, you'll find mountains of journals to grade, final compositions to meticulously critique, projects to ponder, grades to average, bubble sheets to fill out. It's not a very social time of the year. Therefore, the crafty English teacher paces due dates (and sticks to them) over the course of the grading period. As a result, the paper load doesn't get too overwhelming at the end, and the teacher isn't buried under a pile of last gasp attempts by students who have turned in slack facsimiles of "way" overdue work.

So the key is to treat yourself kindly by avoiding this kind of hysteria. Have a fair and rational ration of "final due dates" sprinkled over the course of the grading period. Undoubtedly, this will afford you a more pleasant "Teacher Planning Day." Having all of your record keeping on a computerized grade book also helps a great deal. Before I utilized this tool, I used to spend my planning day with calculator and ratty grade book in hands.

Respectfully,
Mike

Classroom Management

Randy seems poised to begin teaching with an awareness that his first subject is always his students. While many beginning teachers are concerned primarily with whether or not their students "like" them, Randy has moved beyond a focus on himself to a genuine concern for what he might be able to do to promote the students' social and personal comfort and their academic growth. Through his questions and reflections, Randy demonstrates that he understands the relationship between using effective classroom management routines and establishing an appropriate learning environment for middle-school students. He discusses many separate issues, from the physical setup of the classroom to holding students accountable for how they spend their class time; from how to share computer time (and seems to suspect that seven computers should be more than ample, even when they are "ancient," if instruction is arranged to allow students to rotate on and off computers as a part of a set of workstations that they visit) to how to make movies worthwhile in terms of educational goals. Yet all of these issues have a common thread: Randy is exploring the issue of how teachers balance student choice with student responsibility, student freedom with teacher direction. He does an excellent job of framing many of the concerns that may seem mundane when one looks at them from outside of the beginning teacher's classroom window, but which are issues that demand attention when we move into the classroom itself and look around us from that perspective. We can find embedded into his e-mail messages the following collection of ten tips for successful classroom management that Randy has collected:

- Arrange desks and tables in the classroom to allow for movement and clear visual contact with all students.
- Post a clear set of instructional and behavioral expectations and rules on the classroom wall, for easy reference.

- Have an established system that allows teacher and students to take advantage of a small number of computers in the classroom.

- Incorporate a variety of activities during each class period, with opportunities for middle-school students to move around the room during the class.

- Implement an established system for conducting class discussions in which all students are encouraged to be involved.

- Give students some choice regarding books that will be read, and about what type of response to the book will be given.

- Use specific purpose-setting questions to guide students' attention when they watch a movie (or listen to a guest speaker, go on a field trip, and so on).

- Incorporate individual student-teacher talk time as an essential feature of the curriculum.

- Implement strict deadlines for work related to in-class and out-of-class projects, and stick to the deadlines.

- Develop a specific routine to use when students choose to ignore the management plan that is established for the class.

By drawing on these ten items as a starting place for his thinking about classroom management, Randy will be able to set the foundation for a student-sensitive classroom.

Because of his tendency to focus on what students need in order to participate and to succeed in school, Randy's classroom is likely to have characteristics that are similar to the four recommended by middle-school expert Chris Stevenson in *Teaching Ten to Fourteen Year Olds* (1998):

1. an interpersonal climate in which teachers and students cooperate, and in which students are "respected and enjoy good-natured relationships with adults";

2. a climate in which students' "worth and dignity are assured," their self-esteem is developed and protected, and hurtful teasing, embarrassment, and humiliation are not tolerated;

3. an environment that approximates democracy, and in which the teacher and students recognize that "the key to clear understanding and subsequent collaboration is dialogue";

4. an environment in which mistakes become opportunities for learning, and in which, therefore, "redemption is always close, not closed," so that students who choose to behave badly one day are given a fresh start, or clean slate, the next day. (225)

An Eye Toward Lessons He Can Learn

Randy makes the connection between two aspects of the classroom that work in tandem to result in effective classroom management: an orderly physical layout of the classroom, and carefully planned teaching and learning goals and activities. He notices early in his experience that Mrs. P.'s is a classroom in which a teacher has worked diligently to help students become successful learners. However, like most classrooms and teachers, the situation is not perfect. Randy takes advantage of the opportunities he is given to observe what happens when Mrs. P. is unclear about her expectations for students' learning and behavior. What he sees emerge is bad behavior. For example, Randy recounts an incident in which the class watches the movie, and they choose to misbehave badly. The most obvious source of their failure to cooperate is that they are given no purpose-setting questions to guide their participation—their viewing of the movie. Without an academic purpose, they watch the movie as if they are at home on a Friday evening in front of a VCR. To his credit, Randy did not choose to write off this incident as an example of poor planning or bad teaching; instead, he used it as a lesson.

Another instance in which Randy saw weak classroom management lead to misbehavior occurred during the sessions in which students are asked to spend the day writing drafts of their personal narratives. Mrs. P. seemed to make a common mistake at this point: she told students to write, but did not actively help them write. Instead, she seemed to assume that they would know how to use their class time wisely to draft, revise, edit, get peer input, and polish their papers. Again, though, as Randy notes, when the middle-school students are given no structure, they quickly wander out of bounds. The formula that he learns is simple: Students who are engaged in meaningful classroom activities are less likely to misbehave than those who find no purpose in, or connection to, what they are being asked to do in class.

Freedom Within the Fences

Randy brings up an important issue related to classroom management as it relates to student choice and responsibility in two other ways: (1) he seeks advice about how to promote student participation in class discussions when he asks about the pros and cons of having students jump right in with their idea or raise their hands and wait to be called on by the teacher; and (2) he comments on the lack of enthusiasm that students show toward generating responses to books that they have chosen for their long-term literature projects. The classroom management issue that these instances have in common can be recast as a question about the relationship between students' freedom and teacher's ultimate authority.

Randy might ask the question this way: "How can we encourage participation of all students, without relinquishing to them the control and responsibility for what happens in the classroom?" He might also add a note,

"We are, after all, the well-educated adults who are being paid to be sure that students' time in our classes is well spent."

I like to think about the appropriate balance between student freedom and the teacher's ultimate authority with this analogy: Young adolescents appreciate the opportunity to go out to play in a huge yard, one with lots of variety in landscape, a few obstacles to climb over, some rewards to be enjoyed. But they benefit, too, from knowing that there is a fence along the edge of that huge yard. The fence is not tall enough to keep them in the yard if they want to leave it, but it marks the area within which they can feel completely safe and protected. They enjoy having the freedom to explore, but thrive, too, on the sense of protection that we can provide in well-managed, comfortable classrooms.

Using this analogy, we can envision classroom discussions in which students are encouraged to address each other directly, instead of sending all of their comments to the teacher. Yet this analogy helps us see that we, the teachers, are responsible for being sure that the discussion does not wander too far from its purpose. It helps us see, too, that we are responsible for being sure that everyone plays fairly—all students can participate as equally important voices, and no one is ignored or belittled by others who are "playing in the yard" with them. We can also use this analogy to envision assignments in which students are given a wide range of choices regarding which books they will read, and what kinds of responses to the book they will generate. This view requires that we recognize our teacherly responsibility to make sure that students' choices are appropriate for them as individuals and as members of our class group, and that their responses will demonstrate growth in their thinking. The goal of this approach to management might best be summarized this way: freedom within the fences.

Jim Burke describes his classroom as one in which he and his students "create the world together" (2003). His strategy is to assume that his high-school students can accept and responsibly use choices about where they will sit, how they will behave, how they will spend their time. If students demonstrate that they are not willing to accept responsibilities that go along with choice, he steps in and makes choices for them, but without humiliating them in front of their peers. In other words, Burke recognizes that the adolescents in his classes are humans; he gives them respect, and in most cases they return it to him. In well-managed classrooms, respect is reciprocal.

In addition to Burke's *The English Teacher's Companion* (2003), I recommend Harry and Rosemary T. Wong's *The First Days of School: How to Be an Effective Teacher* if you need help deciding how to establish a positive learning environment and smooth classroom management procedures.

In many middle-school classrooms, and a significant yet smaller number of high-school classrooms, teachers are incorporating cooperative learning strategies as a means of providing some choice and of encouraging individuals to participate. Please see Chapter 13, "Interactive Jazz," if you are interested in how collaborative learning might enhance your classes and your teaching.

The following chapter contains a more detailed discussion that addresses how to handle disruptive student behavior.

11

Behavior Blues

Shakia is in a middle school that has a predominantly African-American population. The school, which is situated in a low-income neighborhood, has had a reputation for poor test scores and "bad" students, but with the work of a dedicated principal, faculty, and county support, it is beginning to turn things around. As an African-American teacher and a young mother, Shakia hopes that she will be able to connect with the students with whom she will work. However, she quickly becomes troubled by classroom management and discipline issues, and focuses on those in her e-mails. She comments on her observations of several teachers, and aligns herself with those who are most clearly in charge of their classes.

Redirecting the Gangsta' Mentality

Dear Mike,

I'm working with a skills class, and the majority of the students are minorities. They're only in middle school, but most of the boys try to act like little thugs and gangsters—even though they can be nice. Basically, the kids are all very sweet and they thrive on positive attention. But most of them don't read very well, and they don't believe that school will help them get anywhere in the long run. So they don't do their homework, and when I ask them about it—they put on their gangsta' face and act like they don't care. As a beginning teacher, I find this very distressing.

Thanks,
Shakia

Dear Shakia,

Since I teach high school, I use Ralph Ellison, Richard Wright, Malcom X, Nate McCall (*Makes Me Wanna Holler*), and even the daily newspaper as vehicles to role-play and think about the decisions one has to make on the street. Adolescent novels that might appeal to middle-school students who want to examine street and gang life—from the safe distance of fiction—include Walter Dean Myers' powerful *Monster* and the teen classic, S. E. Hinton's *The Outsiders*. Through the literature the students can examine the "gangsta'" mentality and the chaos it breeds. They can confront their fears and their bravado by using the printed word and literary characters as their springboards of thought. Truth be told—a big part of our mission as English teachers is to redirect self-destructive thinking and habits. This is not only true with regard to reading and writing, but thinking as well. Hence, we have an opportunity and an obligation to reach out to our misguided students through literature and self-reflection journals and role-playing activities that can help them see themselves in a more positive and hopeful light.

Most of all, don't give up on the hope that they can all change and redefine their lives. You've already acknowledged that "they can be nice." There's an "in" right there and a big advantage. But the biggest advantage you need to have is your own unbridled enthusiasm and willingness to care for them. Create a safe place for them to become more vulnerable to the goodness in your heart.

Respectfully,
Mike

Redirecting Negative Energy

Dear Mike,

Today, I had to give a makeup quiz to a student, because he was absent due to his court dates. For an eighth grader, he is a big boy—at least six feet (I am five-four when I'm stretching). He wanted to do his math homework. I tried to get the paper away from him, and I was physically unable to do it. So Mrs. G. comes up and lays him out, and she gets the homework from him—no problem. She's awesome! I hope that with experience I can be remotely as good as she is.

Shakia

Dear Shakia,

Obviously, Mrs. G. has a rapport with this student that has developed over the course of the year. She has the look, the sneer, the leer, the snap, crackle, and pop that elicits the appropriate response from the student.

As an intern, you will encounter this scenario again. The students will figure that you're not their "real" teacher, so they will try to push your panic button, twist your twig, and snap your bean. As the adult in this mix, you must remain cool—calculatingly cool.

Given this situation, I would refer to my personal credo: "If you abuse, you lose." The student was there to make up his English test. You're not a math teacher. And if you're like me (mathematically challenged), you couldn't even begin to help him with his other homework. Hence, I would probably remind our big buddy that he needed to make up the quiz and should he choose not to—the grade book would reflect the consequence. Enough said. Then the proverbial ball is back in his court where it truly belongs.

If the student then snarls and snaps about "not being ready for the dumb old English test," you might suggest that he get out his book or notes or whatever. Then you could use that time to help him prepare for the exam. You could even offer to meet with him during lunch or after school (in the next day or two) to take the makeup test.

At five-four, Ms. Shakia, you don't have a lot of weight to throw around. As a "soon-to-be" college graduate and an adult, however, you have a ton of persuasiveness and patience to wield. Undoubtedly, a humanitarian approach has a better chance to influence adversaries to become allies.

Respectfully,
Mike

Corralling the Cheaters

Hello Mike,

I had a rather disturbing experience this week. I was grading some papers and noticed the exact same answers from two students' papers. Since it was an essay test and the words were exact, this was an obvious case of cheating. I called it to the attention of Mrs. G., and all she did was issue a friendly warning. She almost made it a comical situation.

In my class—cheaters will have hell to pay.

Shakia

Dear Shakia,

(1) What is this hell to pay? Please explain.

Respectfully,
Mike

Dear Mike,

"Hell to pay" is the students won't get the comical slap on the wrist Mrs. G. gave them. I will fail them for the assignment, and they will be well aware of my presence. Regardless what the assignment, their parents will definitely be called.

Later,
Shakia

Dear Shakia,

Thank you for responding. I think calling parents is a good idea and not making light of the situation is essential. However, I'd be very careful not to embarrass the students in front of the entire class. Making an example of someone doesn't usually produce good dividends. I might suggest a more private conference with both students at the same time. Maybe give them an opportunity to reattack the assignment on their own terms in their own words with a penalty of some ten or twenty points. This enables the students to learn from their mistakes. It also affords them the opportunity to gain insight into an assignment they obviously weren't prepared to deal with properly. Why else would they cheat? Experience has taught me that students need to be called on for errors, but not berated or belittled for anything—even if they're totally off base (and they will be from time to time—many times). Patience is the virtue; forgiveness is the grace.

Respectfully,

Mike

Enforcing Consequences

Dear Mike,

I had my first discipline problem arise. It was nothing big, but my kids were so hyper they would not keep quiet for longer than three minutes. I told them several times to be quiet, but it was Friday and they weren't having it. Finally, Mrs. G. asked if I needed help. I said, "Yes." She expressed to them that they were taking advantage of my kindness and it was making her mad. She told them there would be consequences if they didn't stop. They stopped. Later Mrs. G. expressed to me to be a bit firmer. She said kids will eat you alive, and they must respect your rules. She's totally right. But, it is hard to discipline students when they aren't yours. Plus, I'm not sure how she does it, and I don't want to step on her toes.

Shakia

Dear Shakia,

It's always best to start out tougher (without being a total dictator—be a benevolent dictator) then ease up. It's very tough to get control of a situation once the students have started bouncing off the walls. Once you've allowed them to unleash their super jerk powers, they're like super bouncy balls from hell. And believe me some students have an "inner monster," not an "inner child." However, I am not a proponent of the theory that you shouldn't smile until the end of the first semester. That's a bit too stiff and uptight for me.

From your response, it sounds like Mrs. G. has a rapport with the kids. First of all, she was honest with them in her analysis of the situation and their behavior. Then she explained to them that there would be consequences if they didn't stop. The kids understood on both counts, and the behavior immediately improved. This indicates that Mrs. G. does have a set method of enforcing consequences. It also indicates that she displays patience with her students, warns them fairly, and yet holds them accountable for their actions. The results appear to be very effective and full of mutual respect (students and teacher).

I would recommend that you talk to Mrs. G. to find out what her consequences are, and then try using them yourself. Threatening students without consequences, is an empty promise that elicits no change. So find out the rules and consequences, then enforce them. But, don't get too heavy handed with the punishment part. Remember Mrs. G.'s model. She reminds, warns, and counsels her kids. The creation of a positive community classroom is an ongoing process.

Respectfully,

Mike

Silencing the Chatty Ones

Dear Mike,

The highlight of my week was Thursday, because Mrs. G. let me teach the entire class for three periods. It was the day that I was going over the autobiography paper requirements, and she just let me do everything. We started off each class by taking a quiz on the reading. Then I did my thing, and then we played a name game so I could get to know everybody (I don't usually work with seventh period). I thought that everything went really well.

One thing that I got frustrated with was the way three kids were acting in seventh period. I made one girl move, and they were still talking out for a good part of the day. Mrs. G. said that I was probably just getting tired. I don't know about all that, but next time I will be much more firm and not try to talk over them, which is what I did most of that period.

The cool thing is that I got everything done without any help. I could have been the substitute!

Shakia

Dear Shakia,

Playing the name game is a great warm-up activity. A twist I use is to have the students put an adjective (only clean ones, please) in front of their name that sort of typifies their personality. For instance, you might be Scintillating Shakia or Sassy Shakia or Sensational Shakia, and I might be Mighty Mike, or Marvelous Mike, but never Macho Mike.

For interns, learning the students' names ASAP is a necessity. It's the most effective way to initially wield power in the classroom.

As for the chatty gals—what exactly will you do to eradicate the problem next time? Your answer should be in paragraph form with a thesis statement that goes something like this—"The next time those annoying young ladies try to snap my bean in class by incessantly chatting when I'm trying to teach, I am going to . . ."

Now that I've really gotten your proverbial goat, don't get mad, get even. Let those ideas fly. I'll be patiently waiting.

Respectfully,

Meddlesome Mike

Wielding Your Body Language and Perfecting That Look

Meddlesome Mike,

To answer your question:

The next time those annoying young ladies try to snap my bean in class by incessantly chatting when I'm trying to teach, I am going to warn them one time and remind them about the last time I had trouble with them. Then if it continues, I will separate them again. That should do the trick, since they are such a nice group of kids. What do you recommend?

Shakia

Dear Shakia,

Good answer, but don't forget body language. When students try snapping my bean, I calmly walk over to the trouble spot and quietly impose myself in their area. That usually works wonders. They're less apt to act up while I'm hovering above and around them like some killer bee. Problem solved, I eventually flutter from their area and continue to circulate. (I try to always be on the prowl and not glued to the front of the room.) If the problem continues, I would use your strategy by reprimanding them politely, then separating the chatterboxes.

Another strategy I often employ is to call on them during my discourse. This requires them to participate in the "class" discussion. If I'm lecturing, then I simply call on them to help clarify what's up with my lecture. If they don't have a clue what we're talking about, then it's a playful wake-up call to get with our program. All of these strategies work well with sleepy students, too. Of course, you can't just hover over dozers, you occasionally have to whisper sweet something's in their ears and give them a gentle pat on the back.

Of course, another of your main defenses should be your evil eye. You must work on that one. Accrue your own "looks." A furrow of the brow, an intense squint, a puffed lip, a gnashing of the teeth—these will become your best ministers of defense. So practice them in the mirror. Glare with them at your family, your cat, your parakeet or your dog. Every good teacher needs several "looks" that will freeze any wrongdoers and keep them from transgressing in, on, or around your turf.

Of course, the silent treatment freezes them, too. Stop and wait. Then crinkle up your eyes into a slit-eyed stare. Get dramatically bent. Rest assured, order will be restored promptly.

Respectfully,
Meddlesome Mike

Dear Meddlesome Mike:

I think I'm really beginning to gain more confidence in myself as a real teacher. Mrs. G. had to leave the classroom for a little while, and I felt utterly at ease with the whole thing. Most of all, I tried to keep the students on task with their assignments. I walked around the class and observed how far along they'd gotten. I saw two girls passing notes to each other, and I walked around to the one who was reading the note at the time. I tapped on her book which startled her a little because she was so absorbed in the note. It was kind of funny.

Shakia

Dear Shakia,

I appreciate the way you handled the note thing—the girls responded. Quite often, body language speaks volumes. That's why circulating the room is so important. You can playfully throw your weight around a little; make your omnipresence known. The important thing was—you weren't taciturn, and you didn't publicly humiliate anyone. You tapped the book gently to redirect the girl's misspent energy.

Respectfully,
Mike

Calling a Bluffer's Bluff

Dear Mike,

Today, I used your advice and called on a student who didn't seem to have his homework, and who appeared to be writing the answers down in class. He tried to cover by guessing at the answers. Maybe I shouldn't have called on him at all (in another e-mail you talked about not humiliating students), but I didn't want him to think that I didn't notice. When he tried to turn in his homework at the end of class, I told him I wouldn't accept it for obvious reasons. He didn't argue, but I felt a little uncomfortable. Did I do the right thing?

Shakia

Dear Shakia,

Sometimes you have to call a student's bluff. When a student is off task in class, one of the best ways to get their attention is to mention their name in the middle of the point you're making.

For instance, "In the prologue to *Cannery Row,* Shakia, why do you think John Steinbeck is comparing the bums and no-goods to saints and sinners?"

This is a technique I use repeatedly. While it does bring a bit of attention to the disruptive or alienated student, it also is an effective way to "call" my "little lost sheep" back into the fold. In your case, the kid (no pun intended) was actually trying to bluff his way through a homework assignment. By letting him know that you knew that he was unprepared and trying to "pull it off" by "pulling the wool over your eyes" (how's that for an extended metaphor?), you quietly sounded your authoritative snap and wielded your authority without coming off as too heavy handed.

Another option would be to quietly go over and stand next to the student, then pick up his "love note" or "makeshift" homework. As a parting shot, give him a little body language (the all knowing, slightly evil eye) to let him know that he needs to come in out of left field, and get with the old ballgame. Remember, you're the skipper and the ump—so call them like you see them. At this point, I'd say you're calling them pretty swell.

Just remember—every situation and every day is relative, so there's no one set solution to every problem that pops up. Therefore, you need a bunch of different tools on your tool belt and strategies and countermoves in order to contend with the space cadets and malcontents.

My very best overall, global approach, though, is to always have the kids' best interests at heart. Care about them when you correct the errors in their ways. And always let them understand that you don't hold grudges, you just expect them to do their very best.

Respectively,

Mike

The Positive Redirection of Negative Energy

Dear Mike:

Friday we had a spelling bee. It was GREAT! Mrs. G. said my use of the students' names was very effective in maintaining their attention. She also noted that I used a lot of positive comments, even when they missed a spelling word. When a boy who had been sent out to the hall the previous day started to be disruptive, I gently reminded him that participation alone in the spelling bee was worth 35 points, so he may not want to risk being sent out of the room again. I really earned applause from Mrs. G. for that tactic.

Shakia

Dear Shakia,

Sounds like the spelling bee was a huge success. I'm also really jazzed by the way you handled the student who had previously gotten into trouble. Staying positive with the young fellow and reminding him of the positive aspects of participating in the class is a much better tactic than to shake your finger at him and remind him of how bad he'd been the day before and how you weren't about to take any more of his shenanigans today. Quite often, positive reactions inspire positive actions, and it is the most humane way to begin any reprimand.

Respectfully,

Mike

Consistently Respecting Consequences

Dear Mike,

Today I got to observe a gifted language arts class, then I observed a sixth-grade social studies class. While observing the gifted class, I picked up on a couple of effective classroom management techniques. While the teacher was helping a certain group of students, the rest of the class began to talk loudly and misbehave. In response to this, Mrs. B. said, "The following students have a date with me tomorrow at seven a.m." Then she wrote a few names on the board, and the class became quiet again. In other classes, this might not have worked, but I think it did work in this one because the students knew that Mrs. B. was serious and would carry through.

I have begun to realize that this is probably the most important aspect of maintaining classroom management. Students need to know that you are serious about your rules, and that you will follow through with consequences. If you establish this early on, then you won't have to write names on the board all year long. Just the mere mentioning of the fact that they will be punished if they continue to misbehave will make them discontinue.

On the other hand, you may have a teacher like the one I observed in social studies. This teacher's approach was to ignore misbehavior and simply scream her planned lesson to the few attentive students. I had a headache after two minutes in the class. This observation furthered my belief that if there is misbehavior occurring in the classroom, the teacher should stop everything until they get attention from the students then continue. I don't know how the attentive students were able to learn in this environment. It seemed as if the teacher only wanted to get through this class period and "cover" his material.

Shakia

Dear Shakia,

Consequences are important, idle threats only create more chaos. Of course, no matter how consistent the implementation of consequences, problems will surface and resurface. After all, Mrs. B. did have to write some names on the board, and some kids were going to have to be there at seven a.m. the following morning (along with Mrs. B. apparently).

But you're totally bingo about stopping the lesson when disturbances become a detriment to your ability to teach and the students' ability to learn. That doesn't imply that you should become obsessive-compulsive with your role as a member of the police force, like Barney Fife with some incessant screaming, "Nip it!" No, indeed. When students see that they can "shock the monkey" and get you to jump at every little annoying thing they dream up, then they'll spend most of their time devising ways to rattle your cage. So as you've seen with Mrs. B., consistency coupled with consequences is the key.

Respectfully,
Mike

Making the Punishment Fit the Crime

Dear Mike,

I visited another class the other day, and boy was I impressed! Ms. K. had a system. When a student misbehaved in some way shape or form, they were issued a "prompt." A prompt is a warning. Five warnings equal a time-out session of two minutes. In time-out, a student is not allowed to participate in the activities of the class. Surprisingly this works well with the students. One of the students explained how he felt "left out" while in time-out. For that student, the technique was effective. For others, it was not, so they continued to be issued more prompts until they had ten prompts. When a child had this many, he was put in time-out and given sentences. This reminded me of when I was in the fourth grade, and I had to write the dictionary for punishment. It drove me nuts, but it didn't teach me anything. Anyway, the class ran well and the students were willing to participate in the grammar activity.

Shakia

Dear Shakia,

Obviously, most of the kids in this class knew the limits and only a few tried to push it. Thus, the class had more order and less chaos. I'm with you, however, on the writing sentences part. Your analogy to your fourth grade dictionary experience proves my point. We don't want kids to look at reading, writing, or researching (dictionary, encyclopedia, etc.) as punishment. Ms. K.'s original plan is more to the point. The punishment (not being allowed to participate) fits the crime (being disrespectful to the class). We should never give kids the impression that books and writing are "sentences" for punishable crimes.

Respectfully,
Mike

Using the Honest but Firm Approach

Hey, Mike,

I did another required observation in a class that is not a language arts class. I sat in Mr. Q.'s eighth-grade science class to observe his methods of discipline. I've seen these same skills kids in Mrs. W.'s social studies class, and I couldn't believe they were the same kids. They act completely different for Mr. Q. I think it's because he treats them more like adults. It also may have to do with the fact that he's a black male who refuses to take any crap. The students worked in groups, researching a review sheet he handed out to supplement their studies for the test he's holding Friday. I couldn't believe how on task these same students were. They sat in groups of four and five and helped one another find the answers. If the student couldn't handle sitting with the group, he was removed and forced to work separate from the others. I respect Mr. Q. for his laid back atmosphere and his honesty toward the students. I think this is why they respond so well with him.

Mrs. W. (the Special Ed teacher) isn't personal with the students. The few times I've helped teach in Mrs. W.'s class, I realized that students respond to me being human rather than her acting almost like a robot. The students were more receptive with me since I tried to get everyone involved. If a student didn't have a pencil,

I made sure he got one, etc. All kids need is a little personal attention. Mrs. W. seems to have just given up on some of these kids.

Shakia

Dear Shakia,

By watching Mr. Q., you were reminded of the importance of really respecting students. Not only does Mr. Q. "not take any crap," he doesn't dish any out, either. That's why Mr. Q.'s learning community seems so together. Of course, I'm sure a few occasionally stray from his fold, but his job as the keeper of the sheep (bleat, bleat, bleat) is to a be a goodly shepherd. He refuses to label or ostracize any "would be" bad sheep among his family of learners.

By realizing this, you've learned the most valuable lesson for educational effectiveness—students crave positive attention and human connections, and you want to provide them with that. For that, I am thankful. You've demonstrated my favorite interning objective.

Respectfully,
Mike

Showing Your Tender Heart

Dear Mike,

Today was a normal day back in the English domain (a break from social studies). The students did a skill builder then we read "The Mustache" by Robert Cormier in class. It was a very interesting story. Mrs. G. just lost her grandfather about two weeks ago, so this story was very touching to her. She expressed to the students how she felt about this story, so if there was anyone caught not paying attention while the story was read, they had to do a writing assignment. The moral of the story is to always try to tell someone that you care or that you love or forgive them, because it might be too late and you won't have a chance later. The students loved this idea. Many bragged about going home to tell their mothers that they loved her.

Shakia

Dear Shakia,

Your connection to the Cormier story reveals your tender heart. I'm glad Mrs. G. shared some of her own grief with the students. I believe it is our duty to show students how human and humane we are. We expect that from them in writing and in reading, so they need to see it demonstrated and expressed by us as well. However, I'm not too fond about threatening kids with a writing assignment if they don't pay attention—especially, in the context of such a humanitarian theme. It seems a bit ironic and contrary, eh?

Respectfully,
Mike

Picking Which Hills to Die On

Dear Mike,

For the past couple days students have been just working on drawing and coloring still life pictures to go with the poems they wrote. It has been kind of a break and has given me the opportunity to walk around the classroom and mingle with the kids, seeing their work, and talking with them some. These kids are just so cute. Some of the things they say just make me smile no matter what mood I am in. I love it when they come up to me to tell me about something they did, or something that happened to them. It lets me know that they respect my opinion. I also love it when they show me a poem they wrote or a book they are reading. It makes me feel good to know they are learning something and want to show me.

Today, though, one of the little boys did kind of get me a little disgruntled. We were passing out the writing journals. A couple of students were up helping pass them out. He proceeded to get out of his seat, and then placed the plastic bin that is used to hold the journals on his head and wandered around the classroom talking and shouting. I walked over to him and removed the bin from his head and asked him to return to his seat. Of course, he had to get his journal first then he sat down. I felt frustrated. He still got his journal, but did not listen to me. Granted, he sat down, but not when I told him to.

What do I do in situations like this? I felt like he didn't care what I said because I was not his "real" teacher. It is funny how the classroom environment can change from one minute to the next. One minute, everyone is sitting, writing in the journals. The next minute while you collect the work, several students get out of their seats and start talking to one another. Before you know it, there is chaos.

I only hope I can establish some form of control when I do have my own class. I want to be able to quiet the class without raising my voice, or I want to be able to shoot a child a look when he or she is acting out of line and he or she will stop. Today I got to see what it felt like to be ignored. I got over it, though. It was good for me. It allowed me to sit down and think about the importance of these things and how I want to be treated by my students.

It is funny, though, because by the end of that class that same little boy was talking with me about his picture and searching for my approval. I guess it just goes to show, you can't take anything to heart. These kids are moment to moment and as an adult, I have to be careful not to forget that.

Shakia

Dear Shakia,

Reread what you've written. In your own words, you walk through the stages of your pleasure and your rage. You did great! You didn't overreact or get into some power trip. As field generals, we can't afford to constantly battle with the kids. We have to carefully choose which hills to die on. On this occasion, you were brilliant. You made yourself clear and by the end of the period, the little bucket-head journal boy was doing just what you'd always hoped he do—dabble in paint and poetics and share the results with you.

With enough patience, even little devils sprout angel wings. Of course, we must remember that when their wings start flapping too fast, the room flutters with the sound of chaos. But this, too, shall pass. As you indicated, that's why we're the adults. We have patience and we must continue to have patience—or we will become patients in a teacherly nut house.

Respectfully,
Mike

FROM ANOTHER ANGLE

In her email exchanges with Mike, Shakia voices concern about the aspect of teaching that has troubled every student teacher with whom I have worked during the past fifteen years: discipline and control in the classroom. Part of her concern revolves around how she will establish herself as the teacher, especially given her small stature and short tenure in the teaching role. Unlike many beginning teachers, she does not seem interested in establishing herself as one of her students' friends. Instead, she wants to be an adult whom they trust. Her comments cover a wide range of topics, including her reactions to students' "gangsta' attitudes," to her vow that those who cheat will have "hell to pay." Yet in all of these comments, Shakia is engaged in an essential exploration of her own notions about what it means to be responsible for the feel and functioning of a classroom.

As Mike acknowledges, students like to find the limits that new teachers will tolerate by pushing until the teacher pushes back. Could an inexperienced student teacher like Shakia have been fully prepared for the discipline-related problems she encountered while student teaching? Could you? I don't think so. No English education program, or any teacher preparation program, will prepare you for every kind of discipline problem that you will face. Yet there are steps that you can take so that you will be ready to act, not merely react, when the calm of your classroom is violated by misbehavior. Here are some questions that I would encourage Shakia to think through as she works toward assuming responsibility for her own classroom; you might find it helpful to begin to formulate answers, too:

- What is my philosophy regarding teaching and learning, and how will that philosophy inform the decisions that I make regarding how to handle discipline issues?
- What is the difference between off-task and on-task misbehavior, and how will I respond to each?

- How will I define and respond to nondisruptive misbehavior? How much nondisruptive misbehavior can I tolerate?

- How will I define and respond to disruptive misbehavior? How will I deal with it? How much disruptive misbehavior will I tolerate?

- What kinds of nondisruptive misbehavior and disruptive misbehaviors can I expect to find among middle- and high-school students?

- What conditions promote misbehavior among students?

- How might I prevent misbehavior that interferes with classroom activities and that undermines a positive classroom environment?

- What should I do if misbehavior becomes aggressive or violent?

All teachers need to take time to think about what they expect from students, and how they can provide a classroom atmosphere that will accommodate their goals. Shakia might want to review some of the models for classroom discipline that she has read about, now that she has a real frame of reference for thinking about those models. What follows are very brief descriptions of three discipline models that I learned about when I was a classroom teacher. Each was presented in a series of inservice workshops and promoted as the best solution to classroom management at one time or another. (Inservice workshops are an example of professional development opportunities. You go to a location identified by your county school board and participate, usually during after school hours one day a week or during the summer or on planning days, in an educational workshop with colleagues from your school and other schools in your county or district.) I introduce the discipline models that I was taught in various inservice workshops here merely to provide evidence of the range of models that exist, the fact that discipline is an issue for beginning and experienced teachers alike, and to emphasize the importance of one absolute regarding teacher preparation: teachers need to have a discipline plan in mind when they begin their first class; the issue is too important to leave to chance, whim, or desperation.

1. *Assertive Discipline* (associated with the work of child guidance specialist Lee Canter, and his wife, Marlene, a teacher of people with learning disabilities). In this model, the teacher tells students what she expects, regarding their behavior, then gives students warnings before punishing them for misbehaviors (if they continue to misbehave after the warning). The warnings are done quietly; the teacher simply jots down the name of any offending student, without comment, on the board. If the student misbehaves further, the teacher adds a check beside the name. For each check, there is a predetermined consequence (one check equals a ten-minute, after-school detention, two checks equals a call to parents, and so on). The *Assertive Discipline* model is based on the premise that teachers have the right to determine the atmosphere of the classroom, and that students can be taught to adhere to the teacher's rules. There is no arguing when a rule is broken; the teacher assertively applies

predetermined consequences for any type of misbehavior. In reviewing the Assertive Discipline model, Clifford Edwards (2000), an authority on classroom management, notes weaknesses, including the fact that Assertive Discipline reacts to, but does not prevent, misbehavior, and that its use of negative consequences or punishment "stimulates rebellion and promotes the very behavior it is designed to eliminate." It seems that Mrs. B., who puts students' names on the board and uses prompts, may be implementing a type of Assertive Discipline.

2. *Teacher Effectiveness Training* (associated with clinical psychologist Thomas Gordon). This model is based on the premise that instead of rewarding good behavior and punishing bad behavior, adults need to work toward "achieving a positive influence on children," because "having an influence on children is entirely different from controlling them" (Edwards 2000, 153). Proponents of this model argue that there is considerable evidence that suggests that students who are punished for bad behavior do not develop and use self-regulating behavior strategies when adults are not around. Gordon claims that what when they are faced with power-based discipline, like what is found in most traditional classrooms, teens are likely to exhibit "coping" behaviors including these: resist authority, rebel, disobey, be insubordinate, retaliate, vandalize, hit, break rules and laws, throw tantrums, lie, deceive, bully, boss others, give up, become fearful or shy, cheat, or use alcohol (Edwards 2000, 152). The teacher's role in *Teacher Effectiveness Training* (TET) is to identify students' needs, offer solutions that will meet their needs and the teacher's needs or help the student engage in problem solving, and listen actively as the student explains the problem from his or her perspective. TET teachers understand that all behaviors satisfy a need, and to that end, teachers learn to ask several questions about a problem situation. Examples of the kind of questions that TET teachers would ask include these: "When would be an appropriate time to address this problem? What is the first step you need to take to solve this problem? What are some alternative solutions to this problem?" (Edwards 2000, 155). A problem with this model lies in the time that must be devoted to individual discipline problems. Even when the conversation about the problem can be deferred, the misbehavior interferes with the academic momentum of the class.

3. *Choice Theory* (associated with psychiatrist William Glasser, who first became famous for his "reality theory" of behavior). The *Choice Theory* model is based on the premise that all of us have these four human needs: the need for love, for control, for freedom, and for fun. The teacher's role is to be sure that these needs are met for each student. The need for love is commonly met by giving a student extra attention; when the need goes unmet, the student may act out and misbehave. The need for control can be met by allowing students some choice in terms of what happens in the classroom. The curriculum, assignment deadlines, and room arrangement are examples of three areas in which student choice might be offered. When their need for

control is left unmet or not taken seriously, students may make choices that appear to their teachers to be irresponsible. The need for freedom can be met by allowing students to express themselves in a variety of ways, without the kinds of restrictions that teachers often impose. Students learn responsibility through exercising this kind of freedom. If left unmet, the need for freedom may result in rebellion. The need for fun can be met when students engage in academic tasks that are truly satisfying, as opposed to merely entertaining. If the need for fun goes unmet, students lose interest in learning.

These descriptions provide only a glimpse at the kinds of discipline models that exist. My best advice for beginning teachers is to read about several, then zoom in on those that are most compatible with your philosophy of teaching and learning. Regardless of the model that you choose or create for implementing in your classroom, there is one variable that does not change: Be clear about your requirements, and consistent in the application of your rules, and in the consequences for violating them. If you are clear and consistent, the only person with whom a student can be upset, if he or she violates a rule and has to pay the consequences, is him or herself.

Recently, I watched a student teacher deal brilliantly with a student who was guilty of disrupting the class by making a rude and embarrassing comment to one of his classmates. The student teacher pulled him aside and quietly said, "Please repeat to me what you said to Ruby." When the student mumbled, "Oh, I just called her a name," the student teacher insisted, "No, look at me and tell me exactly what you told her." He replied, "I said, 'You look like one of those big old cows I saw at the fair last night.'" The student teacher then asked, "Which of our class rules does that violate?" (without commenting further on the cruel remark, thereby taking away some of the sting of the comment). The student noted the rule, then, upon prompting, was able to tell the student teacher what the class-determined consequence for breaking the rule was: he would have to come in at lunch and clean the desks. Notice that in this scenario, the student teacher turned over responsibility for the problem behavior to the person who had manifested the problem—the student, then let him work through the consequences of his misbehavior.

Behavior management is an aspect of teaching that we will never be able to perfect, because our reactions are necessarily situational. However, as student teachers and beginning teachers, you are in a prime time to begin to determine what kind of classroom environment suits you best, and which discipline models will be most useful as you work to achieve that environment.

I have found these texts helpful when I have needed to review classroom discipline models:

Charles, C. M. 1992. *Building Classroom Discipline: From Models to Practice*, 4th edition. New York: Longman.

Cangelosi, James S. 2000. *Classroom Management Strategies: Gaining and Maintaining Students' Cooperation.* New York: John Wiley and Sons.

Edwards, C. H. 2000. *Classroom Discipline and Management.* New York: John Wiley and Sons.

Wolfgang, C. H. 1995. *Solving Discipline Problems: Methods and Models for Today's Teachers*, 3rd edition. Boston: Allyn & Bacon.

12 *Setting Parameters*

Throughout her internship, Shari puzzles over the plight of an angry young male in her high-school creative writing class, who demonstrates antisocial and self-destructive behaviors. In her e-mails Shari questions her idealism and compulsion to reach these troubled students, and Mike consoles her by sharing his own compassionate experiences as a former teacher in a middle-school lockup facility.

When a Student Goes Too Far

Hello Mike,

I'm fascinated by the creative writing class for a number of reasons. Primarily, the dynamics are different than standard classes simply because of the subject matter. Twenty-five students sharing an interest in an art brings a more personal feel to the classroom. Perhaps, this is what contributed to the profound impact Thursday's event had on me (and the rest of the class as well).

To begin with, there is a particular student we'll call "Lo." He is an outspoken, stereotypical "angry black male" whose comments shock me daily. I have to note, though, I am equally surprised by the sensitivity with which Lo offers encouragement to other writers in the class. But that is irrelevant right now.

Every day, two students give writing prompts which the students all write about for fifteen minutes each. The following day, before the first new prompt is given, students volunteer to share their writing from the previous day.

This past Monday, Lo issued the prompt: "Kill someone in the class." The following day Lo offered to share his. He then proceeded to read his entry throughout which most of the students were killed (although that did not even touch the horrifying aspect to this piece). Basically the theme running throughout the story was Lo issuing Mr. O. a slow, humiliating, painful death. This included (at various points) shooting out both of his kneecaps, grabbing Mr. O. by his "scrawny neck," forcing him to swallow sleeping pills before sewing his mouth shut, and pouring alcohol on his wounds and eye sockets.

My take is that Mr. O. should not have allowed Lo to offer such a prompt. Overall, though, I think Mr. O. handled the situation expertly. He did not react in anger, as I think I would have most certainly done had someone spoken of me in such a way. Calmly, Mr. O. followed Lorenzo's piece with a short discussion on going too far. He stressed the fact that he does not like to put constraints on the students' writing, but that as far as what is and is not appropriate "sharing material," some discretion should be used. I think Mr. O. demonstrated a great deal of self-control and wisdom in his means of dealing with this. He did not single out Lo, and he cited a few other incidents of students going overboard. Later, Mr. O. told me he intended to speak with Lo personally before class the following day, but I must say that in observing this turn of events I learned an enormous amount about how a professional must act in such a personal environment.

Unfortunately, this was the prelude to my first experience with standing before the class. I was supposed to assign both writing prompts for the day. The first time, I felt like I stumbled over my words a little, paused a few times, and certainly did not use the eloquence I had demonstrated in the run-throughs I played in my head. After the first fifteen-minute writing, I asked a couple of kids what they had written. Doing this seemed to make all the difference in the world. I quickly figured out that talking with the students rather than at them put me in such a more relaxed state. I feel like the students, also, appreciate this more personal level. I certainly need to remember that when my next opportunity in the front of the class arises. Hopefully, that will not be too long from now.

Shari

Dear Shari,

I'm surprised Mr. O. didn't put the quietus on Lo's journal diatribe before it made it to the blackboard. Giving students this kind of a task is empowering. However, the teacher must make it clear that this is an institution of higher learning, where a righteous level of respect (for self and others) must be maintained. Obviously, Lo's prompt was way out of line (his own response was even more bizarre). For these reasons, topics should be submitted and conferred upon before the class is subjected to such weirdness.

Don't kid yourself. There are plenty of angry and disillusioned students out there in a rainbow of colors with a wide range of agendas. Our job isn't to stifle their "creativity," but to hold them to a higher standard both linguistically and spiritually than is out there on the streets and in the movies and on TV. We're art teachers. Literature is there to inspire us, not degrade us. We have to be the bearers of good intentions. Great writers don't compose thoughts to degrade or demoralize their fellow man, whether they be fourteen or ninety-four. As John Steinbeck so aptly put it, "It is the duty of the writer to lift up, to extend, to encourage." As teachers, we should ditto this mentality for the study of English as an art. Hence, we have to keep our guard up because we are the guardians of the Muse.

I also really appreciated what you said about talking to the students and not at them. Communication is best served in that manner, and we are there to model good communication.

Respectfully,
Mike

Teaching At-Risk Students

Dear Mike,

Nothing too exciting happened in my creative writing class, except I learned a little more about Lo—the writer obsessed with violence and drugs. Mr. O. gave me a little background, including the fact that Lo recently moved down from New Jersey to live with his grandmother. Apparently, Lo spent some time in jail in Jersey, and he told Mr. O. that he's through with that kind of life.

This very scenario is the reason I want to teach—I want to be someone who helps kids like Lo stay "through" with that kind of life. I suppose it is because of this that I was quite concerned with the fact that Lo was not in class Thursday. It felt strange—his absence was certainly conspicuous; the dynamics of the entire room were changed. That Lo was not in class may not be much to write about, but I feel it is worth remembering that I spent the entire period wondering where he was.

Shari

Dear Shari,

For the first three years of my teaching career, I worked in a minimum security, lockup facility for middle-school aged boys from all over the state of Florida. On the surface these guys appeared pretty scary. I faced apathy and rage on a daily basis. Of course, my "clients" had good reasons to feel alienated and to "act out." The majority of them were refugees from broken homes. Most had been emotionally, physically, and sometimes sexually abused. In school, they had been stamped and labeled ESE, EH, LD, ADHD, SLD and other combinations of varying exceptionalities. Naturally, such labeling provided the school system with a tidy way to ostracize and segregate these "troublemakers" from the mainstream. Not surprisingly, most of their school records were as abominable as their criminal records. They had been chronically truant, they had failed several grades, they were reading at least two or three grades below their age level, and they had been repeatedly suspended and expelled. As for their brushes with the judicial system, their rap sheets were several pages long, and they had been convicted for big time crimes, such as assault, battery, grand theft, rape, and attempted murder.

Of course, the great irony was that these young fellows weren't unteachable, and they weren't unreachable (after all, they were locked up; they had to come to school). What I soon realized was that the majority of them were just like me and you. They wanted to love and be loved.

That's what really gets me excited about your reflections. You realize that the most exciting and important subject you teach is each student. Teaching English runs a pale second.

Respectfully,
Mike

Suspension or Detention?

Hello Mike,

Lo is back after being suspended again (Mr. O. does not know for what), and there is tension accompanying his return. Due to excessive absences, Lo has already failed most of his classes, including the creative writing class. Unfortunately, this leaves him with little incentive to put any effort into anything. He spent both days this week talking under his breath and antagonizing Mr. O. There were two incidents when Mr. O. acknowledged comments made by Lo (when I say acknowledged, I mean that he did not hide his shock, nor did he attempt to ignore Lo) and the class immediately got excited and out of control. Both times it took several minutes to get everyone back on track, and even then it was obvious that everyone was distracted.

It is becoming more apparent to me how vital the teacher's role is in facilitating discussion and instruction, while weeding out digressions and distractions. I am also seeing how easy it is to allow a student to take control of the class and belittle your authority. It's kind of scary. Either way, I'm quite concerned about Lo, as well as others who are surely in similar positions. Why are students punished for skipping by being told to stay home? That's a reward! And all that results is the students getting pushed further and further away from an education. I get so frustrated seeing Lo sitting there, trying to be a bad ass while Mr. O. is lecturing.

I just want to shake him and say, "You're so young! It's too early to screw it all up!"

Shari

Dear Shari,

Your concerns about Lo "as well as others in similar positions" are valid. It would make more sense to give them an in-school suspension—a quiet study hall or a "no talking" zone—where they could focus on "makeup work" for the time they're missing in class. Thus, the punishment would fit the crime. They abused their privileges in class, so they're extracted from that environment and placed in a more controlled environment wherein they must stay abreast of their studies so when they return, they have makeup work in tow. As a result, the main thing they missed was the opportunity to be in a more educationally and socially stimulating environment. The county used to run a program like that, and several schools still operate in the same fashion. It definitely makes more sense than excommunicating street kids back to the streets then allowing them to return with little or no chance for success. Obviously, if all they can do is fail when they return, then why should they try to do anything but screw up life for everyone else? Go figure.

However, Mr. O. has got to look out for the interests of his overall class, too. Lo's continual outbursts and distractions may at some point become too burdensome for the class to bear. All students have a right to learn in a safe environment, and as teachers we have to ensure that safety issue. Either way, it's a tough call.

Respectfully,
Mike

Working with Seriously Troubled Students

Dear Mike,

Mr. O. told me that Lo has been absent for several days, and his name had appeared on the suspension list. Mr. O. did not know why. I don't know if this sounds naive or silly or maybe even immature, but his absence (especially knowing there was punishment for something involved) was driving me nuts. I feel like somebody needs to do something, and I fear that Lo is getting criticism and not counseling. Of course, I know that Lo probably wouldn't even recognize me if I passed him on the street, much less even know my name, but I feel compelled to do something or at least to find out if somebody is doing anything. So what is doable? And what is stepping over the line? By giving it this much thought, am I already stepping over the line?

On a larger scale, I wonder what this says or implies about my future. Am I being silly or unrealistic? And does this compelling drive to save the underdogs get better or worse? What do you do with students who are obviously dealing with more than finding the right homecoming date? And how often are such troubled students going to be appearing in my classroom? Sorry I'm bombarding you with all of these questions.

Shari

Dear Shari,

The day you give up on the underdogs and quit caring is the day you should turn in your teaching certificate. Seriously, somebody's got to give a damn about these troubled troublemakers. Most of the time, few do. Even the kids, themselves, don't often care. They're not only self-destructive; they can be dangerous. That's why it's important to remember and realize your role. You are their teacher. You can't be everything to everybody. But you can be the most compassionate, caring, and engaging teacher a student could ever want in a classroom. When he comes back, let him know how much you missed him and how the class didn't seem the same without him. Based on the thoughts you're sharing with me, these are not abstractions; these are facts. What they symbolize to me, Shari, is your commitment to the students. When a teacher frets over the future of her lost souls, I rest assured that those students have fallen into the hands of a good caretaker.

Remember, though, you won't reach them all, you won't teach them all, and you won't save them all. But don't ever let that stop you from trying or believing that you might. That's why we do what we do. I've lost plenty of students. Some have dropped out. Some have gone to jail. Some have had babies at fifteen. A couple of them committed suicide. One was killed in knife fight, and there were a couple DOA's from drunk driving. For various reasons, many fail. But we still have to teach them, and try our best to reach them. That's why we do what we do.

Respectfully,
Mike

When It's Time to Let Go

Dear Mike,

After a stealing incident that occurred Thursday (three people independently came up to Mr. O. and said they'd witnessed Lo snagging someone's lighter), Mr. O. wrote the first referral he'd written in five years. He showed it to me, and asked if I thought he was being clear. Mr. O.'s referral comments noted that he'd been pushed to the end of his patience and good-will and was finally having to take into consideration the rights of his other students. Seeing how the referral was under the heading of "theft and intimidation," I guess I'm being forced to acknowledge that Lo has in fact been interfering with the other students' sense of well being. So I suppose I think Mr. O. was reasonable in offering a referral, but I can't help but wonder what else could have been done.

How long and how hard does one try before giving up and handing a student over to the lions? Or are the authorities the lions? I saw Lo in the hallway and tried to smile—a weak attempt at encouragement. And he responded with a "why-are-you-smiling-at-me" look. I'm kind of curious to see if Lo is in class on Tuesday. According to reports Mr. O. has been hearing, he didn't seem to think that Lo would be around much longer. I was disappointed in the obvious pleasure this gave Mr. O. I know—that's easy for me to say.

Shari

Dear Shari,

I'm afraid Mr. O.'s right. When a student continues to be a problem for the class, then a teacher must make a tough choice. In 19 years, I've only cut one student out of my class. The kid was hell-bent on sabotaging the class. To put it mildly, he wrote degrading papers; he made disparaging remarks; he led uprisings; he made a mockery of every assignment. Basically, he was demonstratively vehement in each and every interaction concerning me and the class. Naturally, he was exceedingly bright, but all of his brilliance was misspent projecting his malice. If it sounds like I took it personally, you're right. Even though, I advise my student teachers not to take things personally (à la all the negative vibes, cutting remarks, whining, complaining, ugly looks, and strange noises)—in practice sometimes our beans simply snap and our hearts shatter. I'm not proud of the fact that I failed to reach this kid, and I had to mull it over for quite some time before I eventually expelled him from the class. Unfortunately, I had been pushed by the student to make the same decision as Mr. O.—the class was more important than this individual whose main objective appeared to be sabotage.

Hopefully, it won't ever happen again to me or Mr. O. or to you, either.

Respectfully,

Mike

PS—Sometimes the authorities have to be lions, but such is the nature of the beast.

FROM ANOTHER ANGLE

The very first time the cooperating teacher left me alone with a group of twelfth graders during my student teaching internship, soft-spoken, impeccably dressed Xavier stood up, dropped his jeans, and mooned me. His action was an exclamation point that marked the subterranean level of respect I had, at that point, garnered from his class. The scene was hysterically funny to everyone in the room except me. As an intern I was humiliated. Worse, I had no repertoire of remarks or reactions that would help me get through the event and laughter, then get back to trying to teach. Looking back on that afternoon, I realize that Xavier's unexpected challenge represents one of the most troubling issues that inexperienced teachers face: balancing the teacher's need for respect and authority in the classroom with students' rights to express themselves freely.

Can teachers encourage students to express themselves freely, and also insist on what Mike calls "a righteous level of respect" within a classroom? If the teacher allows for free expression of ideas, then reacts negatively when students express views that are not popular or respectful of others, does that teacher undermine the very classroom atmosphere that he or she has attempted to create? On the other hand, if the teacher allows students to express troubling or threatening ideas in class, is that teacher guilty of disrupting a productive, low-threat classroom environment, one in which all students feel that they are safe?

These questions, and the discussion they should provoke, might be situated in a broader discussion, one that looks critically at the elements of effective student-sensitive learning environments. Creating and maintaining a student-centered classroom is difficult. Prospective and beginning teachers need to realize that an environment in which adults and teens share responsibility for decisionmaking and learning will not spring up, full-grown, overnight. That kind of comfortable and productive environment demands a lot of gardening work—a lot of planning, seed planting, fertilizing, pruning, watering, weeding, and talking. The issue of how we establish and maintain healthy, challenging, yet safe and supportive classroom relationships and environments is one that connects all aspects of teacher education, one with which educational theorists, researchers, and practitioners, regardless of their political and philosophical persuasions, are concerned.

Learning to teach is, necessarily, a process, one that only begins with preservice education. Let's look at Shari's situation again. Her struggle to decide if Lo should have been given permission to share aloud his paper, an essay that is about killing his classmates and brutally torturing then killing the writing teacher, Mr. O., is complicated. Most of us would agree that the topic should not have been allowed. Even in classroom situations when the teacher gives students "free choice" in creating topics for their peers to write about as part of the instructional format, common sense would suggest that this student's topic choice negates the classroom contract. Nevertheless, Shari is, as an intern, a "visitor" in this classroom as well as a teacher. She does not feel comfortable going against Mr. O.'s policy; if he does not stop Lo, she feels that she cannot, either. She recognizes the value of giving students some topic choice, but obviously worries about the particular choice, "Kill someone in the class." She understands that the call for violence will induce emotional tension, at the very least, in the classroom. She therefore is complicit in Mr. O.'s decision to give Lorenzo a voice, even when it is an inappropriate one. She agrees with Mr. O.'s rationale: that teachers should use activities in which "students learn from each other." However, she is concerned with the hidden curriculum, as well as the explicit one, that emerges when this practice is carried out in the classroom.

In an example of the kind of problem preservice teachers are expected to solve, Shari must weigh the theoretical ideal (student participation in topic choice) against the classroom reality (a student makes a seriously flawed choice that might prove dangerous for others). Shari looks on the positive side of the situation: she voices support for Mr. O.'s decision to speak in general terms instead of directly to Lo about "going too far" when choosing the topic for the class to address. She admires Mr. O.'s determined effort to demonstrate "respect for diverse perspectives . . . in planned learning activities," but has trouble reconciling that freedom with the actual outcome, a paper in which "openness, mutual respect, support" are glaringly absent.

Later, in Shari's second assessment of the situation that involves Lo's violence-laced paper, we see a picture of the classroom that seems to be more romanticized than it is realistic. She has learned that he moved to town to live with his grandmother after spending time in jail, and that he has vowed to leave a bad life behind. With this knowledge in mind, Shari writes, "This very scenario is the reason I want to teach—I want to be someone who helps kids like Lo stay 'through' with that kind of life." While we may admire and share her wish to have a positive impact on students like Lo, we may also suspect she will prove to be more altruistic in theory than she will be able to be in practice.

After another few days pass, Shari observes a bored, malcontent Lo; on this day, he chooses to contribute only antagonistic remarks that serve to distract his classmates and teacher. Shari demonstrates the preprofessional competency of "recognizing problems" when she makes an observation about how easily students can take control of classrooms in ways that disrespect their teachers and classmates. However, she has no real opportunity to "research solutions and evaluate outcomes" in this short exposure to a classroom situation. Has she actually demonstrated, then, competence regarding problem behaviors and attitudes? Probably not. Although she recognizes the problem in Lo's behavior, she does not see that the teacher could have prevented this particular problem. She has not made a connection between the assignment format (students are allowed to contribute writing prompts, and are not required to have the teacher approve their topics) and the resulting situation. Shari will probably need to live through several problematic experiences before she is able to determine her own stance regarding how to best handle situations like the ones Lo participated in and provoked.

Educational theorist Eliot Eisner (1998) states that "competence in teaching" should be related to "the kind of education that we think students should receive . . . what we want teachers to be able to do," and that teachers' work should relate directly to "the aspirations we hold for our children" (206). He draws our attention to the fact that no theory can account for every circumstance a new teacher like Shari will find herself in, and encourages us to think in terms of the "highly contextualized and particularistic decisions" that teachers must almost constantly make (208). He would be likely to remind Shari that "There is no single best way to teach" (209), and suggest that she learn to rely on her own "artistry and intuition" instead of predetermined definitions of correct teacherly behavior. Harvard professor Catherine Snow acknowledged, in her presidential speech before the American Educational Research Association in 2000, the value and limitations of a teacher's personal knowledge:

> Personal knowledge, knowledge based in one's own experience and practice, is an irreplaceable source of wisdom. In fact, the best teacher-education programs may turn out to be those that insist that teacher education candidates have personal experiences with child learners before they start to acquire the research-based knowledge that is also such an important part of their education. But personal knowledge is also a limited source of wisdom . . . It must be compared to knowledge from other sources, connected with knowledge based in research, and interwoven with knowledge derived from a theoretical perspective to be made useful. (8)

It seems that neither Shari nor Mr. O. was reaching beyond her or his own instincts in this situation, and their failure to do so might have led to a serious, even dangerous, situation for everyone in the classroom.

Eisner and Snow are right—there is no one right way to teach, and teachers must rely as much on their instincts as on their carefully drawn plans. And yet, the situation that is disconcerting to Shari is probably troubling to you, too. It reflects a serious problem in preservice education: Shari is left in an extremely vulnerable position in this circumstance. You probably would be vulnerable in the same situation. Like you, she is learning to negotiate classroom management with students and a cooperating teacher, and thus is open to many ideas. She wants to believe that the teacher used the best judgment in handling the situation. She wants to give students as much freedom as possible, and believes that older high-school students should be given almost free reign. She has difficulty seeing that one student's decision to express himself cannot take precedence over the right of the entire class to feel safe.

As a teacher, you will not be able to abdicate your responsibility for making the "tough call" when that is the call that is required. Shari seemed to assume that preventing Lo from creating any prompt he chose, and reading aloud any essay he composed, would infringe on his rights within the classroom. What she did not realize is that his actions infringed on the rights of all of his classmates and his teacher to feel safe and positive in the class.

This situation, and the concerns it generates, leaves troubling questions for you and your cooperating teachers and colleagues to consider together. Some of the questions you might want to address include these:

- How might your cooperating teacher better support you as you test your wings as a new teacher?
- If Shari had been the only teacher in the class on the day that Lo read his violent paper, how might she have responded? How might Lo's classmates have reacted?
- Would the adolescents' opportunity to learn, in this context, have been sacrificed if Mr. O. had turned over the class to Shari, a novice teacher, in that particular situation?
- How would you have responded, if you were Lo's teacher?
- What kind of help would you need from your cooperating teacher, in a similar situation?
- How might you have structured the assignment differently, in order to avoid a problem like this one?
- At what point would Lo's continual outbursts and distractions become too burdensome for you and the class to bear?
- All students have a right to learn in a safe environment, and as teachers we have to ensure that safety. What would you do to ensure students' emotional, social, and intellectual safety in this situation, or in others that raise similar concerns?

For further reading, I recommend Eisner's book, *The Kinds of Schools We Need: Personal Essays* (1998) from Heinemann, as well as the following texts that deal more specifically with issues of classroom management, and teaching behaviors that promote cooperation and an environment that is conducive to learning:

Cangelosi, James S. 2000. *Classroom Management Strategies: Gaining and Maintaining Students' Cooperation*, 4th edition. New York: John Wiley & Sons. I especially like this text because it offers a balanced approach to classroom management. Cangelosi introduces the perspectives of several theorists and schools of thought, ranging from Kounin's "Withitness Approach," to Glasser's Rational Choices model, and the Behaviorists' Conditioning Responses. There are management scenarios in each chapter; in most, both children and adolescents are features in separate scenarios. These verbal pictures illustrate how teachers handle tough situations, demonstrating the management model that is the focus of the chapter. The book prompts discussion about how a new teacher can be prepared for many management and discipline issues, and why and when certain models would be appropriate, without suggesting that there is one correct way to interact with students in classrooms.

Moore, Kenneth D. 1995. *Classroom Teaching Skills*, 3rd edition. New York: McGraw-Hill. Less systematic in its review of specific models of classroom management and student behavior than the Cangelosi text, this book is, nevertheless, valuable. In it, Moore highlights the significant role that the teacher plays in students' behavior and performance. Moore's Part Three, which focuses on "Instructional Skills," begins with a chapter on communication, then moves to motivation, reinforcement, questioning, and then to classroom management. I like the way that Moore ties together the elements of good instruction and planning with appropriate behavior and positive school performance among teens. New teachers who feel like they are alone in classroom discipline concerns might find this book, with its self-tests and answer keys added, particularly useful.

Graham, Peg, Sally Hudson-Ross, Chandra Adkins, Patti MacWhorter, and Jennifer McDuffie Stewart. (Eds.) 1999. *Teacher/Mentor: A Dialogue for Collaborative Learning.* New York: Teachers College Press and Urbana, IL: National Council of Teachers of English. This book is a wonderful text for those who want to take time to mull over the student-teacher relationship. It does not outline specific strategies for collaborative learning; instead, it is a collection of essays from the perspectives of those involved in secondary English student teaching situations: mentor/student teachers (the latter are called "teacher candidates" in this text); teacher researchers (a role that can become overwhelming when it is an added requirement for student teachers, but that would help student teachers explore issues such as the impact of Lo's behavior on the environment for writing in Mr. O.'s class); the "teacher candidate," and finally, all members of the "collaborative community." We are fortunate that this text is situated in English language arts courses; it speaks to all teachers, but more directly to those of us who are in the same field as the editors and contributing authors.

13

Interactive Jazz

Sarah is an energetic intern raring to try new and inventive things at a local middle school in a zone that caters to families with average incomes. Sarah is very creative in her approach to literature and composition and she thrives on the notion of having a more interactive class. Luckily, her mentor, Mrs. Z., encourages her by giving her a fair amount of leeway and freedom with regard to her lesson plans and class activities. The outcome is a rather vibrant interning experience that results in a meaningful experience for Sarah, the students, and her mentor.

Getting into Groups

Dear Mike,

Mrs. Z. had the students using group work to cover a poem filled with imagery. Mrs. Z.'s theory was that the students would have more fun working in groups and also be more successful. She was correct. The classes were a little hectic, but the poems came out great.

The format went as follows. After sitting down, the students were given a minilesson on imagery. We defined it, gave examples of it, and read poems that contained imagery. The class was then given an optional guideline to follow. Some used the guideline, others were more creative. Again, it was a bit hectic, but it was worth the effort. Most of the poems were excellent, and the students enjoyed the interaction.

After the classes, I told Mrs. Z. I planned to use group work for my poetry lesson. She said that she enjoyed group work, but she only uses it occasionally because it's noisy and it wears her out. Personally, if the noise is related to the work being done, I don't mind. I think it's also very important to know that once your class is in the group work mode, your control is significantly decreased. Despite that risk, I think students enjoy interacting with each other, and it's a great stimulus shifter, which prevents the students from becoming bored. Perhaps, too much group work can be exhausting, but hey, I'm young. That should not be a problem.

Sarah

Dear Sarah,

I have found that group work is especially effective with poetry. I like to have the students cowrite, coedit, coproduce and coread their productions. I also agree that by having a specific objective, such as imagery or similes or metaphors or onomatopoeia, it helps put a focus on the task at hand, which in turn helps with your evaluation of their final product. Thus, a guideline or rubric is important. Therefore, I'm not so sure that I would allow them to abandon the objectives entirely. I think it's an invaluable quotient for determining their "mastery" of the literary element. Although, I do agree that we need to leave a lot of room for imagination (within the boundaries of good, clean fun). You probably don't want them to get too down and dirty. If you let them, they will—just for the shock value and cheap thrills of being "as nasty as they wanna be."

Kudos to you, though. You're right! Group work is highly interactive, so it makes things lively and fun. However, don't think that the "teacher's control is significantly decreased." It's just different. You need to circulate; keep close tabs of what's happening (or not happening) and articulate what needs to be accomplished without imposing too much of your stifling direction. When they're floundering, though, or when they're totally off task, you've got to reel them in.

Respectfully,
Mike

Switching Gears and Staying Active

Mike,

This week, I observed a neighbor teacher's class in action. The teacher I observed was Mr. Mc. Mainly, I wanted to see how he changed the stimulus during class and accomplished closure. His way of initially getting attention was to speak above the students. Not a method I prefer, but I really do not have a better idea just yet. Once the class was listening, he let them know what their expectations were for the day. Overall, Mr. Mc. did not change the stimulus too often. He had them study for an open book test and work on some extra-credit crossword puzzles. The students were mainly in the "student as a silent reader" mode until they took the test.

After the test, the students became observers, watching a film on African safaris. Their closure here was to make a safari collage out of what they saw on the film, and in the books on Africa they had been studying. All in all, I liked his methods of control and work distribution during class. But I could see where stimuli changing would have done him a world of good, because there were times when the students began to get a little happy in their seats.

In two weeks I'm supposed to have a lesson plan to include in Mrs. Z.'s poetry unit. I'm really nervous about that, mainly because I really have little idea what I'm going to do. I'm contemplating doing something on the similarities of music to poetry. You know, the themes, meter, the purpose behind writing it. After a lesson plan, I was going to have them bring in the lyrics to their favorite "appropriate" song for homework, and have them write about why it's tops with them, and to identify the theme of it. This way, they are writing about something they like, and they can have homework that really is not difficult. It's sketchy right now. Let me know what you think.

Sarah

Dear Sarah,

Variances of stimuli are critical. Some experts say that the activities should change every 15 minutes or about the length of a TV show before the commercial break. After all, we are dealing with the TV/video generation. (But I wouldn't suggest sticking too closely to this time table.)

For openers, Mr. Mc.'s intro does illustrate the importance of using your voice to assert yourself. Remember, though, volume isn't the key to an effective speaker. An animated voice relies on a more assured tone and timbre. It is never monotone or predictable. It can be your best friend and weapon. Giving the students the day's agenda is also a good way to begin class. Lay your objectives out on the table, so the class has a clear cut course of action to follow.

Where Mr. Mc. and I really differ is on his reliance of inactive passivity (although, granted this was a one-day, one-shot deal). My preference is for more action and interaction. Too much silent reading and crossword doodling compounded by TV watching is just too controlled for my tastes. I prefer to interact with my class and to have them interact with one another.

So my advice is to think interactively. Don't think that students are only on task when they are quiet (Plus—they may get "too happy in their seats"). So jazz up your poetry lesson. I think that coupling poetry and music sounds (no pun intended) like it has plenty of interactive possibilities. Just be sure to illustrate the thematic aspects before you have them bring in "their favorite song." Of course, the best way to accomplish this is by modeling your own top tune for them. Show them how it's done—don't just tell them. This will get them tuned into what you want them to do, and it'll get them tuned into you.

Consequently, when they bring in their song to share, they can't stare at you blankly and say, "I didn't really understand *your* assignment. But this song has a really rad beat and I just like it." You should probably also clarify some guidelines for appropriate material or such classics as "Cop Killer Boogie" and "My Bitch duh Ho" will pepper your classroom. You probably should have them write out their responses and practice delivering them, too. Or you'll hear a lot of "Well, you know, like, I just, like, really like this tune, you know, 'cause like, it's like really meaningful to me, like when I'm down, and I need to like be, like, lifted up and feel better. You know, like sometimes how it gets, like when everything seems so like way-bad and everything?"

But whatever you do—don't forget the performance quotient. Make it part of your objective. Get them up and have them share their reflections about their favorite songs. And have them respond to each other by giving feedback and asking questions after each presentation. It's really the most important thing we do. It's not only interactive, it's really, really, really fun.

Respectfully,

Mike

Rocking the Classroom

Dear Mike,

On Tuesday, I observed a cool lesson. Mrs. Z. played "Ironbound" by Suzanne Vega and gave each student a copy of the lyrics. After she played the song once, she asked them to start writing about what they saw in the song. She hinted to them to look for symbolism. Once they started writing, she played the song again. As they were writing, she walked around the classroom and made comments to people, highlighted stuff she liked, etc. After about ten minutes, she called on a random student to share his ideas. After she had called on two more, kids began volunteering their thoughts and ideas and the class erupted (positively) into a room full of ideas. It was very exciting because I was participating, but having a hard time coming up with stuff until they started coming up with ideas. Once we got going, I came up with some stuff and was able to share my ideas, too.

I really like this idea, and I wonder why she doesn't do more of this type of learning. Most of the time, the students are either reading or taking a quiz or test.

Sarah

Dear Sarah,

I call it interactive jazz. The kids get jazzed; the teacher gets jazzed; the house rocks. Less tedium and more jazz is what I hear you saying we all need (students and teachers alike). So turn up the heat, cook and design, then improvise on some interactive jazz.

Respectfully,

Mike

Varying the Stimuli

Dear Mike,

Here is my plan for my poetry lesson. I am going to teach Langston Hughes' poem "The Weary Blues" by showing a short video of his life. Then I am going to get on a chair in the back of the room while soft blues music is playing, and read the poem aloud (in character!). I'll have a dramatic student read the part of the piano player with me.

After a discussion about the poem, the students will get in a comfortable spot and draw an image of what the scene looks like to them with that really thick sidewalk chalk to give their pictures that smoky feeling.

The next day I'll show the video of Wycleff's "Gone 'Til November." We'll discuss the similarities between Hughes and Wycleff, and then I will have them talk about poetry in music. For their assignment on that day, I will ask them to get into groups, and write their own lyrics, and for the daring ones, I'll have them perform it in front of the class.

What do you think of my lesson? Any suggestions?

Sarah

Dear Sarah,

Bravo! You're hitting some hot licks with your interactive jazz! I also appreciate how you're mixing learning styles by varying the stimulation—audio, video, music, artwork, et al.

My only suggestion is to make them all share. It's important to get everyone involved in the performance aspect of the lessons. That's the most essential portion of this interactive equation. Overall, though, you're cooking.

Respectfully,
Mike

Interacting with Poetry

Dear Mike,

I took your advice and had every group perform their "Weary Blues" poems. They were so cool. Mrs. Z. was very impressed and pleased. She even did a similar activity today. First, they read a Shel Silverstein poem about chores that contained a lot of alliteration. Then the students listed chores, and what they shared and what they hated about each chore on the board. For homework they made up their own poem using alliteration, and then today they read them aloud. I was really impressed with their poems. It took the whole class period for everyone to read, but it was well worth it.

Sarah

Dear Sarah,

Kudos to Mrs. Z.!

Her lesson contained several key elements. First of all, it was entertaining. Shel Silverstein's silly stuff is super (notice my alliteration). It engages the audience. Secondly, she had a clear literary objective (alliteration). In addition, the lesson was somewhat interactive—the students brainstormed, shared ideas, and cooperatively participated in a prewriting activity. Then, of course, they modeled the writing, using both a thematic element (chores) and a literary one (alliteration). Finally, the students were given ample time to write (overnight) and they were required to share their products in class—which is a very, very essential ingredient when creating a cooperative learning environment (we must share and share alike).

As you noted, the readings took all period, but it was well worth it. Amen, Sister Sarah. Most students have fun writing poems, and sharing them is even more fun. And fun is what schools need more of (focused fun that is).

Writing poems can also be a fabulous way to have the students respond to Lit. For instance, I've been driving my eleventh-grade college prep students pretty hard lately. They've read *Catcher in the Rye* and *Cannery Row* back to back these nine weeks, and they've had to write several lengthy essays in response. To lighten up the mood, I had them write a free verse poem (we've also been studying Whitman) about one of the characters, settings, or themes from either novel. We had our "poetry show" yesterday, and it was amazing. The students had written some really beautiful and insightful stuff. I got goose bumps and tears several times; it finished our week on a most bodacious note.

Respectfully,

Mike

Getting the Students to Teach

Dear Mike,

Today, Mrs. Z. asked me to take one of the students into her office for tutoring while the rest of the class worked on grammar. This was a really good opportunity because I had not had a chance to work one on one with a student yet. It is much easier to stand in front of the class and say "Does everyone understand? Okay, let's move on" than to sit with one student who is having problems and really doesn't understand.

The student needed a lot of help with different types of pronouns, but instead of having her sit and do grammar exercises, I had her try to teach me the types of pronouns. Of course, I allowed her to have the book in front of her for reference. She would look at the examples in the book then she would try to describe the different cases (reflexive, interrogative, etc.) to me in her own words. I could tell that this really helped her a lot. I could almost see her coming to an understanding of these parts of speech. Although it was a little frustrating, waiting for her to come up with a definition sometimes—overall, it was a great experience.

The next day, Mrs. Z. had me lead both classes for the entire period. Unfortunately, she also apprised me of the lesson plan as I walked into the classroom. It was okay, because we were doing a rather fun activity (at least I tried to make it fun—I guess it's debatable). Since the class is taking a field trip to the Legislature in about a month, each student had a packet of handouts on "Parliamentary Procedure." Mrs. Z. wanted me to simply read through this packet aloud with the class. For the first couple of pages, we just read through the different procedures, and I fielded any questions. Then I noticed that the class was getting bored and some students weren't paying attention, so I changed it up a little. Instead of reading through the rules aloud, I asked them to read the rules silently, then whoever felt like they understood the concepts could try to present the information to me and the rest of the class. This got them all to read, because none of them could pass up an opportunity to get the attention of the class. After a couple of failures to follow procedure, the class really began to understand, and they were having fun doing it (not bad for an ad-libbed activity).

Sarah

Dear Sarah,

I'm very impressed with your intuitiveness. In both of your activities (the one-on-one tutoring and the classroom lecture), you accentuated learning by having the students teach and explain the lesson. This is the most effective way to measure if someone "really knows" something. Obviously, to teach it you must know it. (Makes teaching kind of a scary prospect, eh?) You have "discovered" a most illuminating teaching tool. Plus, it's more fun than just reading aloud what's already in front of the kids.

Respectfully,
Mike

Making a Game with the Grammar Monster

Dear Mike,

Mrs. Z. asked me to create a fun lesson-game to present, dealing with the grammar that the students are studying. When I started, I was afraid that the group thing I designed would get a little out of hand and would be difficult to manage. But, I had anticipated these difficulties beforehand, and therefore the transitions went pretty smoothly.

For example, before the students started moving into their groups, I told them that the group that gets together first (quickly, yet SAFELY) will get to share with the class first. Well, they didn't even know what they were sharing yet, but that was enough incentive for them. Once they were all in their groups of four, each member was given a part of the sentence (subject, helping verb, main verb, and direct object) and they were to create a sentence combining each of their respective parts. Of course, I had to remind them that the object here was not to create the silliest or most disgusting sentence, but rather the most correct sentence. It was a good thing that I said that, because some students definitely felt compelled to write the more bizarre style sentences. I gave the groups about seven minutes to work on the sentences then we began to share them in class. A couple groups had written incorrect sentences, but that was actually good because it gave me another chance to go over direct objects. When I gave them a second chance to write sentences and switch around the parts, all of their sentences were correct. I saw this as a success in learning.

After class Mrs. Z. remarked that the group work went a lot more smoothly than she had anticipated, and I agreed.

Sarah

Dear Sarah,

You're mighty slick. What impresses me the most is your nose for sniffing out trouble spots and snags. Your usage of "mob" (I mean, child) psychology was quite effective. Students enjoy competition, even if the payoff's dinky or they don't have a clue of the activity. It's that "Me, first" mentality.

I also appreciate the way you anticipated the grotesqueness and the silliness that such an activity would undoubtedly elicit—(if the little darlings were left to their own demonic devices). The students responded; they were on task; they came up with stellar products; they showed a mastery of your objectives. Such a success! I'm so very proud and impressed.

It's very commendable that you are trying out "new" and "fresh" approaches (games) with a rather stiff subject (grammar). It's also very admirable that you're tackling group work. A lot of warhorses shy away from groups because the students get a little noisy when they are interacting, but interacting is the key to a certifiably sound communication class.

Respectfully,

Mike

Using Speeches to Get Close

Dear Mike,

Since I know how much you love music, I'm sure that you will appreciate this. A student gave his demonstrative speech on the guitar and after explaining the different parts of the instrument and how to position the hands, he played (and sang) "Wonderwall," "One Headlight," and another song that HE HAD WRITTEN! He received three standing ovations from the class. I couldn't believe how talented he was!

Of course, there is very little I can do with the classes because they are giving their speeches for the next week. They have been a lot of fun to watch, though.

Sarah

Dear Sarah,

I once read about a secondary school teacher who still does "show and tell" with his students because it gives them a forum to explain, demonstrate and share a bit of what they're all about. I wish I could have seen the singer-songwriter. It must have been goose bump cool. And believe me I've gotten a few of those over the years from amazing student performances. In fact, every nine weeks I require some sort of formal oral presentation in my classes. It's a great forum for cultivating classroom magical moments. It also keeps the class interactive and jazzy.

Respectfully,

Mike

Combining Art and Literature

Hey, Mike,

   I'm teaching next Tuesday. I'm going to have the kids read a story by Arthur C. Clarke for homework and we'll go over it some at the beginning of class. Then I'm breaking them up into groups, and we're going to break out the crayons! I want them to draw images from the story. This works well I think since the subheading the story's under in the book is the "Setting" section, and the author uses some pretty vibrant images that the kids should hopefully pick up on. Well, we'll see. Mrs. Z. doesn't do much hands-on work, so I think the kids will like the change.

Sarah

Dear Sarah,

   Sounds fun. But don't be surprised if it gets hectic or chaotic. Make sure you write your objectives on the board and talk about them clearly before you break them up into groups. Let them know what you expect from them as a final product. Ask them if they have any questions, then go for it. If it gets a little chaotic, don't freak. Circulate continually. Check out what they're doing. The students will dig the variety of experience, but they'll be lively. So be prepared. It's going to be fun.

Respectfully,
Mike

Hey, Mike,

   I'm wearing a big grin! I had control yesterday (power!) and taught my lesson on Arthur C. Clarke's "If I Forget Thee, Oh Earth." I was pretty scared at first, but determined not to show it. Initially, I had a hard time getting the students interested in the assignment (tough crowd at 7:20 a.m.), but after I got them into groups, they started getting into it. I circled around examining their pictures, getting the kids on task, answering questions, and just generally talking and laughing with the students. Since the story is a bit dated (more Cold War than nowadays) many of the kids were confused, but as I went around to each group we discussed it. It helped them get a clearer idea of what it was about. It was barely controlled chaos, but a lot of fun!

   Toward the end, I could have used a bit more control. I had a hard time getting the students to calm down and listen politely to what the other groups were presenting. Eventually, I had to make them get back into rows for the final discussion.

   Mrs. Z. said I did a great job and has already asked me if I'd consider doing a lesson plan for a segment of *Julius Caesar* soon. Have to think about it. All in all a very satisfying day (I got some cool pictures, too).

Sarah

Dear Sarah,

I'm so proud.

It was very bold of you to tackle group work again. In my opinion, it's the most difficult to pull off. As you so aptly pointed out, the students can get off task very easily and when it's time for their group to give their presentation, they are often still a little hazy about how they're going to pull it off. So they'll whisper, scratch a few more notes, add a couple lines, and just generally create an annoying buzz in the arena.

Sounds like you handled yourself well, though. You circled the classroom, answered questions, and clarified the objectives. Most of all, you enjoyed the students. You laughed. You responded. You created an atmosphere conducive to true communication.

As for the initial chaos and lethargy you felt from them at the beginning of the morning, perhaps a little interactive, historical brainstorming at the top of the class about the Cold War would have helped access their prior knowledge. Then you could have filled in the gaps with a brief overview of the time period. That might have helped clarify their task once they broke into groups. Overall, though, bravo! You've done so well that the manager wants you to come back up to bat and hit again. Keep me posted. And keep the students jazzed.

Respectfully,
Mike

Rewriting the Script

Hey, Mike,

We're starting *Julius Caesar*. I'm teaching Acts II and III. Mrs. Z. has been more than helpful, but she has a very busy schedule. Not only does she teach full-time, but she also sponsors FOUR clubs! It's a wonder that she has time to sleep! I'd love to have some input for my *Julius Caesar* lesson. I'm having them break into small groups for tableaus, but I also want to incorporate a class discussion and possibly a creative writing assignment.

Until next time,
Sarah

Dear Sarah,

Sounds good to me. Another cool thing to do with antique literature is have them rewrite scenes in a contemporary scenario with today's lingo—including slang. One of my favorite things to do with my ninth graders is to have them rewrite *Romeo and Juliet* hillbilly style (see Figure 13–1). To get them into the mood, I play a recording of Andy Griffith from the '50s where he recounts the play in classic backwoods American vernacular. Then I put the kids in groups and divvy up the scenes. We spend several days on the rewrites, and the students have a terrific time mimicking the Bard with a rural twang. A lot of them get into hayseed

Southern Fried Romeo and Juliet

We will rewrite Act I of the play in Ye Olde Americana—hillbilly style—à la the Hatfields and McCoys via the Capulets and Montagues. We'll keep the same names but the scenario will change—with our climactic act ending at the Capulets' semi-annual Big Barn Dance and Bar-Bee-Cue Pig Feast.

In order to do a most excellent job each group must:

Emulate the essence of each Shakespearean passage in their particular scene (in other words, rewrite almost every "dad gum" line but in a hillbilly vernacular).

Act out the scene for the class with each member of the group participating in character.

FIGURE 13–1

costumes, bring in some recorded bluegrass for background music, and even do a little hoe down dancing. The best thing, though, is that the assignment really forces them to examine the text. As one student observed last semester, you really have to know the material on several levels to go from Elizabethan English to standard American English to Redneck Americana. And as with most interactive assignments, the rewritten plays are a whole lot of fun to watch and perform.

Respectfully,
Mike

FROM ANOTHER ANGLE

Sarah is miles ahead of where I was as a student teacher—or as a beginning teacher, for that matter. First, she understands that English/language arts classes are places that need to be filled with noise, at least a lot of the time.

Early on, I thought a quiet class was a good class. I did have fleeting suspicions that I was not quite right about that equation, and wondered why my "good" students were often unengaged, but I rarely tested it. I was happy when I felt that my voice carried more of an impact than anyone else's, and when it was the one that dominated.

Second, instead of trying to be the one person in the classroom with all of the answers, Sarah is willing to let students learn from and teach each other by using collaborative groups that have focus and purpose. I tried having students "work together in small groups" a few times when I was a rookie, but ran into two big problems: One problem had to do with the nature of the group assignments. Instead of giving each group one problem to solve, I gave them assignments that could easily be broken up into separate parts, so that individual group members worked on individual parts of the assignment problem in isolation, then reported their final results back to their group. That plan used parallel brains, but not shared ones. My second problem was that I failed to account for the fact that group work provoked a lot of noise and temporary chaos. I was unprepared when the class got out of hand and was unable to regain any sense of organization or focus. The vice principal had to come in to see for himself what all the ruckus was about—I avoided him for weeks after that, since he had seen my students in such a disorderly disarray.

Third, Sarah reflects on her misfires as opportunities to learn. I was either too embarrassed to admit my multitude of mistakes, or plain unaware of them. I thought, mistakenly, that preparing for the next class was a better use of time than reflecting on the previous class. Too often, I failed to use what my experiences with bad plans, poor implementation, and awkward communications could have taught me.

Because she is willing to try collaboration in her classroom, Sarah might benefit from adding information about several popular models for collaborative group work to her teaching repertoire. In *Teaching Ten to Fourteen Year Olds* (1998), Chris Stevenson describes collaborative group formats (which he calls cooperative groupings) as particularly well suited "to meet the social and intellectual needs of young adolescents" (233). He asserts that collaborative groups promote "interdependent learning by establishing conditions that require small groups of students to work productively and positively together, face to face, sharing individual responsibility for a group product" (Stevenson 1998, 233). He summarizes research on cooperative learning by pointing to the "general improvement in academic achievement and grades among students working in successful cooperative groups," as well as growth in social aspects of learning, including self-esteem that grows from individual and group accomplishments (233).

Stevenson recommends several protocols, including these: the Learning Together model (Johnson and Johnson, 1988, cited in Stevenson 1998, 234), in which members of a small heterogeneous group work to solve one problem and produce a single product; the Group Investigation model (Sharan and Sharan 1976, in Stevenson, 235), in which students who have agreed to work together as decisionmakers and investigators spend several weeks researching and then reporting on a topic; Student Team Learning models, the most popular of which is Student Teams Achievement Divisions (STAD) (Slavin 1980, in Stevenson, 235–237), in which groups that include low-, middle-, and high-performing students and that reflect the gender and racial mix of the class listen to the teacher present subject matter, then quiz group members on the material prior to a whole-class quiz. After the quiz, individuals receive grades, but groups are also awarded points for the average quiz score, and earn special recognition if the group average is an improvement over the previous quiz score.

In *Whole Language in Middle and Secondary Classrooms* (1994), Harry Noden and Richard Vacca also recommend collaborative grouping. They discuss formats in terms of purpose: inquiry groups, performance groups, and gaming groups. Inquiry groups might incorporate the popular "jigsaw" method, in which each group member learns the group's material, then teaches it to members of another group, or the "rhetorical inquiry" method, in which students' initial responses to literature or other sources are developed through increasingly sophisticated questions from emotional to analytic to evaluative levels (Noden and Vacca 1994, 46–48). Members of performance groups might be involved in coauthoring a drama, engaging in literature-related role-play, creating a class newspaper, conducting peer tutoring, or participating in a class debate (48–51). Gaming groups take advantage of the excitement and enthusiasm produced by games in order to provide short-term motivation for learning. Games might simulate popular television game shows, such as the use of *Jeopardy* as a format for reviewing for a test, or they might imitate a popular board game, such as Clue or Bingo. The benefits of each of these collaborative/cooperative instructional formats, when they are correctly implemented, is that all students have opportunities to talk with each other, suggesting answers, working toward solutions together. Students who have particular learning disorders or disabilities can frequently contribute in ways that more traditional classroom assignments do not allow; for example, despite a problem with processing print texts, a student could be a star as a member of a role-playing group. English Language Learners will have more opportunities to ask for clarification, and to try their language skills in low-risk settings when they are working alongside classmates in collaborative groups. That is what "interactive jazz" in English/language arts all about. Every student has a voice and sings in the classroom chorus. The room swings and sways. Students are energized, and it is a hopping place for a teacher to be, too.

Sarah will, I have no doubt, develop her own models for individual and group contributions to class, too. I suspect that, as a beginning teacher, she will continue to take her work seriously. She will continue to put her students' needs and interests ahead of her personal goals. She will continue to reflect on, and learn from, her failures as well as her successes. She will continue to try new ideas and try them again, with modifications. I suspect that Sarah will be a fine teacher.

REFERENCES

ALLEN, JANET AND KYLE GONZALEZ. 1998. *There's Room for Me Here.* York, ME: Stenhouse.

ALLISON, LIBBY, LIZBETH BRYANT, AND MAUREEN HOURIGAN. 1997. *Grading in the Post-Process Classroom: From Theory to Practice.* Portsmouth, NH: Boynton/Cook Heinemann.

ATWELL, NANCIE. 1998. *In The Middle: New Understandings About Writing, Reading, and Learning.* Portsmouth, NH: Heinemann.

BAINES, LAWRENCE AND ANTHONY KUNKEL. (EDS.) 2000. *Going Bohemian: Activities that Engage Adolescents in the Art of Writing Well.* Newark, DE: International Reading Association.

BAINES, LAWRENCE AND ANTHONY KUNKEL. 2003. *Teaching Adolescents to Write: the Unsubtle Art of Naked Teaching.* Boston: Allyn & Bacon.

BEACH, RICHARD AND JAMES MARSHALL. 1997. *Teaching Literature in the Secondary School, 2nd edition.* Belmont, CA: Wadsworth.

BRADDOCK, RICHARD, RICHARD LLOYD-JONES, AND LOWELL SCHOER. 1963. *Research on Written Composition.* Champaign, IL: National Council of Teachers of English.

BURKE, JIM. 2003. *The English Teacher's Companion: A Complete Guide to Classroom, Curriculum, and the Profession,* 2nd Edition. Portsmouth, NH: Boynton/Cook Heinemann.

CANGELOSI, JAMES S. 2000. *Classroom Management Strategies: Gaining and Maintaining Students' Cooperation.* New York: John Wiley and Sons.

CHAMOT, ANNA UHL AND J. MICHAEL O'MALLEY. 1994. *The CALLA Handbook: Implementing the Cognitive Academic Language Learning Approach.* Reading, MA: Addison-Wesley/Longman.

CHARLES, C. M. 1992. *Building Classroom Discipline: From Models to Practice,* 4th edition. New York: Longman.

CHRISTENBURY, LEILA. 2000. *Making the Journey,* 2nd edition. Portsmouth, NH: Boynton/Cook Heinemann.

CUMMINGS, RHODA AND GARY FISHER. 1993. *The Survival Guide for Teenagers with LD.* Minneapolis, MN: Free Spirit.

DAVIDMAN, LEONARD AND PATRICIA T. DAVIDMAN. 2001. *Teaching with a Multicultural Perspective: A Practical Guide,* 3rd edition. New York: Longman.

DELPIT, LISA. 1995. *Other People's Children.* New York: The New Press.

DORNAN, READE N., LOIS MATZ ROSEN, AND MARILYN WILSON. 2003. *Within and Beyond the Writing Process in the Secondary English Classroom.* Newark, DE: International Reading Association.

EDWARDS, CLIFFORD H. 2000. *Classroom Discipline and Management.* New York: John Wiley and Sons.

EISNER, ELIOT. 1998. *The Kinds of Schools We Need: Personal Essays.* Portsmouth, NH: Heinemann.

ELBOW, PETER. 1973. *Writing Without Teachers.* New York: Oxford.

GERE, ANNE RUGGLES, COLLEEN FAIRBANKS, ALAN HOWES, LAURA ROOP, AND DAVID SCHAAFSMA. 1992. *Language and Reflection: An Integrated Approach to Teaching English.* Upper Saddle River, NJ: Prentice Hall.

GOLDEN, JOHN. 2001. *Reading in the Dark: Using Film as a Tool in the English Classroom.* Urbana, IL: National Council of Teachers of English.

GOLUB, JEFF. 1994. *Activities for an Interactive Classroom.* National Council of Teachers of English.

GOLUB, JEFFERY N. 2000. *Making Learning Happen.* Portsmouth, NH: Boynton/Cook Heinemann.

GRAHAM, PEG, SALLY HUDSON-ROSS, CHANDRA ADKINS, PATTI MACWHORTER, AND JENNIFER MCDUFFIE STEWART. (EDS.) 1999. *Teacher/Mentor: A Dialogue for Collaborative Learning.* New York: Teachers College Press and Urbana, IL: National Council of Teachers of English.

GREGG, GAIL P. AND PAMELA S. CARROLL. 1998. *Books and Beyond: Thematic Approaches for Teaching Literature in High School.* Norwood, MA: Christopher-Gordon.

HERNANDEZ, HILDA. 1997. *Teaching in Multilingual Classrooms.* Upper Saddle River, NJ: Prentice Hall.

JAGO, CAROL. 2000. *With Rigor for All: Teaching the Classics to Contemporary Students.* Portsmouth, NH: Boynton/Cook Heinemann.

JAGO, CAROL. 2002. *Cohesive Writing: Why Concept Is Not Enough.* Portsmouth, NH: Heinemann.

KAYWELL, JOAN. (ED.) 1993, 1995, 1997, 2000. *Adolescent Literature as a Complement to the Classics,* vol. I, II, III, IV. Norwood, MA: Christopher-Gordon.

KENT, RICHARD. 1997. *Room 109: The Promise of a Portfolio Classroom.* Portsmouth, NH: Boynton/Cook Heinemann.

KOHN, ALFIE. 1993. *Punished By Rewards: The Trouble with Gold Stars, Incentive Plans, A's, Praise, & Other Bribes.* Boston: Houghton Mifflin.

KOHN, ALFIE. 1999. *The Schools Our Children Deserve: Moving Beyond Traditional Classrooms and 'Tougher Standards.'* Boston: Houghton Mifflin.

KOHN, ALFIE. 2002. *The Case Against Standardized Testing.* Portsmouth, NH: Heinemann.

MACRORIE, KENNETH. 1988. *The I-Search Paper: Revised Edition of Searching Writing.* Portsmouth, NH: Boynton/Cook Heinemann.

MILNER, JOSEPH O'BEIRNE AND LUCY F. M. MILNER. 2002. *Bridging English*, 3rd edition. Upper Saddle River, NJ: Merrill/Prentice Hall.

MONSEAU, VIRGINIA AND GARY SALVNER. (Eds.) 2000. *Reading Their World: The Young Adult Novel in the Classroom*, 2nd edition. Portsmouth, NH: Boynton/Cook Heinemann.

MOORE, KENNETH D. 1995. *Classroom Teaching Skills*, 3rd edition. New York: McGraw-Hill.

NIETO, SONIA. 2000. *Affirming Diversity: The Sociopolitical Context of Multicultural Education*. New York: Longman.

NODEN, HARRY. 1999. *Image Grammar*. Portsmouth, NH: Boynton/Cook Heinemann.

NODEN, HARRY R. AND RICHARD T. VACCA. 1994. *Whole Language in Middle and Secondary Classrooms*. New York: Harper Collins College.

NOGUCHI, REI. 1991. *Grammar and the Teaching of Writing: Limits and Possibilities* Urbana, IL: National Council of Teachers of English.

OHANIAN, SUSAN. 1999. *One Size Fits Few: The Folly of Educational Standards*. Portsmouth, NH: Heinemann.

OLSON, CAROL BOOTH. 2003. *The Reading/Writing Connection: Strategies for Teaching and Learning in the Secondary Classroom*. Boston, MA: Allyn & Bacon Longman.

PIRIE, BRUCE. 1997. *Reshaping High School English*. Urbana, IL: National Council of Teachers of English.

PURVES, ALAN, THERESA ROGERS, AND ANNA O. SOTER. 1995. *How Porcupines Make Love, III*. White Plains, NY: Longman.

RIEF, LINDA. 1992. *Seeking Diversity: Language Arts with Adolescents*. Portsmouth, NH: Heinemann.

ROMANO, TOM. 1987. *Clearing the Way: Working with Teenage Writers*. Portsmouth, NH: Heinemann.

ROSENBLATT, LOUISE. 1996. *Literature as Exploration,* 5th edition. Modern Languages Association.

RYGIEL, MARY ANN. 1992. *Shakespeare Among School Children*. Urbana, IL: National Council of Teachers of English.

SHAUGNESSY, MINA P. 1977. *Errors and Expectations: A Guide for the Teacher of Basic Writing*. New York: Oxford University Press.

SIMMONS, JOHN S. AND LAWRENCE BAINES. (Eds.) 1998. *Language Study in Middle School, High School, and Beyond*. Newark, DE: International Reading Association.

SMITH, MICHAEL W. AND JEFFREY D. WILHELM. 2002. *Reading Don't Fix No Chevys*. Portsmouth, NH: Heinemann.

SNOW, C. E. (October, 2001). "Knowing what we know: children, teachers, researchers." In *Educational Researcher* 30 (7), 3–9.

SOVEN, MARGOT IRIS. 1999. *Teaching Writing in Middle and Secondary Schools: Theory, Research, and Practice*. Boston: Allyn & Bacon.

STEVENSON, CHRIS. 1998. *Teaching Ten to Fourteen Year Olds*, 2nd edition. New York: Longman.

STRICKLAND, KATHLEEN AND JAMES STRICKLAND. 2002. *Engaged in Learning: Teaching English, 6–12*. Portsmouth, NH: Heinemann.

SUAREZ-OROZCO, CAROLA AND MARCELO M. SUAREZ-OROZCO. 2001. *Children of Immigration*. Cambridge, MA: Harvard University Press.

TRELEASE, JIM. 1995. *The Read-Aloud Handbook*. New York: Penguin.

TSUJIMOTO, JOSEPH. 2001. *Lighting Fires: How the Passionate Teacher Engages Adolescent Writers*. Portsmouth, NH: Boynton/Cook Heinemann.

VENN, JOHN J. 2000. *Assessing Students with Special Needs*. Upper Saddle River, NJ: Prentice Hall.

WEAVER, CONSTANCE. 1996. *Teaching Grammar in Context*. Portsmouth, NH: Boyton/Cook Heinemann.

WEAVER, CONSTANCE. 1998. *Lessons to Share*. Portsmouth, NH: Boynton/Cook Heinemann.

WILHELM, JEFFREY D. AND BRIAN EDMISTON. 1998. *Imagining to Learn: Inquiry, Ethics and Integration through Drama*. Portsmouth, NH: Heinemann.

WILHELM, JEFFREY D., TANYA N. BAKER, AND JULIE DUBE. 2001. *Strategic Reading: Guiding Students to Lifelong Literacy 6–12*. Portsmouth, NH: Boynton/Cook Heinemann.

WOLFGANG, C. H. 1995. *Solving Discipline Problems: Methods and Models for Today's Teachers*, 3rd edition. Boston: Allyn & Bacon.

WONG, HARRY K. AND ROSEMARY T. 2001. *The First Days of School: How to Be an Effective Teacher*. Sunnydale, CA: Harry Wong Publisher.

DATE DUE

GAYLORD

PRINTED IN U.S.A.